Praise for *The Embodied Path*

"In *The Embodied Path* Ellie Roscher guides readers through the familiar and unfamiliar terrain of body stories. Weaving together others' stories and her own experiences, Roscher offers a vivid and diverse collection of body narratives, tangled with the twists and transformations that bodies endure. Readers will be challenged and changed by *The Embodied Path* and its powerful, provocative invitation to enter our own stories: the hidden narratives of suffering and strength held within our bodies."

—**Laura Kelly Fanucci**, author and speaker

"By turns generous, informative, and moving, Roscher's latest is a key offering to those of us who are fully aware that we can do better. Perhaps most important, it is a reminder that we have always been capable of more. The stories here, both Roscher's and those of her collaborators, are an entry to the work Roscher gently but firmly encourages us to undertake, for our own sakes."

—**Yi Shun Lai**, workshop developer and facilitator at All-In Inclusivity Workshops

Stories shape the way people understand themselves and the world they live in. Too often, people are made the objects of those stories, used in ways that support harmful master-narratives. Ellie Roscher demonstrates the power of counter-stories. She provides tools and models for re-authoring ourselves and, in the process, changing our relationships with ourselves and others. In this thoughtfully crafted book, Ellie reminds us that writing is an act of liberation."

—**Lee C. Fisher**, PhD, director of the Minnesota Writing Project

"As a wellness coach, I have witnessed over and over again how the combination of storytelling and powerful questions can open doors to new, or reclaimed, ways of being that lead us back to the home deep inside us. *The Embodied Path* is an invitation to begin the journey, and it provides the tools necessary for wayfinding. Full of diverse perspectives, truth-telling, and opportunities to reflect, this book is a must-read for anyone with a body. It started healing something in me that I didn't know needed to be healed."

—**Heidi Barr**, wellness coach and author
of *Collisions of Earth and Sky*

"Reading *The Embodied Path* was like attending a beautiful dinner party with strangers who become friends. I savored these stories and all the ways the telling eludes the trappings of competition and assimilation for the sake of something true and holy. Ellie Roscher hosts these pages with deep care, calling us back into our skin and helping us listen for power differently. Her honor for the teller does not waiver, so I found myself trusting Ellie with my breath and body too. This book is alive, a wellspring of gratitude, and an invitation to notice incarnation everywhere."

—**Meta Herrick Carlson**, pastor, poet, and author
of *Ordinary Blessings* and *Speak It Plain*

"Ellie Roscher is a sage story-keeper and unleasher. Bare, beautiful, and quietly revolutionary, her book unravels our menacing master-narratives about what a body is for and invites us to feel at home (again) in our own skin."

—**Erin S. Lane**, author of *Someone Other Than a Mother*

"Most books just want you to read them, but this interactive book invites you to heal, grow, learn, process your trauma, write your own story, and find 'coherence in the chaos.' *The Embodied Path* is a brilliant, vulnerable, equity-seeking, cutting-edge exploration of life within our messy and beautiful bodies. Read it and fall in love with your own body, perhaps for the first time."

—**Dr. Jacqueline Bussie**, author of *Love Without Limits* and *Outlaw Christian*

THE
EMBODIED
PATH

THE
EMBODIED
PATH

TELLING THE STORY OF YOUR BODY FOR HEALING AND WHOLENESS

By Ellie Roscher

Broadleaf Books

Minneapolis

THE EMBODIED PATH
Telling the Story of Your Body for Healing and Wholeness

Copyright © 2022 Ellie Roscher. Printed by Broadleaf Books, an imprint of 1517 Media. All rights reserved. Except for brief quotations in critical articles or reviews, no part of this book may be reproduced in any manner without prior written permission from the publisher. Email copyright@1517.media or write to Permissions, Broadleaf Books, PO Box 1209, Minneapolis, MN 55440-1209.

Cover image: Lizaveta Kadol/iStock
Cover design: Olga Grlic

Print ISBN: 978-1-5064-8282-8
eBook ISBN: 978-1-5064-8283-5

For Hanna, Ellen, Jen, and Sally.
Your body stories are brave and beautiful.

Revolution begins with the self, in the self.

—TONI CADE-BAMBARA,
The Black Woman: An Anthology

Contents

Author's Note

The art of embodiment is not new, nor owned by any individual. I honor and acknowledge the teachers before me who sought ways to connect our hearts, minds, and bodies. I am informed by the ancient wisdom of several lineages including Christian monasticism, the eight-limbed path of Ashtanga yoga with roots in Ancient India, and yin yoga, which incorporates principles of Chinese Taoist philosophy.

A few of the names in this book have been changed for the privacy and safety of the participants.

Introduction

There is a deep wisdom in our very flesh, if we can only come to our senses and feel it.

—Elizabeth A. Behnke,
quoted in *My Grandmother's Hands*

I started gymnastics when I was four years old, inspired by Mary Lou Retton's gold medal performance in the 1984 Olympics. I loved her teammate Julianne McNamara. She had strawberry blonde hair like me. At my first practice, I studied the older girls and followed every directive from the coach. After, while putting on my shoes, I asked my mom, "Can I come back tomorrow?"

In between practices, my dad got down on his hands and knees in the living room, while I adjusted my hair and leotard like the girls on TV. I rubbed my palms together, took a deep breath, sprinted across the room, and catapulted over my dad's back. The imaginary crowd erupted in applause. My endorphins surged. I waved to my imaginary adoring fans and sauntered back to take my second vault.

I was competing by age seven and won the Minnesota state meet in my age group and level at age nine. I practiced fifteen hours a week, traveled for competitions, and dreamed of moving to Texas to train with Béla Károlyi. In gym class, clad in my plaid Catholic school uniform skirt, I pummeled the boys in pull-ups.

Then, when I was thirteen, I fell. While practicing a new tumbling pass the night before flying to Michigan for a meet, I over-rotated and took the brunt of the landing on my outstretched left hand. My elbow dislocated and fractured. Bone chips flew off the joint.

I knew it was serious by the looks of horror on the faces of my teammates and the panic in my coach's voice saying, "The bone is trying to break through the skin!"

In the ambulance, the shock wore off enough for me to realize that I was not flying to Michigan the next day. My competitive season was over. My gymnastics career might be over. For an eighth-grader with big dreams, these realizations were tragic. I wallowed.

In the emergency room, a team of medical professionals buzzed above me. Someone cut my leotard off my body. The pain was consuming. What I didn't know at the time was that the displaced bone cut off blood flow to my hand. Dr. Gannon, the square-jawed orthopedic surgeon on call, struggled to restore a pulse to my wrist to keep the tissue alive. He eventually manipulated the joint enough to get blood back to my hand, and everyone seemed to settle down a bit. Five shots of novocaine in my armpit numbed my arm and sedated me. I woke up with a bright orange cast and rhythmic throbbing in my left arm.

After a series of casts and months of painful, thrice-weekly physical therapy appointments, my progress plateaued. Each time I went in for a checkup, the white matter on the X-ray was brighter and thicker. The range of motion in my elbow was severely limited. For an adult, an arm that doesn't bend or straighten all the way may hardly register. But for a young gymnast, it seemed an insurmountable and unacceptable obstacle. I sat in Dr. Gannon's office, confused and anxious to get back to training. In a sport with a short shelf life, time was ticking. I was losing my edge. I was feeling sorry for myself.

Then, my story changed.

Dr. Gannon looked me in the eye and said, "I need you to understand. Your injury was more serious than I let on. In the emergency room, I almost had to amputate your arm."

He explained his methods to revive circulation to my hand, having nothing to lose. He was not completely sure why it worked. "I know you are frustrated with how slowly your healing is going," he continued, "but actually, your body is healing *too* well. Too quickly. The joint is calcifying to ensure it never breaks again."

My left arm locks out bent, and I cannot touch my left shoulder with my left fingers. If you cupped my elbows in your palms, you would feel that my left elbow is significantly bigger than the right. My body is a physical manifestation of my fears, my intensity, my perfectionism, and my drive toward overachievement. My body didn't stay broken long enough. It rushed the healing, averting vulnerability to create stability. In the striving, it became rigid. It clung. It skipped "supple" and went straight to "stuck." On the other hand, it is remarkable how my body took care of itself, bracing and fortifying to protect itself from harm.

In Dr. Gannon's office, my disposition went from self-pity to gratitude in a matter of moments. I was a victim one minute and a survivor the next. Frustration melted, evolving to patience. Abhorrence became wonder. I walked out of Dr. Gannon's office that day with a new story. I walked out with the posture of someone acutely aware that she could have just one arm, but instead—despite the odds—she had two.

This book isn't about what happened to my elbow. This book is about the story I tell about what happened to my elbow, and how that story has helped me live a more embodied life.

The moment Dr. Gannon told me that he did not amputate my arm, my narrative around my elbow trauma changed. Since that moment, I have been in tune not only with my body, but with the story of my body. I continued to enjoy competitive gymnastics through college with a permanently bent left arm. Gymnastics empowered me to view my body with a sense of joy. Embodied gratitude moves through the world differently than embodied bitterness.

Decades later, I am still actively grateful to have two arms. I am aware of the vulnerability of our breakable, mortal bodies, which helps me stay awake to my life. Being a woman who menstruates monthly, a parent who breastfed her babies, a marathon runner, and a yogi, I marvel at what my body can do at every life stage. My body knows how it feels to climb a mountain, run for four hours straight, and flip on a balance beam. It stores memories of throwing a curve ball, dancing at my wedding, and absorbing fetal kicks. My body has endured miscarriages, sexual assault, and cesarean sections. My skin carries prints of toddler snuggles and gentle caresses from my spouse. My scars form a topographical map of my life, telling the imperfect tale that only I know as lived experience.

As my wounds heal, the stories that live in the scars encourage continued vulnerability, unfolding, and expanding. When we break, we can break open in a way that grows self-love, wisdom, and compassion. I seek not perfection, but wholeness. I revise my body story with new information and insight, applying meaning where I did not see it before. Weaving the story of my body into my being helps me integrate more fully into my body, inhabit my body, and live an embodied life.

For years now, I have invited my writing, theology, and yoga students to tell the stories of their bodies too. I encourage fellow peacemakers to make peace in their own bodies, to start the revolution in their beings. It is rigorous, vulnerable, and profound work. It is simple but not easy. It is one tool of many available to walk the embodied path toward healing and wholeness.

This book contains a curated selection of body stories, as well as some of my own. My stories appear in each chapter not because I think my stories are more important and deserve more airtime but rather to invite readers to see themselves in each theme and chapter too. We do not have one exhaustive story. I vary the length, style, and formality of my stories to model that variety is possible and encouraged. There is no one right way to construct a story. I also did not want to ask a participant to do something I was not willing to do myself. Many of my stories explore difficult moments, which is not a criticism but rather a love letter to my body, my sports career, and my embodied path.

I interviewed collaborators, translated what I heard to the page, and worked with them on edits. You may sense a varying level of intimacy in the essays, which reflects how long I have known the person, their chosen level of engagement in the process, and how much of the person's body story I had access to. The partnerships felt holy. There were times I heard something or wrote something that felt both new and true to the person. In the intentional time set aside to reflect on their bodies, they had fresh insights and discovered new threads. I learned so much by listening, crafting, and drafting, and collaborators told me they felt seen and validated in the process.

In my work crafting and sharing my body stories and inviting others to do the same, a myriad of benefits emerged, of which I will focus on four.

First, crafting our body stories forges meaning and expands identity. Many things happen to us that do not make sense. We get sick, we get assaulted, we live with depression. Telling a story about these things will not help them make sense. Some suffering we endure will never make sense. Yet, with time, we can choose to look back at our lives and craft stories that make meaning. The way we make meaning will influence who we are and who we become.

Not all moments carry equal meaning. We mine our memories and find the ones that hold weight and carry a charge. We make a meaningful story by choosing those moments, putting them in some order, raising themes, and assigning importance. We shift our role to narrator. Observing our memories and crafting a story from them is empowering. The stories we tell reveal why we think our lives are worth living, adding dignity and hope. Claiming coherence in the chaos, folding the hard moments into a narrative, brings worth as we transcend the superficial and momentary. Our lives take on a significance bigger than ourselves.

Forging meaning can give you the vocabulary you need to fight for your freedom, dropping the constraints the world puts on you. Andrew Solomon says it this way: "There is always someone who wants to confiscate our humanity. And there are always stories that restore it." Forging does not make the suffering right, but it can, with time, give it a role. Some of our present joy grew from past sorrows. My elbow injury, for example, gifted me the joy of knowing I was living with two arms and amplified what my body can do. Sharing stories is the foundation of identity and allows us to show up in society as who we really are, not despite who we really are.

Many stories in this book are about the multiplicity of our becoming, about our identity expanding in all directions. You do not need to become something to be becoming; becoming has its own inherent value. Becoming is not a linear process with a destination. In terms of race, ability, sex, sexuality, and gender, for example, our sense of identity does not move on a spectrum from one thing to another. Instead of growing like a tree in a linear, progressive, and ordered way, we experience becoming more like a rhizome, which, as Elizabeth Grosz explains, is "an underground—but perfectly manifest—network of multiple branching roots and shoots, with no central axis, no unified point of origin, and no given direction of growth—a proliferating, somewhat chaotic, and diversified system of growths." Our becoming does not have beginnings and ends, but a series of middles that live in us as a meshwork. More grass than a tree.

The people I interviewed reminded me time and time again that creating and sharing our body stories connects us to something beyond ourselves. Our stories help us cope and thrive. They expand society's view of what it means to be human. We are the main characters of our own stories, and we can consciously fall in love with our lives and our bodies as they unfold, expand, and become.

Second, crafting our body stories carves space to process trauma. Everything that happens to us happens to our bodies. Trauma lives in our bodies, and our bodies can go to great lengths to protect themselves from harm. Often, our bodies will know things before our brains do. And often when we think our brains are finished processing trauma, our bodies tell a different story. Healing is hard, but so is not healing, and healing from trauma cannot be rushed.

Trauma therapist and somatic abolitionist Resmaa Menakem explains trauma as a defensive maneuver, a protective response to an event that it perceives as dangerous. Trauma is a response to an experience that was too much, too often, too fast, and you experience the world as unsafe. Your system got overwhelmed. There was not enough room for your body to process it. We can internalize the trauma, storing it in our bodies, where it can remain untended to. A trauma-informed person will not ask you, "What's wrong with you?" They will ask, "What happened to you?" You are not defective. Your body has an amazing ability to protect you and survive. In *My Grandmother's Hands*, Menakem reminds us that our bodies hold the trauma from our lives and unhealed dissonance and trauma of our ancestors.

If you are working through body trauma, do it with trained professionals. Trauma tries to hide and forget. Yet our living memories shape and inform our present selves. Trauma does not communicate with logic or rationale. It lives, as Bessel Van der Kolk says, outside "the tyranny of language." Trauma has no access to cognition; it can't put words to a story. It is not reasonable, articulate, or rational. We will experience it as urges, revulsions, and charge, and a feeling that the world is unsafe. The breath and body practices are in the chapters to invite us to be in our bodies and be still enough to have an alternative body experience that does feel safe.

The work of this book, being tied to words, should happen in a time and place where you feel safe and calm and when you are ready to attach words. Carving out time to listen to others' stories and tell your own can be one of the tools you have to create space enough to process and slowly, ever so slowly, move through clean pain toward healing and wholeness one layer at a time. As bell hooks writes, "The longing to tell one's story and the process of telling is symbolically a gesture of longing to recover the past in such a way that one experiences both a sense of reunion and a sense of release."

Third, crafting our body stories works to dismantle the hierarchical separation between the mind and the body. Plato and the Stoics, who deeply influenced Western thought, were skeptical of the body. Stoics valued lack of passion as the highest virtue. The mind's job was to control the body and suppress emotion. Plato said sacred love was that of the immortal soul and profane love was that of the body. He did not believe the senses inform the soul. Mind–body dualism considers the body dirty and mortal, something to be transcended. Self-control, lack of emotion, living in the mind, and denying the body became the goal of spiritual enlightenment and divine favor. So the highest place in society was held by the elite males, politicians, and philosophers who could live and work in the mind. Women and laborers were inferior, bleeding, breastfeeding, and living and working in the body.

Mind–body dualism is central to Western thought and originates in the Christian ethic that celebrates suffering, self-denial, and self-control, and also material achievement. We cannot be too loud or take up too much space. Pleasure and desire are stifled. This dualism remains alive today in our mind-over-matter mentality. Yet mind–body dualism is simply not working. Our bodies are wise, and we can only override their signals for so long. We cannot think our way out of a feeling problem. Ignoring our bodies delays healing. By inhabiting our messy, powerful bodies, we can contend with both the trauma that has happened to us and the trauma we have inherited. This book invites us to stand in opposition to mind–body dualism. It works to dissolve the lines between the mind and the body that dismiss the connection and power of our bodies. Engaging in this work, you may experience real barriers, especially if you identify as White, male, heterosexual, able, Western, or Christian, in part because of the stronghold of mind–body dualism. Be patient with yourself. Some of the barriers may be very old. Honor your ancestors and engage in the work of subversive embodied storytelling.

Fourth, crafting our body narratives as counter-stories can shift dismissive and limiting master narratives. Dominant culture can have an exploitative view of people in marginalized groups, creating stories that can damage the identity and limit the agency of folks in the marginalized group. I will call these stories master narratives. Master narratives treat individuals like a group. They tell us who we are and who we are not, setting standards that require conformity and assimilation. Master narratives are used to justify oppression and maintain the status quo, and often disregard place and community and push for linear, redemptive arcs. Master narratives in our society would have me believe that, as a woman, I am inferior to a man, that my value depreciates as I age, and that I'm fragile and not resilient enough to contend with my own Whiteness or reject the misogyny I've internalized. I have learned helplessness to unlearn, and creating a counter-story can help.

Narrative damage can be narratively repaired. We can tell counter-stories to the master narratives. Counter-stories are told to resist, repudiate, subvert, contest, and undermine the master narrative. They don't buy what the dominant culture is selling. The narrative acts of insubordination set out to shift the oppressive master narrative and, in so doing, can create more freedom and agency in the storyteller by shifting their identity, which can shift the perspective of the dominant group if taken up. Counter-stories create opportunities for narrative resistance and repair.

This is a book of counter-stories. It is a book that believes stories can help individuals, institutions, and society be less cruel. It is a book that believes in solidarity and self-creation. The people I interviewed told me how freeing it was to realize their bodies have a story and that they have agency over the story they claim. The counter-stories already shifted the identity of the participants, and they hope, in sharing them, the stories may also shift something in you. As a reader, you are invited to be open to the stories shifting and widening your perspective. As a participant, you are invited to construct your own body story as a counter-story to share. Hearing and understanding each other's stories will accompany us toward personal and communal peace.

How to Use This Book

So let us pick up the stones over which we stumble, friends, and build altars. Let us listen to the sound of breath in our bodies. Let us listen to the sounds of our own voices, of our own names, of our own fears. Let us name the harsh light and soft darkness that surround us. Let's claw ourselves out from the graves we've dug. Let's lick the earth from our fingers. Let us look up and out and around. The world is big and wide and wild and wonderful and wicked, and our lives are murky, magnificent, malleable, and full of meaning. Oremus. Let us pray.

—Pádraig Ó Tuama,
Daily Prayer with the Corrymeela Community

While you read, I invite you to listen with your whole being and join in. This book is a tiny sampling that should not be seen as exhaustive or representative. Our body narratives are as varied as we are. Each person offered the version of their story they were ready to tell, speaking for themselves and not representing a group. Each story is a two-dimensional snapshot of a wildly sacred and ongoing human narrative that could be easily expanded to its own book, and it would still not be complete.

This book is being published in one moment in time that has a sociopolitical context, and the words the participants use reflect that. I venture that the language will sound dated in fifty years. Our language expands as our understanding of our layered identities expands. People use language to name their experience, which is an act that has agency, and yet it also lacks agency in the fact that language is always evolving and so are we. The word choices you see in these stories are a collaboration, and the diversity of word choice points to our age and the sociopolitical context in our becoming.

Go Slowly

Read this book slowly and with care, perhaps just one story a sitting. Listen deeply. Notice what sensations come up in your body as you read. Where do you feel a sense of restriction or expansion? What stories surface in your own body?

There is a difference between our jobs and our work. Part of our life's work as humans is to drop into our bodies and inhabit them. There are real barriers to that work, and this book encourages you to find flow around those barriers to a place where you know, listen to, and deeply respect your body and the bodies of others. It will not happen overnight. It is a daily, moment-to-moment invitation to opt in and approach your body with curiosity and reverence.

Work through the Reflection Questions

Don't just consume the book. Interact with it. Use the reflection questions alone, in pairs, or in a group to go deeper, metabolize it, and make connections with your body. This book is an invitation to learn from other people's body stories, and it is also an invitation to compare and foil your stories with theirs as you craft your own. Our society will do better if we inhabit our bodies and bring them more fully to our conversation circles.

Work through the Writing Prompts

It's your turn. Sometimes you don't know what you think or feel until you write it down. Writing can heal us. Things that may prove difficult to articulate can be given a voice through writing. A blank page is a great listener.

Telling your body story counters the master narrative that wants you to live perpetually in your head. Learn from the wisdom of your body. Spend time crafting your body story. Spend time sharing it. You are worth your time.

If possible, don't type these exercises. Use paper and a writing utensil. Don't worry about grammar, punctuation, or spelling. If it helps, set a timer, maybe for seven to ten minutes, for each writing prompt and write without overthinking for the time allotted. Choose specific moments, walk around old memories, and get into the details. Try writing in the present tense to access the richness of memories and hold them close. Don't worry if your story is not linear or redemptive. Bring in a sense of culture, place, and community.

To hear the quiet inner voice speaking its truth, silence and stillness help. In her *Harvard Business Review* article "Writing Can Help Us Heal from Trauma," Deborah Siegel-Acevedo asserts, "A certain kind of guided, detailed writing can not only help us process what we've been through and assist us as we envision a path forward; it can lower our blood pressure, strengthen our immune system, and increase our general well-being. Expressive writing can result in a reduction in stress, anxiety, and depression; improve our sleep and performance; and bring us greater focus and clarity."

Unlocking the memories in your body loosens blockages and creates flow. Putting language to the suppressed memories can set them free and dissipate the power they hold. When we write out our stories, we create some physical distance from them, transferring them from our bodies to the page. There, we can see them and contend with them. We can walk around the memories 360 degrees from the periphery and meander through them, getting a new view and fresh perspective. With the raw material on the page, we can revise it, shape it, heighten themes, and mold it like a potter. We become the author, the narrator, the main character, and the audience member in the front-row seat.

As bell hooks writes, "Writing was the healing place where I could collect the bits and pieces, where I could put them back together." In this way, our story "emerges as a narrative of resistance, as writing that enables us to experience both self-discovery and self-recovery."

Claim the role of author in your life. Do writing that is just for you. Distinguish between private and personal. You don't need to go somewhere you are not ready to go, and you don't have to share your story unless you are ready. People who shared for this book were ready to tell me their stories. We were in right relationship. If and when you are ready to share your stories with people, do not feel the need to share everything, and share only with people with whom you feel safe.

Keep in mind the stories in this book were written over a long period of time. They were edited professionally. Your story doesn't have to be grammatically perfect or creatively crafted. Let the story be as beautiful, messy, and unedited as real life.

Work through the Body and Breath Practices

Your body has endured a lot. Mindful and self-soothing practices will help us metabolize our pain and mitigate the feeling of getting overwhelmed. Spend time in your body. Tend to your body. Your body is your home. It is where the stories reside. Your body is where you experience pain, joy, and pleasure, so your body is where the healing, repair, and transformation happen. We can unlearn helplessness by doing something with our bodies. Do anything that is not nothing. Dare to inhabit your body more fully.

Getting stories unstuck and contending with them can produce in us a supple strength. We can live and move and breathe in the balance between instability and rigidity. More flow is possible.

Be Kind to Yourself

Your body has a story. Crafting and sharing your body story can help you inhabit your body more fully. The embodied path can lead to healing and wholeness. The idea is quite simple. The work is exceedingly rigorous. Be kind to yourself. Go slowly. Slower than you think is possible. How patient can you be with your practice of unfolding, expanding, and becoming?

Healing is essential to our individual and collective wellness. Healing and meaning-making is hard work. Take yourself seriously, and don't take yourself too seriously. Drink plenty of water. Take breaks. Get rest. Resting is not quitting. Sleep.

Did you ever get growing pains in your shins when you were a kid? I remember that aching so well. Growing hurts. You are outgrowing your former boundaries, your restrictive stories. You cannot be contained. Dare to believe the world will benefit from your freedom, your agency. We want you inhabiting your body, awake to your life, healing, growing, strong and whole. When you inhabit your body and when you tell the stories of your body, you can live in more freedom, with agency. When you listen carefully to the stories of other people's bodies, our society's limited and harmful narratives can shift, breathe, and become more. Individually you can, and communally we can, heal toward wholeness.

One

Bodies Break
Living with Limitation

To be 'well' is not to live in a state of perpetual safety and calm, but to move fluidly from a state of adversity, risk, adventure, or excitement, back to safety and calm, and out again. Stress is not bad for you; being stuck is bad for you. Wellness happens when your body is a place of safety for you, even when your body is not necessarily in a safe place. You can be well, even during the times when you don't feel good.

—EMILY AND AMELIA NAGOSKI,
Burnout: The Secret to Unlocking the Stress Cycle

While pregnant with my first child, I experienced a body fatigue I had never known before. I was nauseated all day, curled in on myself. While awake, I longed to be sleeping. While upright, I dreamed of being horizontal. I dragged myself through the day. Then I got shingles, and I gave up trying. Rest was nonnegotiable. I spent hours on the couch not really watching *The Good Wife* or *The West Wing*, chosen in part because of the sheer number of episodes. I had never moved so little for so long. I felt depressed and isolated on the sidelines, like I was waiting to live my life again. Like those hours, days, weeks, and months didn't count. Like I didn't matter.

It felt like when, as a young athlete, I had to sit out of practices and competitions while my injuries healed, watching my teammates, pining. Or right after COVID-19 stay-at-home orders, when I quit my job to facilitate online learning for my children. I grieved the loss of my public life and the value placed on contributing.

Our society is structured around the productivity of the strong. Our master narratives would have us believe that weakness should be overcome and avoided at all costs. The master narratives of the dominant culture value young, healthy, able bodies. They encourage us to deny our mortality and strive for unattainable perfection. Bodies that are marked by physical, emotional, or mental limitations are discarded and isolated in little and not-so-little ways.

In other times and places, people believed illness was a divine judgment and punishment, so people who were sick deserved it. Lepers were quarantined in colonies. Folks living with mental illness were sent away to asylums where they were not seen or heard. Societies were built around efficiency and speed, and those who did not belong were removed. Residue from this broken and fearful logic remains. People with illnesses such as lung cancer, HIV/AIDS and diabetes, and mental health issues like depression and anxiety are blamed and judged. Society creates distance as if we could catch these ailments like a cold.

The COVID-19 outbreak gave and continues to give us an opportunity to contend with our flawed assumptions around body limitations, contagiousness, and worth. We are all on the dynamic, ever-shifting continuum of ableness, illness, and wellness. We all take on dis-ease and claim strength where we can. Looking back on the moments I felt sidelined, I can see my value. The stories were defective, not me. Exploring themes of wellness and ability in our bodies can shift our societal structures so that all bodies have value and are accommodated fully into mainstream society. Nature needs diversity to thrive.

The body narratives in this chapter explore the themes of sickness, wellness, and ableness. They create agency in the narrators while putting pressure on the narratives that value speed, production, and survival of the fittest. We experience suffering when our bodies present limits. It's a reminder of our ultimate mortality. Individually and collectively, we will benefit from slowing down, listening, and learning from our amazing and imperfect bodies. There is strength in gentleness and wisdom in the vulnerability of human limitation.

Over-Achiever

It was the last gymnastics competition of the regular season. The team, having congregated around the chalk bin during bars, moved to hover at the end of the vault runway. The five varsity athletes took off their grips and three of the five replaced them with wrist supports. They ceremoniously caked their palms and feet with chalk, then bounced in place and swung their arms to keep their muscles warm and alert.

Of the four apparatuses, the vault is arguably the most dangerous. In 1988, American gymnast Julissa Gomez died after being paralyzed from a fall on vault. In 1998 at the Goodwill Games, Chinese gymnast San Lan's vault crash resulted in her paralysis. The vault used to be the men's pommel horse with the handles removed. In 2001, the thinner vaulting horse changed to a longer, wider vaulting table to help prevent severe and fatal injury. The new apparatus model is four feet long and three feet wide. Women tend to vault with the table about four feet above the ground, but slight alterations are made for each gymnast, factoring in the height, power, and speed of the athlete as well as the difficulty of the skill being performed. Because of its shape, gymnasts have nicknamed it The Tongue. On the end opposite the springboard, several blue mats are stacked to cushion the landing.

I carried the springboard from the uneven bar area down the vault runway and centered it precisely, six feet, four inches from the vaulting table.

There were two people with me: Tierney, the spunky red-headed assistant coach, and Amy, a senior who was on probation from competition for her failing grades. Tierney and I set the table for Maggie (the superstar who superstitiously always had to go first), meticulously counting off seven visible notches on both uprights. Tierney and Amy tinkered with the four-inch landing mat while I double-checked the distance between the springboard and the vault. Maggie gave me a thumbs up.

"Three-minute touch warm-up begins now," a voice announced over the PA system. Maggie powered down the runway, her neck tendons showing as she sprinted. She executed a 540-degree flip, from handstand on the table to standing on the ground, soaring well over our heads in a piked position with perfectly pointed toes.

"Nice, Maggie," I said. "Open your shoulder angle a little bit more and press your thighs together on your landing."

I spun to look down the runway. Bri was rubbing her palms onto her shiny purple leotard at the far end.

"Table at five, eight-incher in tight," I directed. Tierney and Amy jumped in like a NASCAR pit team. I moved the springboard six feet, two inches away from the vault and signaled to Bri to get her feet in front of her on her hurdle. She nodded with intense eyes and waited.

I crouched down and hooked my right shoulder blade under the front ridge of the vault. Tierney was in the back. I tried to turn the front spin lock and tugged on the rusty spring-loaded pin. Nothing. It wouldn't drop. I grabbed the notching above the base, left hand above right, and tried to manipulate it from under the table. Unbeknownst to me, Amy pushed on the top of the vaulting table with all her weight. The table dropped hard, pinching my right hand between the notched upright and the base of the leg. I panicked and yanked my hand free. Blood squirted from my fingertip and the center of my palm.

"Shit." I sprinted across the floor exercise mat toward the trainer stationed by the stretcher in the hallway. Lightheaded, I watched the girls finish their warm-up vaults while the trainer boxer-wrapped my hand.

I coached the rest of the meet, trying to keep my hand above my heart. When pain surged, I blinked very slowly and held my breath for a moment. By the time the team was bundled and in the bus for the long ride home, any remaining euphoria had worn off.

Palm readers will tell you that the right hand is controlled by the logic and reason of the left brain. It is influenced by education and experience, reflecting the objective, linear, masculine, outer self. I was annoyed that it was my right hand that was busted. I couldn't believe I grabbed the notching.

I got off the bus and drove myself home one-handed, arriving a little before eleven. Dan met me at the door, confused that I buzzed to be let into our apartment.

"We have to go to the emergency room."

"What happened?"

I held up my bloody, wrapped hand and let out a pathetic yelp.

In the emergency waiting room, I put my head on Dan's lap and closed my eyes. Being in acute nerve pain all night was rubbing me raw. A little before one in the morning, I got called back. A man in blue scrubs pointed to a gurney for me to sit on. I bit my lower lip and clenched my jaw as the man cut off the wrap.

"Okay, we're going to need to clean this thing off. How long has it been bleeding?" he asked.

I was so tired. "About five hours."

My palm was a sausage-bloated pile of swimming red. The tip of my right ring finger had an oval almost the size of my fingerprint of missing skin. Right below my ring finger on my palm, a two-inch-long, half-moon shaped opening sat atop a swollen mound of flesh. In both wounds, what looked to be tissue or fat was clearly visible.

Dan threw up. Twice.

Eventually, the doctor came in. "Hi. I'm Dr. Hawkinson. What do we have here?"

"A vaulting table crashed on my hand," I said.

He left the room and came back with supplies that included a long needle.

"This is going to hurt a little. I need to inject the anesthesia just under the surface of your whole palm. It's going to take multiple injections. Hang tight."

He positioned the needle at a low angle, parallel to my hand, inserted it straight into the gouge in the center of my palm, then rotated the needle around the circumference of my palm like the hand of a clock.

"Okay. I'll let it set and be back in a bit to look."

I released the clenched muscles in my neck, jaw, and abdomen. I didn't look when the doctor dug around in my hand and finger, not peeking when he gave me the prognosis.

"We actually can't do anything for you tonight. On the pad of your fingertip, there isn't enough skin to pull back together to stitch. It's going to have to grow back together on its own. What happened with your palm," he demonstrated with my left hand, "is that when it got crushed, the pinky side swelled more than the thumb side, so the skin broke open vertically." He made his pointer and middle fingers pop open like scissor blades. "Once the swelling goes down, the skin should grow back together nicely. It's too bloated right now to check for damage of the nerves, tendons, and ligaments. I'm going to refer you to a hand specialist. Keep it wrapped, soak it daily in soapy water, and go see the specialist as soon as you can. Any questions?"

My body was tired from the healing. In my mind, I personified the micro-communities of cells at the edges of my open skin regenerating, building a bridge toward each other. The soaking and rewrapping got easier every day, and when the nerves were a little less vulnerable, I explored my hand. I could see what I thought might be connective tissue through the holes, and I watched my palm turn from black to purple to blue to green to brown to yellow. I watched my palm deflate and the lifelines and print patterns re-emerged.

By the time the two wounds had sealed, there was a two-inch mound stationed in the middle of my palm. Over the several weeks of healing, an over-expression of collagen created a densely packed, cross-linked fiber arrangement, like the builders had constructed a bird's nest instead of a bridge under my skin. The mound was tight and itched and changed color throughout the day. I had nightmares that ants were laying eggs under my skin. I could feel it when I grabbed the steering wheel, turned a doorknob, or shook a hand. I rubbed the new growth absentmindedly, trying to either make it go away or welcome it to my body. I wasn't sure which.

When I went to see the specialist for my final appointment, he looked at it and tilted his head.

"Huh. Looks like a hypertrophic scar formed as the wound closed. You're going to need to go to therapy to see if you can break it up."

My right hand excelled at producing granulation tissue. My body overcorrected. Again. I had less than nine months to unheal. The breakup of collagen in my hand, which should be natural, needed to be forced before the maturation phase of wound healing closed it for good.

I drove downtown to see an occupational therapist who specialized in hands. A young woman with straight, black hair and a white coat pointed to a chair and walked around the table to sit opposite me.

"Okay, let's take a look," she said as she reached for my right palm. "Wow." She meticulously and curiously explored the mound for a few moments. "Let's see what we can do."

She put a dollop of shea butter on the lump and grabbed a metal tool that resembled a wrench handle. She rubbed the butter over my scar and chiseled the wrench back and forth over the collagen clump.

She shook her head slowly and without looking up said, "Your body heals too well. Too fast."

My body speaks loudly to get my attention. Stys, migraines, canker sores, and shingles have tried, with varying degrees of success, to tell me it's well past time to slow down. Healing can't be rushed. Neither can love, nor art, nor justice. My mind is wired to prioritize speed and efficiency above all. My body brings me back to the truth, repeatedly whispering over and over again, *Slow down. Drop in. Listen. Dwell. Be here now. Don't miss it.* I rub the little bump on my palm whenever I grow impatient with my journey. It is a worthy endeavor to tend to my body, listen to it, and trust that the lessons it has for me will bring me back home.

What activity do you rush through? What is one thing you can do to listen to your body today?

The Sick and the Well

One of the demarcations of society is between the sick and the well. Living on the side of the sick, yet often passing as well, Kevin intimately knows the intricacies of the demarcation. If you saw Kevin on the street, you wouldn't guess that he struggled with and felt sidelined by his compromised health for half his life. He faces decisions in the most mundane moments. Should he perform like the sick person he is or the well person he appears to be? Should he hold the door for someone or have the door held for him? Should he disclose his illness and risk losing control of the narrative? Risk them saying, "Oh, God I'm so sorry"? Risk receiving their pity but maybe also their compassion? His illness is almost unmarked, yet significant. It is and is not an intimate thing. He constantly negotiates physical space with healthy bodies. He decides what story to tell and thus what identity to claim. It's mostly altogether too much, and he resides in his head not as relief, but necessity.

When Kevin was twenty-one years old, in his senior year of college, he was strong and tan. He worked two jobs and excelled at school. He biked everywhere and dated a lot. He felt young and invincible, as so many college seniors in the dominant culture do.

Then, out of the blue, his kidneys failed. The failure was idiopathic, with no known cause.

Soon thereafter, Kevin's mom donated one of her kidneys to him. The doctors talked about the transplant as something that would get him back to normal. Back to being strong and tan, young and invincible. The kidney failure challenged his sense of vitality, but he believed the transplant would get him back on track.

Four months later, Kevin was back in the hospital getting a biopsy done on his transplant kidney. The medical professional doing the procedure used a needle the size of a coat hanger. He kept going back to get more tissue. It felt like breaking through tough, thick fabric, layers of rubber. Unpleasant would be putting it mildly. After the biopsy, Kevin returned to school without telling the story. They called to tell him he had a tumor in his kidney that had to come out.

As he prepared for the surgery to take out the tumor, Kevin had an overwhelming sense of calm optimism. This procedure would work, and he could return to normal. Young and invincible. On the well side of things.

Anesthesia knocks out the pain but also memory, so the next few days were hazy. He came out of the anesthesia just long enough for the doctors to apologize that the procedure didn't work. They had to take the whole kidney out. He was, again, without a working kidney. Kevin comforted them, telling them it was okay. He was driven by bravado and an irrational sense that it would all work out. Playing the good patient, he didn't have to dwell in his vulnerability and his mortality.

The doctors removed the transplant kidney. As he waited for another kidney, he did a whole year of dialysis. The stories he tells are about biking to dialysis. He wanted to locate himself as an able body in a room full of sick people. He sat next to an eighty-nine-year-old man named Abner and thought, "What the fuck am I doing here?"

Kevin continued in the role of good patient, constructing a story about himself that was more palatable. He tried claiming insider status with health care providers, moving himself away from liability, helplessness, and dependency. He located himself as the patient with whom nurses could be straight. He wanted the nurses to experience their time with him as a breath of fresh air, a break from their more difficult and cranky patients as the temporary one who was just a visitor, always on his way out. He was desperate to be the fun one, as to not be grouped with the morbidly ill.

Sixteen months after Kevin's first kidney transplant, his uncle Bruce matched as a donor. Bruce agreed to donate his kidney, which finally put an end to Kevin's need for dialysis multiple times a week.

Kidney failure is not a disease that brings a sense of imminent crisis. It is a slow burn of not-okay-ness. One intense exception to the subtlety came days after his second transplant. His body was rejecting Bruce's kidney. His creatinine levels dropped precipitously but bounced from 1.7 to 1.9, then 2.1, indicating vascular rejection of the kidney. It is sometimes treatable, but not always. Doctors gave him a drug that was so new that the nurses were reading about it as they were administering it to him. The 2.1 fell back to 1.9. That tiny fall showed the possibility and then eventually the certainty that the extreme treatment worked. The transplant took. But then he got sick and started throwing up. Having not slept and unable to drink, so wildly uncomfortable, he wondered for a moment if this was the end. For the first time since his kidneys failed, he allowed himself to think, *Maybe I don't make it through this. Maybe this is it.*

He did recover, and with Uncle Bruce's kidney working, Kevin's body was yet again not in acute crisis. He was also not well. He got his eyes checked because he was having a hard time focusing. He was chronically tired. He started taking a whole handful of drugs, including blood pressure medication, calcium, iron, and vitamins B, C, and D, having no idea he'd be taking them for years to come. He got gout. A benign cold turned into pneumonia and a long hospital stay. He was cold all the time. In the winter, he wore a stocking cap, two pairs of pants, several layers on top, and a scarf indoors. He integrated the layers into his disheveled high school English teacher persona. During harsh Minnesota winters, layers could be mistaken for creature comfort instead of a reaction to perpetually high blood pressure and low hemoglobin. People didn't treat him like he was sick, even when they knew he was.

When Kevin confided in people about his illness, the only response he could digest was someone telling him how well he was handling it. Yet that sent him deeper into his striving to be seen as healthy and to distance himself from the sick, the vulnerable, and the clearly mortal. It was exhausting.

The worst side effect from having a transplant kidney was warts. Because of the immunosuppressants Kevin took, coupled with low kidney function, his immunity was compromised. His body couldn't fight off warts growing and spreading like other bodies could. Every three weeks for nine months, he went to laser treatments. The procedure used lasers to heat up a layer of tissue, so the blood vessels exploded. It felt like a rubber band being snapped against his fingertips over and over and over again.

Kevin confided in his mom once that it was hard, so she accompanied him to an appointment. She didn't say anything or comfort him. She didn't need to. Her simply being there took enough of the burden away that he saw the situation clearly. It was like a switch flipped. He started crying in the waiting room and said, "I can't go back there. I can't do it anymore." Before that moment, it had never occurred to him that he had the option to stop. Good patients don't question or complain. His mom helped advocate for him to use lidocaine and try a new method, cauterization, which removed the warts in two comparatively painless treatments.

Nine years after Uncle Bruce's transplant, Kevin's ankles started swelling again. There were little cellular rejections here and there, but for the most part, he was okay. He was okay. Everything was okay. His okay-ness felt spiritual, the way some people might believe God is looking out for them. It was an innate sense of optimism, or denial. Maybe both.

Then the following year, three months after getting married, Kevin got pneumonia. In the hospital they did a scan and found cancer in one of his native kidneys. They needed to take it out, which is a very invasive and painful surgery. Once it was out, they found a second kind of cancer in it that is bilateral. He had to heal from the first removal so they could remove the second native kidney too. Meanwhile, Bruce's transplant kidney was failing, but they could not give Kevin drugs because of the cancer. After his second cancerous native kidney was removed, his transplant kidney was so low functioning that he started dialysis again.

Over a year of dialysis, two kidneys in and three kidneys out, Kevin was teaching high school English. He took extra classes and student-taught to get his license. He took PhD classes. He taught summer school. He never took a break. Maybe it was his White-bodied masculinity telling him to be productive. But more likely, it was the fact that he had a shorter time line. He got a slow start because of his illness, and will have a shorter life because of it too. And if he stayed in his mind, the mounting layers of trauma from each wart removal, each hour on dialysis, and each surgery could be kept at bay.

Kevin went to dialysis for fourteen hours every week for another full year. He was often the youngest patient there by decades. At first, he tried to be productive while hooked up, but eventually gave in to watching Netflix. When he was on dialysis at age 21, Kevin thought of it as a cure that would get him back to normal. Now on dialysis at age 36, he understood it was a treatment postponing the inevitable. His sense of perpetual okay-ness dimmed.

After months of gently inviting folks to get tested to see if they might be a match, a teacher at Kevin's school named Jackie matched as a donor and agreed to donate a kidney. Kevin was very sick and felt that time was running out. He left dialysis for the last time before transplant surgery full of urgent, clinging hope. He was so desperate to be done, to have those fourteen hours a week back, to feel better again. The day before his scheduled kidney transplant, the hospital social worker called. Jackie's last test showed a positive crossmatch. She was no longer a compatible donor and the surgery was canceled. He felt despair in his bones. In his teeth. For the first time since his kidney failure fifteen years prior, he allowed himself to wonder, *Why me? Why is this happening to me?*

Going back to dialysis after the canceled transplant surgery was hard because it was easy. People did not react to his returned presence with surprise or horror, but a sense of calm inevitability. He felt the permanence of the treatment. The technician simply said, "Oh, good to see you again. Take a seat." They were just doing their jobs, but it was his body. His life. He pulled up the shittiest Netflix show he could find on his iPad and settled in.

Kevin's community rallied around his desperation for a kidney. Ben, a young man who did not know Kevin but saw a post about him on Facebook, got tested. He called Kevin and said, "I think I might be the guy." Kevin was deeply relieved. Later in the conversation, Ben mentioned possibly going on a trip before the surgery. "Would that be all right?" he asked.

There was that demarcation between the sick and the well. How could Kevin explain what he had been through? The years of taking a handful of medications every day, the warts, the surgeries, the seemingly endless hours hooked up to a dialysis machine, the fear of a slow and miserable dissent into deeper illness from long-term kidney failure.

"Well, no." Kevin answered and admitted, "I am anxious about that."

A week after the phone call, Ben donated his kidney to Kevin. Kevin felt good right away, but he had felt good after the other two transplants as well. The true sign that a body has accepted a transplant happens around day 100. Kevin threw a party at his home 100 days in. He exuded genuine elation. Ben's kidney worked in his body better than his mom's kidney or his uncle's kidney ever did. His creatine went down, and he backed off the blood pressure medication until he did not take it anymore. His sperm count went up, and after struggling for a while, he and his wife got pregnant with their first child. His hair curled. He started sweating. He put on weight. His physiological body felt different, like he was in possession of it. It allowed him to pretend that he wasn't a transplant patient.

At age forty, Kevin feels remarkably healthy. He takes five medications a day, which, he laughs, seems like a normal volume of drugs. He is no longer concentrating on living through the next year of his life; he has room to think about enjoying the next thirty years. For the first time ever, he is experiencing the mundane, non-catastrophic, mediocre "I'm getting older" feelings. The "my kids are growing up too fast" feelings. The boring feelings that may inspire him to buy a motorcycle. Those are compounded, however, by the "I will probably die long before my wife" feelings and the "I hope my kids grow up to be happy adults and I get to be around long enough to see it" feelings. Because of his children, he is much less okay with the idea of dying at age 60. There are still reminders that he is, indeed, a transplant patient and always will be. He still resides on the sick side of the sick-well divide.

Yet he sees his illness as a gift. Being a man who is aware of his limitations has softened his heart. He has access to what it's like to be an old person. He knows he is mortal. And for twenty years, a community of people has actively rallied around him. People tell him he is doing a great job just for staying alive. In high school, he wanted to be a celebrated person. When his kidneys failed, he thought to himself, *Well there you go. Are you happy now, asshole?*

With a renewed sense of health came anxiety in Kevin's body. It carries weight. When Kevin is physically suffering, he doesn't feel anxiety. When the physical crisis stops, the anxiety returns. These days, he is uncomfortably anxious most of the time. One theory is that the anxiety is a physiological response to having a healthy body. During his years of dialysis, he put a lot of energy into staying alive, enduring the moment, withstanding the pain, and healing from trauma. Now his body doesn't know what to do with that extra energy. He can't quite settle into life without fight-or-flight mode kicking in. Like an old, worn-in companion, he prefers the physical suffering to the anxiety.

When he slows down, Kevin's anxiety heightens, which is physically uncomfortable, so he doesn't slow down. The discomfort feels like going through withdrawal. His flight from stillness feels like an addiction. He wants to slow down and explore the discomfort. He wants to address the anxiety while deliberately avoiding addressing the anxiety. The double bind has become one of his quirks. A badge of honor. His unused yoga pants sit in the corner, taunting him.

Even writing his dissertation was slow enough for anxiety to present itself. Chewing helped, so he ate Rice Krispies cereal while he typed. When he was finishing his PhD, his wife asked, "When will this be done?" Pregnant with their second child, she wanted more time to relax with him and be a family. He completed the PhD, but the overworking wasn't done. Because he curbs his discomfort with something as benign as eating a lot of cereal and as virtuous as getting a PhD, he gets away with it. He tries to outrun and outthink the anxiety. Daunting waves of trauma are hibernating just below Kevin's neck.

Stable health gave Kevin access to the witness perspective. He is, as Gatsby says, simultaneously "without and within." He worries about his kids' kidneys. To think of his son Jack going through what he did is disarming. To think of Jack going through it is to better understand himself going through it. When Kevin is in crisis mode, when it is happening to him, he can navigate it. He can become the good patient. The young guy at dialysis. When he imagines it happening to his son, when his role becomes that of a witness, accompanying Jack, it allows space to acknowledge the pain, vulnerability, and a sense of mortality that will steal his breath.

Kevin has lived half of his life chronically ill. He moves through the world of the well almost unmarked, but when things get quiet, he knows he is a visitor. Chronic illness is his home, maybe more so than his house, the present moment, or his body. Chronic illness has a culture, a language, and rules. Unlike well people, he knows intimately and profoundly how hospitals distort time and space. He knows what the normal range for a white blood cell count is, and what CBC and BMP stand for. His body is covered with scars from incisions, ports, catheters, and skin treatments. The scars tell a story, pointing to a catalogue of loss, reminders of physical pain, bursts of adrenaline, and endless hours of being restricted by the beeping machines that were keeping him alive. The scars are ultimately superficial. They do not tell the story of the anxiety, how Kevin fills silence with working and chewing. How he fears meditation. His mind races to obscure, to move away from vulnerability, fear, and loneliness that lurks below the surface for a chronically ill man who today has one kidney inside him working remarkably well.

To heal, to curb his anxiety, Kevin wants to be a witness to himself. He wants to picture himself the way he sometimes pictures his son, offering his younger self affection and courage, room to feel and be scared and say it is hard. It's easier to live it, to be close to it. To pull away and be the storyteller is to create enough distance to see it, feel it, process it, and possibly get to the other side of it where there might be more agency and freedom. And sharing that story maybe, just maybe, will dissolve that demarcation between the sick and the well enough so that we all might remember our vulnerability, interdependence, and mortality. We can all offer ourselves the tender companionship we would offer a child. So that we all can see, even for a moment, the sheer wonder of it all.

> *Take the witness view of a time you were sick and offer yourself some tender affection. What is one thing you can do to relationally traverse the demarcation between the sick and the well?*

Folding to Unfold

Deep into December, Caren was in Boston, visiting her son and his family. Bustling around the apartment, trying to be helpful, her mind raced to thoughts of the new year approaching. What would 2020 bring?

"Mom, are you coming?" her son, Aaron, called from outside. He and Caren's grandson, Reed, were anxious to get to the Children's Museum. Her husband Kim was outside, too, looking at his watch.

"Coming!" she yelled back. She grabbed a large garbage bag from the kitchen and lugged it outside to deposit.

At the top of the apartment stairs, Caren's foot caught in the garbage bag, and in that moment, a series of irreversible things unfolded, seemingly in slow motion.

She thought, *I cannot catch my balance.*

She fell down the stairs, toward the sidewalk, headfirst.

She thought, *Why? Why the garbage bag?*

As Caren hit the sidewalk, she thought, *This is not going to be pretty.* Her glasses flew off. Her head bled. Her wrist hurt. *What did I just do?*

Aaron and Kim rushed to her aid with horrified looks on their faces. A neighbor brought ice. A group of people encircled her, coming up with a plan to get her to the emergency room. But Caren was the helper. She was not the one who needed help. The role reversal felt abrupt and embarrassing.

In the emergency room, the doctor and nurses offered Caren focused attention and care. She was taken by it. She was far from the most urgent case, but they treated her like she was. Each time she retold the story of *just tripping over a garbage bag* to a medical professional, the trivialness of the bag gained weight. Replaying the accident, Caren realized that by extending her hand as she hit the sidewalk, she had saved her head from injury beyond the seven stitches above her eyebrow. The accident could have been much worse.

She focused on her wrist. It was burning with pain.

The doctor diagnosed a boxer's break on Caren's dominant right hand. She left the hospital with a large cast, her mind swimming with questions. *What am I fighting? What is in my garbage bag? How can I slow down? How can I receive help graciously?*

Caren didn't have to wonder about how to slow down for long. Her life came to a crashing halt. When you can't pull up your own pants, when you are in throbbing physical pain, when you are a writer who literally cannot write, you must ask for help. Caren's identity as hypercompetent and independent hit a wall. She felt vulnerable, and worse—old. Caren wondered, *How can I shift out of the negative and find something positive from this experience?*

She decided to focus on gratitude—and the feeling grew. She started with her right hand. Each morning she thanked her hand for saving her from what could have been a severe head injury. The more she thanked her hand, the more she welcomed her healing season as a chance to practice gratefulness in the space that opened in her days.

Eventually, Caren's cast came off. Then the splint came off. She headed to therapy, anxious to get back to normal. Underneath the surface she wondered, *When you are broken, do you ever really go back?*

In physical therapy, Caren marveled at the muscles she took for granted. It was thrilling to be able to clench and unclench her fist again. At the end of her first session, her therapist said, "Let's think of some ways you can exercise your hand. What do you like to do?"

"I like to fold origami cranes."

"Perfect. That's perfect," she said. "Make as many cranes as you can."

In 2016, Caren published a nonfiction book called *Sachiko: A Nagasaki Bomb Survivor's Story* that went on to win multiple awards. Sachiko was six years old on August 9, 1945. Her country was at war, and she didn't have enough to eat. She was playing outside when an atomic bomb exploded only a half mile away. In the months that followed, her hair fell out and several family members died. She dedicated her life to studying peacemakers, overcoming, and living into healing.

Caren first heard Sachiko's story in 2005 and was haunted by it. She leaned in with the fierce curiosity and compassion of a writer. Sachiko and Caren became friends, and Sachiko asked Caren to write and share her story in the United States so that no one else would have to live through what she had endured.

In researching the book, Caren traveled to Japan five different times. Sachiko taught Caren how to fold origami cranes. Many children in Japan know how, and they send cranes to Nagasaki and Hiroshima to usher in peace and healing. One peace park has a space the size of a football field designated for disintegrating old cranes. They compost the cranes and make them into recycled paper so children can keep folding them into cranes again and again.

The crane symbolizes long life, health, and hope. Origami cranes are not easy to make, and early cranes, wrought with mistakes, might not be exactly beautiful. Eventually a muscle memory sets in. It becomes a meditative practice. Folding a crane is a lot like becoming a peacemaker. It takes time. You make mistakes. The process and the product are beautiful and vulnerable. And it's a lot more fun if you learn from someone else.

Folding cranes to strengthen her hand was medicinal for Caren. While she folded, she thought of Sachiko and her resilience. While she folded, she let go of the garbage bag. Her fall could have caused a lot of serious damage, and it was preventable. *I need to pay attention*, she thought, *I have too much left that I want to do with this life.*

Caren folded cranes while watching *PBS NewsHour*. She could make six cranes in a normal news cycle—eight if the news was bad. The cranes centered and grounded her, allowing her to take in the pain ringing from all over the world. She made cranes into bouquets and mobiles and tucked them into thank-you cards. She kept them in her purse and handed them to people she encountered in the grocery store or post office as random acts of peace. Unexpected, the cranes stopped people and inspired smiles. Workers carefully placed them somewhere special, in view, as if there had always been a nest there waiting to be filled. She created these human moments of connection from her own healing.

While folding her cranes, Caren gained trust in herself again. She welcomed in the space necessary to heal, knowing it was not going to happen fast. She stayed present to the moment and brought a renewed and deliberate thoughtfulness to her days. It took tripping over a garbage bag to learn to let go. It took crashing to wake up. And it took folding cranes to remind her how beautiful and delicate life can be.

Caren is a writer. She starts forming a story around a moment almost as it is happening. As she was falling down the steps, she already sensed she was living a moment that would appear in her body story. She looks for living, breathing metaphors in her days. She pays attention to moments that feel alive with energy and potential. She believes in the power of meaning-making. She knows that we choose the version of the story we internalize, and that choice affects our identity and outlook.

Telling her story created space to process. Editing it reminded her of the lessons she learned while healing. How soon we forget, the master narratives pushing us to hurry up and carry on. Creating a counter-story shifted Caren's identity around her age and ability. Her story shifted her from the aging, broken, sidelined person who couldn't do her job to a person who was granted the gift of time to reflect, learn, and create peace. Instead of rushing to heal and get back to normal, she chose to unfold and grow into a new person who is more aware, grateful, and more at peace with each folded crane.

> *Take a moment to offer your body gratitude for what it can do. What is an activity you enjoy that encourages slow, deep listening?*

The View from Here

When Rebecca was five, her family moved into a picturesque 1950s house on Appletree Lane in Deerfield, a suburb of Chicago. Two years later, her youngest brother was born. When he was four months old, Rebecca became disabled.

Rebecca went to a friend's pool party and came home exhausted. She told her parents she felt tingling all over, like her limbs were falling asleep, and that she wanted to take a nap. Her parents thought she was trying to get attention, adjusting to having a new baby in the house. She descended to her basement bedroom to sleep, and when she woke up, she could barely crawl back upstairs. Her body was weaker. She told her parents, "I can't feel my arms."

"Are you joking?" they asked.

"No. And it's getting hard to breathe."

Her parents took her to the hospital, and she was paralyzed from the neck down within twenty-four hours.

Rebecca was diagnosed with transverse myelitis, a rare disease diagnosed roughly 300 times a year in the United States. The severity of her acute case and the permanent damage it caused was even more rare than the diagnosis. Two weeks prior, she had had the flu. Instead of attacking the flu, her body attacked the myelin sheath on her spinal cord. It is like the deterioration that happens to a person with multiple sclerosis over years, but with Rebecca it happened over the course of hours.

She woke up in the intensive care unit on a ventilator. She couldn't move, she couldn't talk, and she couldn't feel her body. She was seven.

Rebecca came off the ventilator after two weeks to the surprise of her doctors and the relief of her parents. She spent a month in the hospital and two-and-a-half months in the best rehabilitation center in the country. In rehab she learned how to let caregivers take care of her. She learned how to drive her wheelchair, type, and turn pages with a mouth stick. Her parents learned how to adapt their home and care for her there. Her mom is a teacher, and her dad is an architect. It was as if they had been preparing for this crisis for years.

She lost a lot of weight from muscle atrophy, but also because she could not keep food down. Her body was struggling from disassociation and adjusting to her new reality. She probably would have benefited from eating several small meals very slowly throughout the day, but at the rehab center she ate three larger meals on a tight schedule. When she left to move back home, she was thirty-six pounds, one pound away from needing a gastrointestinal tube.

At home, Rebecca's parents counted calories and took their time at meals. She drank high-calorie shakes and whole milk. She could eat as much butter as she wanted and took a liking to KFC. Her weight rose and they shifted their focus to getting her back to school.

It was 1992, two years after the Americans with Disabilities Act was passed, but change was slow, and to this day enforcement is a challenge. The school had never had a student in a wheelchair before and did not always grant proper accommodations. Local doctors and lawyers advocated for Rebecca's family, and changes were made. Before her return, the entire school gathered in the auditorium to watch videos of Rebecca in her wheelchair, with splints on, using her mouth to type and turn pages, so they would be prepared. Her parents wanted to curb confused or frightened stares. They taught the students how to be her advocates. It was still the Rebecca they remembered; she would just stay sitting down.

Rebecca's transition back to school was seamless and her schoolmates continued to be a supportive community for her. At her high school graduation, she got a standing ovation as she accepted her diploma, and she was able to receive their love and admiration because the entire community had rallied around her and her family. They showed up at fundraisers to raise money for her equipment and wheelchair. They babysat Rebecca's three younger siblings when she had appointments and health complications. The crowd continued to stand—something she would never do again. She felt grateful and proud.

Her mantra became, *This is hard, but it's not bad.*

At her ten-year high school reunion, her caregiver observed, "Rebecca, we were there for three hours and no one treated you strangely. No one stared." Sadly, this was unlike Rebecca's experience out in the world at large. Because they had all grown up together, they treated her like a person who happened to stay seated.

Rebecca has learned to live independently. "In terms of folks with disability, I'm kicking ass," she said, then added, smiling, "I mean, not literally, but I'm kicking ass." She moved seven hours away to attend college at Mizzou. She studied art, creating with her mouth. She learned graphic design and ran her own graphic design company upon graduating. She married a man with cerebral palsy who uses a manual wheelchair. He represented the United States in the Australian Youth Paralympics in wheelchair basketball, winning a gold medal, and went on to play in college and adult leagues. They moved into a condo they designed together. For $250, they wired their house with Amazon Echo. For the first time since she was seven, Rebecca could turn on the lights by voice and operate the television remote with her phone. It was a small joy. When she was a kid, her family considered spending $5,000 for a similar system, but decided against it for practical and financial reasons. Now, because able-bodied people are willing to pay for these conveniences, driving the cost down, she can finally afford it.

One in five people in the United States has a disability. Yet Rebecca said, "We are left off the list. We are always an afterthought. Politicians won't say the word disabled." She explained, "Elderly folks are just considered old, not disabled, but they need similar services and support too. If we just created universal spaces from the beginning, life wouldn't be so hard. There are structural barriers, cost barriers, and attitudinal barriers. It does not cost money to give more access to a gay person, for example, but I have unique needs that are expensive. We are also the minority that any person could join at any moment. We deserve accommodations and almost no one acknowledges us. They send us to nursing homes and forget about us. They send us away. We feel invisible."

It is very expensive to be disabled. Rebecca's caregivers cost upwards of $50,000 a year, which only covers help getting up, eating, bathing, and going to the bathroom. Medical care, equipment, medical supplies, food, and shelter are additional costs. So is care for travel or eating at a restaurant. Caregivers in Illinois get paid $15.50 an hour, just above minimum wage, so many of her caregivers are unskilled and unreliable. She explains, "Even though my husband and I both have good, full-time jobs, we are living on the brink of poverty. If I were to make $250,000, then a fifth of my salary would go toward my care. That might be doable. If I earn $100,000, half goes to care, and that is not sustainable."

In the 1980s, there was a push to support folks with disabilities to stay in their homes rather then send them to nursing homes. Federal and state funding go to support accommodations for folks with disabilities, so each state is a little different depending on the state funding. Many states have income and asset limits to qualify for government support. In Illinois, Rebecca only has an asset limit. To qualify, she and her husband cannot have more than $17,500 in assets, not counting her condo or her car.

Rebecca laid out, "I can make money, unlike folks in other states with an income limit, I just can't save it. How am I supposed to build an independent life with these restrictions? I would love to save money for kids someday, but I can't. It makes me so angry. Why did the state support me going to college just to tell me it's better to not earn a wage and live in poverty so I can qualify for support?

"In our country we only value people as worthwhile humans if they can economically produce. But society is not built in a way that

I can be productive. We use a medical model, which focuses on curing people. I can't be cured. If we were to adopt a more social model, we could embrace the diversity of all bodies and realize all bodies work differently and have value. Then we would invest in policies that support the independence and thriving of people with disabilities. Even though I am made to feel like it, I am not the problem. The system is the problem."

Rebecca went to law school to change the problematic system.

In 2011, she started taking classes part-time at Loyola Law School in Chicago. While training to be a lawyer, she needed a lawyer's help to get the accommodations she needed, like a table high enough for her to type with her mouth. She graduated with a health law certificate. She didn't want to be pigeonholed as a disability rights lawyer and activist, even though she enjoys that line of work immensely. It was the principle of the matter. "People think we are only capable of working in a disability field, which is so limiting. I am more than my disability."

Rebecca graduated from law school in 2015. Her entire extended family came to support her. The administrators asked her to be on the stage, so they didn't have to use the lift during the ceremony. Reading of the names began, and she settled in. Her last name began with W. When they got to her name, they forgot her. The two names after hers were read and the crowd was invited to applaud for the graduates. Rebecca was livid. Crying, she yelled repeatedly over the clapping, "You forgot me! You forgot me!" She was so tired of feeling invisible. Of being forgotten.

The chancellor realized his mistake, calmed the applause, and called her forward. She rolled her wheelchair toward him, seething with anger and embarrassment. All 5,000 sets of eyes were on her. People in the audience thought she was crying for joy and pride, not disgust. They rose to their feet, giving her a standing ovation. Unlike at her high school graduation, it was a standing ovation she absolutely did not want.

"They didn't know me. They didn't know that I had a bed sore during my third year that required surgery or that I came to class via FaceTime from a hospital bed for weeks after I had surgery to correct it. They were clapping for me because I am in a chair. It felt like inspiration porn."

When she approached the chancellor, he reached out to shake her hand. Realizing his mistake, he leaned in to greet her instead and inadvertently turned off the power to her wheelchair. She couldn't move. She had to repeat, "You turned off my chair!" a few times before he heard her and responded. "It was so humiliating. One of the most painful moments of my life. I had to remind myself over and over, 'You are not the problem. You are not a problem.'"

Rebecca failed the bar exam the first time she took it. For an accommodation, she was offered double the standard amount of time. That meant that, instead of two eight-hour days of testing, she had four. "I am typing with my mouth. One letter at a time. It is so physically and mentally draining over four days. It was too much." The test was only offered twice a year, so she decided to retake the bar exam the next time it was offered, even though she had had sepsis and emergency surgery to remove a kidney stone the week before and nearly died. The test cost $800, and she was drowning in law school debt. She couldn't afford to skip it. She failed again, and three more times after that.

She was ready to give up, but then Rebecca got a good job in the city law department that offered great health insurance. It was just the motivation she needed to take the test one more time. On her sixth try, she passed. Finally, she could write "Esq." after her name. Finally, she would get the respect she deserved. Those three letters frighten people, which feels both powerful and sad. Millions of people have disabilities without "Esq." at the end of their name. What can they do to be seen and taken seriously?

Rebecca has spent a significant amount of time in the hospital. She is an expert in her own care, and yet she is often disregarded by health professionals. They won't let her consent to her own surgery, or they do not ask her if she has an advance directive. Her care changes when she tells them she is a health law attorney. It is an important tool in her arsenal.

When Rebecca passed the bar, she was elated for about a week. Then anxiety started creeping in. It was time to look for a job. "I dread the job hunt," she said. "It's such a demoralizing process for me. During an interview, they can't see past my chair. My disability is front and center. They think about how expensive it will be to accommodate me. It doesn't matter that I am the most loyal employee because I am afraid to quit and lose income. It doesn't matter that I am the best problem-solver because I have to be to get through each day. It doesn't matter that I successfully hire, coordinate, and manage six caregivers. Those things don't show up on my resume. The only jobs I've gotten have been after phone interviews when they don't see my chair. The rejection is more paralyzing than my paralysis."

COVID-19 has made job interviews easier for Rebecca and her husband. It is making the bias of in-person interviews even clearer. On Zoom, potential employers can't tell that her husband is in a wheelchair. They see him, not the chair, and listen to his answers instead of thinking about their culture, their stairs, and their bathrooms. After going ten years without a job offer from an in-person interview, he was offered two remote jobs within six months. In his current job as a paralegal, he told them about his disability on his own terms. As the finishing touches were being applied to this book,

Rebecca accepted her first job as an attorney at Chicago Volunteer Legal Services.

Job interviews and remote work are the only things COVID-19 made easier for them, however. Rebecca has 13 percent lung capacity. She cannot risk getting sick. On the day of our interview, she had been in isolation for 586 days. Before stay-at-home orders, Rebecca overheard a coworker talking about a bug going around her family. She left work, scared, and hasn't returned. She didn't leave her condo at all for the first seventy-four days, and now does so sparingly. They had one caregiver come in the morning to transfer Rebecca from her bed to her chair, the only thing on her care list that her husband can't physically do. Rebecca drove sixty-seven miles to get her first and second dose of the vaccine, then recently got her third dose locally. "I write a post on social media every single day, even if it's just a sentence, to remind people that I am here, that I can't go out in public safely until we all commit to protecting the community. I am in the community. I do not want to be erased. I do not want to be forgotten."

At the beginning of the pandemic, Rebecca remembers scientists in the media saying, "Don't worry. The only people dying of COVID-19 are old people and disabled people." According to the Illinois Department of Public Health, 25 percent of the people in Chicago who died of COVID-19 lived in long-term care facilities, but disability activists estimate the number to be much higher. Elderly people, and people like Rebecca, who can't easily get out. People you don't see because they don't go out. Because they've been put away. Because society won't change to support their needs to move and live with ease.

She is not the problem. She matters inherently.

We need new policies to support and protect Rebecca and her community. When the current policies were written, the world was different. Folks with disabilities are living longer. They need affordable long-term care. They need more accessibility, and they need the help of folks with fewer literal barriers. It's hard for Rebecca to fight when 60 percent of election poll locations aren't accessible and mail-in ballots are under attack. "I can't sign my name or mark my ballot because the tables aren't high enough," Rebecca said. She sighed, exhausted, and repeated yet again, "All because I sit down."

Rebecca is an amazing storyteller with deep conviction and well-deserved rage. She invited me to see her barriers that I take for granted. It is my job to keep looking and seeing, to join her in her work to change the systems for her ease and because she is not the problem. She is brilliant, brave, funny, and resourceful. We will all do better when she does better.

> *Who in your community gets isolated or sent away? What is one thing you can do to see them and advocate for a system change?*

Our bodies get sick and break. Our bodies fall short and disappoint. Ultimately, our bodies will die. They are needy and demand our attention. They are imperfect, quirky, asymmetrical, and unpredictable. Through it all, we decide if we approach our bodies with frustration or curiosity, with animosity or compassion. We decide if we tell a body story steeped in what our bodies can't do or in what they can.

Ableism tells a master narrative around who is normal and who is lacking. It tells stories about which bodies are valuable, disposable, or desirable. People usually think of disabilities as individual problems, limitations, or flaws rather than problems, limitations, or flaws in the system that limits our ability to live unencumbered.

Disability justice frameworks place the onus on the systems to change, not the people. The poor urban planning that leads to the absence of a ramp is the problem, not the person in the wheelchair. These frameworks are also shifting the accessibility conversation beyond logistics, beyond inclusion and diversity, to justice. As we make the world more accessible to more people, to more bodies, we need to question the system that would be built with inaccessibility as an option. Disability justice workers urge us to see that we are all interdependent. All our bodies have limits. None of us gets through the day without assistance. Yet some bodies are labeled as disabled, and others are not. How can we reimagine bodies and relationships in a way that normalizes limitation and centers interdependence? How can we take a closer look at the line that divides the sick and the well? Maybe your body story can help.

Reflection Questions

* What did your body experience while reading these stories? Did any of them resonate with you and your body's story?
* What is the coolest thing your body can do? What is something you really enjoy doing while your body is active? While your body is still?
* Talk about a time when you were sidelined from society. What is something "chronic" that you carry with you and manage? What are the tools you use?
* When you have experienced brokenness, how does the urge to bounce back, rush healing, and get back to normal show up for you? What opportunity does the brokenness present to learn, grow, and unfold into wholeness?

* How do your physical health and mental health relate to each other? What is something we would know about you by looking at your body? What is something about you that we cannot see?

* Talk about a time that one limitation led to an increased capacity in another way.

* What has your body lost? What has been taken away?

* How do you feel your worth tied to productivity? What is something you live with and will live with long-term that has no cure?

* Which bodies in society are you taught not to see? Who gets sent away?

* The stories we are born into are important, influential, and powerful. Draw your family tree as far back as you can. Identify the storytellers in your family and ask them to tell you stories. Listen hard. Where did you come from? What stories from your ancestors shaped you? What stories that get told about you do you reject? Claim?

* What are the master narratives in your birth family, found family, place of work, media, and society at large around limitations—physical and mental illness, injury, aging, and death? Are body limits talked about, integrated, or ignored? Are bodies viewed as lacking or is focus placed on our systems?

* Do you have any counter-stories that could alter the perception of the dominant culture? How do we as individuals and our community benefit from telling and listening to more stories that challenge myths of independence, wellness, and ability? How might our narratives become healthier and more interesting? How might your identity shift? Who might benefit from an increased sense of agency and freedom?

Writing Prompts

Divide your page up into four quadrants. Choose four of your five senses and label the four sections (ex: SAW, HEARD, TASTED, TOUCHED, SMELLED). Spend 30 seconds on each of the quadrants, listing things you have noticed and experienced in your day pertaining to the different senses. This exercise warms up your brain to write and helps awaken your senses so you can live in your body more often and notice what you are noticing.

Write about a time you literally or figuratively fell and decided to get back up again.

Write about a time when you came face to face with the limitations of your human body, maybe through illness or injury. What part of your ability or health were you taking for granted? We are dependent on so many things and people to survive. We break. We are mortal. And we heal and adapt. We are resilient. We survive. What is your story of living with limitation?

Breath Practice

Find a comfortable seated posture with a tall spine. Gently seal your lips and breathe through your nostrils. Notice air entering and leaving your nostrils without altering your breath. Simply notice that you are breathing. After a few breath cycles, empty out your lungs and begin a five-count inhale and a five-count exhale. Continue for about ten breath cycles and then return to your natural breathing.

Body Practices

Hum. Find a comfortable seated position. Gently press into your two sitting bones and lift the crown of your head toward the ceiling. Place your chin parallel to the floor. Close your eyes and relax your face. Inhale through the nose, and with each exhale, hum. Hum in a low pitch from deep in your belly, feeling the vibration in your chest and the back of your throat. Keep the sound smooth and consistent. As you hum, notice if you want to rock, stand, or place a hand on your body to ground yourself. Allow the sound and rhythm to soothe you. Continue to hum for a few minutes. Put your note out into the universe.

Choose a part of your body where you experience limitation, or a body part you have been rough with either physically or verbally through self-talk. I may choose, for example, my left elbow that can't straighten. Think about if and how you dismiss it, think negatively about it, or exist in your mind so you don't have to face it and your limitations. Take some time today offering it gentle affection. Massage it with lotion or body oil. Think about how that body part contributes to the whole, your ability to be an active person. Acknowledge what it has taught you. Offer it gratitude. If necessary, apologize and commit to healing your relationship with your body through affection and elevated self-talk. Allow it to be part of your process to forge meaning and expand identity. Invite it back in as a teacher and part of your healing and wholeness.

Two

Bodies Connect
Expanding the Love

We will not end white-body supremacy—or any other form of human evil—by trying to tear it to pieces. Instead, we can offer people better ways to belong and better things to belong to. Each of us can also build our own capacity for genuine belonging.

—RESMAA MENAKEM,
My Grandmother's Hands

At a recent yoga training, the facilitator had us sit facing another person, our knees almost touching and our eyes closed. The practice would be to hold each other's eye contact in silence for a several minutes. When the facilitator invited us to open our eyes, I instinctually leaned forward without realizing it. She cued us to stack our shoulders over our hips, and I leaned back. In that moment, I felt a deeper alignment in my body that opened a sense of expansion in my being. I had more room to hold my partner's gaze. I had more space to offer her. It felt like I could have stayed in that posture of connection, holding expansive space for love, forever.

I think about this moment a lot. My tendency is to pitch forward, literally and figuratively. I jump ahead to the future. I hold my mind in higher esteem than my body. I lead with my ego and my intellect. I lean forward to guard my chest, protect my heart, and hide my abdomen. I lean forward because I want you to know I am here, I am with you, I've got you. I lean forward to ingratiate myself to you and put your needs first. I lean forward because I do not want you to think by pulling back that I am pulling away.

In the yoga exercise, when I did pull back, I was not pulling away. I was pulling myself into alignment so I could exist from my core. It brought ease and expansion. In wanting to connect with my partner, I was hindering the quality of my ability to connect. My tendency is to pitch forward. My mindful work is to pull not away but back into alignment so I can connect more deeply and authentically.

We were born social, designed to be in relationship. Babies need to be held to survive. We crave closeness, intimacy, and a true sense of belonging. We do not walk the embodied path in a vacuum by ourselves. Although the work can benefit from quiet time alone to feel, write, and process, the work is not solitary. We want to belong to our own bodies, and we want to belong to each other. We want to belong to a beautiful and body-affirming community.

The body stories in this chapter explore how our bodies are astounding tools of connection. Not by escaping our bodies, but rather more fully entering our bodies, we can live from our core in a way that makes real, deep, and true connection with others possible.

Instrument of Connection

I consider myself neither a poet, composer nor musician. These are merely tools used by sensitive men to carve out a piece of beauty or truth that they hope may lead to peace and salvation.

—GIL SCOTT-HERON,
liner notes in *Small Talk at 125th and Lenox*

The night before an Everyday Everybody concert, Stephane opened his closet and selected a sequined jacket. He tried on his entire ensemble from hat to shoes, letting his wife watch and offer feedback. Before every show, Stephane gets into his performing body and addresses imposter syndrome with a strategic wardrobe. When Clark Kent puts on his cape, we can still see him, but he also becomes Superman. Stephane looked at his reflection, sparkling. Game time.

The performance was atypical. Due to COVID-19, the concert streamed online. Stephane couldn't see the audience. He couldn't feed off their energy. He couldn't even see his bandmates, all streaming in from separate rooms. It was nearly impossible to get lost in the moment in an online concert, and yet, there were advantages too. Every viewer had a great seat and could appreciate all the components of the large funk band working together. The fans deeply appreciated the offering after months of stay-at-home orders and a desire to consume and engage with art. Even standing alone, mediated by the screen, Stephane's physicality commanded attention, exuding lead man performance energy effortlessly.

Music was prominent in Stephane's childhood home in Canada. His mom played David Bowie, Michael Jackson, Bob Marley, and James Brown in the house. She loved music, sang loudly, and always joked about never remembering a lyric. His dad sang pop music while doing home projects and played the Dave Brubeck Quartet cassette tape on family road trips. To this day, Stephane can sing all the parts on their *Time Out* album. Stephane's family listened to a lot of jazz,

Cameroonian folk music, and R&B. At family events, they played and sang together, calling themselves the Cameroonian von Trapps. Stephane's grandpa and uncle on his dad's side were choir directors who loved singing Christian hymns and spirituals. His grandpa on his mom's side played guitar and, through repetition, passed down his favorite hymns. Stephane took piano and violin lessons as a kid, but traditional lessons never stuck.

In 1997, when Stephane and his family moved to the United States, his cousin moved in with them and taught Stephane guitar. Steph's fingers ached from calluses, but he kept playing. He watched Michael Jackson's Live in Bucharest concert, which his mom had recorded on VHS in 1992, again and again, studying his two-hour performance. Meanwhile, Stephane started competitive soccer and excelled on the field.

As a Third Culture Kid, Stephane was raised to believe music and sports did not offer sufficient academic and professional stability. His parents encouraged a more traditional path that served them as immigrants to Canada and then the United States from Cameroon. Work hard in school. Get a good job. Have a family and a purpose. The musicians and artists in his family were the outliers. He felt a subtle pressure to choose a linear path.

Stephane attended a French international school with kids who traveled the world. His ear for music was stoked there. He kept learning through osmosis and peer pressure. His friend Yannick's dad taught them both, and they benefited from a healthy rivalry. Over a landline telephone, his friend Kyoko taught him how to play "Dust in the Wind" in ninety minutes. He copied other bands and played covers to get ideas for progressions. He spoke in moods and colors. He trusted his ear.

In the high school talent show, he played "Redemption Song" by Bob Marley and the Wailers. From his vantage point today, it was a bit of a technical failure. There was one microphone placed somewhere between his mouth and his guitar, not quite capturing his voice or his instrument well. He was walking off the stage before the audience realized he had finished. Regardless, he was up on stage, in front of the entire student body, performing with his voice, his guitar, and his body. His peers remember the performance to this day.

Shortly thereafter, Stephane's friend James told him, "Look, I found this great band from the UK. The front man is a British Nigerian. You're going to love them." They went to The Black Cat in Washington, DC, to see Bloc Party. The concert marked him. He saw a Black man leading a White band and thought, *"Oh, I can do that. I'm allowed to do that."*

By college, Stephane was playing varsity soccer and playing in two different jam bands called Seize the Sound and Quiet Hours Tom. While playing covers, he started writing and composing his own songs too.

In addition to Michael Jackson, Stephane studied Prince, Lenny Kravitz, Jimi Hendrix, and Kele Okereke from Bloc Party. He analyzed Prince spin in heels and jump with a twenty-pound guitar in unyielding outfits all while conducting and giving cues to his band. He absorbed how James Brown hit six splits in a row. He tracked Michael Jackson from his role in the Jackson 5 to his solo career. Michael Jackson didn't hold an instrument. He *was* the instrument. Stephane was drawn to multitalented, triple-threat lead men who danced, sang, and held the crowd, who took their job to entertain seriously, who gave their entire body up to the craft. Aspiring to do the same, he started seeing his entire body as his instrument. From then on, music and movement would always be inextricably linked.

Stephane approached the stage like a soccer player. In soccer, there are twenty-two people on the field moving strategically. Each person has a defined role. Only one person is touching the ball. What you are doing when you don't have the ball is what makes the difference. In soccer, Stephane played with kids two and three years older than him. He had good balance and excelled with both feet. He had good vision of the field, anticipation, and instinct. Being a younger, smaller guy, Stephane's advantage in soccer was that he never stopped moving and was always aware of his surroundings. If his team was tired, he knew he could be the conduit to birth a second wind. He saw soccer as a full-body sport that demanded intense endurance.

Like his soccer team, his band is an ecosystem. He likes playing with big bands that require lots of collaboration and expression. He loves bringing a slew of people together on a project. He can be in the center of a large band pulling strings, turning 360 degrees to communicate, utilizing his voice and movement toward his performance, exuding the balance and physicality it takes to sing, play, dance, conduct, and engage with the crowd, all in a sequined jacket. He wants to put on a show, and he does.

In his work life at the World Bank, Stephane was a bit more buttoned up at first. More private, measured, quiet, and reserved. Eventually, his front man stage presence influenced his work persona. He has become more colorful and outgoing there over time. On stage, it's his job to run the full concert and give an emotive, inspired show. He wants your heart to pour out. He wants the audience to get their money's worth. That same mentality shifts the quality of energy he brings to his day job as well.

When Everyday Everybody formed, music became more than a hobby. It started out as a social project. The band members met on Craigslist and liked playing together. They played house parties and then eventually opened for bigger bands at local venues. They gave themselves a name, gained a following, and traveled outside their city for gigs. They got a booking agent and an accountant and created an LLC. They hired themselves out for weddings, made flyers, brought along photographers, and got serious about social media. As the band gained popularity, their capacity to hold current grew. Album sales rose, listeners spanned more geographical space, and concert venues got bigger. They gained a following and eventually the audience members were singing along, bringing their personal experiences of the songs to the new moment. The spotlight was on the band, on Stephane. Everyone at a show sent their energy toward the stage. It felt like excitement and panic at the same time. The band grew capacity to ground, grow, absorb, and continue to transcend their bodies, inviting the audience to do the same. The boundaries dissolved. The musicians and the music became larger than life, connecting with people throughout the venue at such depth that the energy exchange felt metaphysical. A few years ago, they performed sixty times in a year, all while holding other full-time jobs. It's a huge sacrifice, but a few formidable moments keep bringing Stephane back.

During Everyday Everybody's first major run, they opened two nights—one at the Brooklyn Bowl and one on their home turf in DC—for Everyone Orchestra, an improv band. Stephane and his band played their hearts out. They always like to give the folks who attend the opener a good show and show respect to the main band by providing momentum and setting the stage. Everyone Orchestra invited Stephane to join them onstage during the second set. He hesitated, but then told his bandmates, "If I say I believe I have what it takes, I have to try." His bandmates knew he was nervous. On stage, it didn't show. He created the lyrics on the spot as the lead vocalist. They watched him come out of himself with a sense that he was doing what he was made to do. It was a mountaintop professional moment for him.

In the afterglow of the show, a man approached Stephane and introduced himself as Kevin. He was in recovery, living in a half-way house, and had requested a pass to go to the concert. "You brightened my day, man," he told Steph. "I got the night away and came to the whole show, not knowing what to expect. Your band was great."

In that moment, Stephane realized, "Every time we perform, somebody has come for a reason to get something. Like when I saw Kele Okereke. My duty as a performer is to honor that and give them my art. They may need exaltation or salvation. Every performance I think, *Don't hold back. Someone out there needs this.*"

Later, Everyday Everybody preformed three nights in a row in Durham, North Carolina. They sang "Revolution," a song about the need for change in the current civil rights movement. It was inspired by the killing of Trayvon Martin:

> *Bodies choking on pavement in the morning*
> *Bullets flying before the ink dries in the news*
> *Don't send your soldiers overseas while your civilians fight the war*
> *Mothers are scraping their knees*
> *Lifting their babies off the floor*

After the show, a woman and her child approached Steph and his bandmate Sara and said, "You described how I feel every time I see a Black child die. You put power in those words. Thank you for that."

People leaving Everyday Everybody's shows were different from when they arrived.

A good performance is one when Stephane stops thinking. He's in the groove, totally in his body. He gets out of his own way. If you really watch, you can see a distinct look on his face that conveys that he is exactly where he is supposed to be, open and vulnerable, being real with his art for us to see, hear, and experience. He gets to the raw place where his art is bare. The beauty comes out. We witness him in the zone and can't help but participate in the moment.

Feedback from fans who are moved by his commitment inspire him to keep creating. Stephane always hopes his lyrics feel authentic to people. The erasure of Black bodies is still happening; there are still forces that seek to divide rather than unite. So many people struggle with loneliness and feel like they are the only one feeling alone in a world with 7 billion people, and his beliefs and vision can be conveyed in lyrics. Then the band creates a sonic landscape to give the lyrics light, color, and grounding.

Normally, Stephane expends 25 percent of his tank on the first few songs to get the fans to come with him into the zone. Then he makes sure to save enough so that the last 10 percent of the show feels like the first 90 percent. But now and again, Everyday Everybody will use a show to work through different energies. A riff off a standard show, a gradation of transcendence. They go in with negative energy and use it for an explosive, hard hit of creativity. There is no respite. They go all in with no breaks from beginning to end, seamlessly traveling to another place through music, inviting the audience to come along for the ride.

Multi-instrumentalist, artist, engineer, and producer Al Evans is also the drummer and cofounder of Soulive. Stephane met Al the night he played with Everyone Orchestra. Al wrote a song called "As Far as We Know" and heard Steph's voice on it in his head. He recognized Steph's talent and invited him to make solo music in addition to his work with Everyday Everybody. Steph channeled the persona that came alive when he was improvising with Everyone Orchestra, and Brother Goodlove was born. The songs are deeply relevant and timely and are rightly striking a chord.

Stephane is the first to tell you he is not the best vocalist or guitar player technically. He does, however, know how to use his voice, his guitar, and his body as tools to interact with the energy of the audience for a moment of connection. He invests in the moment and plays each show as if it were his last. Steph knows how to get a crowd close, how to get them jumping, singing along. Every detail is tended to, including the clothes. The clothes are an extension of the art. He is playing for the person in the back of the room, for his teenage self, for Kevin, for the person who needs something from the show and may not even know it. Stephane becomes an amplified version of himself—his voice, his guitar, his movement, and his clothes. It is his job to fill the room.

Stephane has memories from growing up of looking his best for family outings and church on Sundays. For shows, he shows respect to his upbringing and to the paying audience by looking sharp. At game time, he dresses up as a student of the musical traditions and heroes who inspire him. It's a uniform, part of the equipment. He is telling a story and conveying a persona, a culture, and a freedom of expression.

When the uniform is on and sound check is complete, Stephane spends time in the crowd. He wants to get the pulse. He asks, *What do they need from me?* Then he and the band members take a nature walk around the neighborhood, taking in the context. They huddle up, and Steph offers a pep talk. They welcome the organizers to bring their hopes for the show into the circle. They share their feelings and intentions. They remember that the songs are bigger than them. Then they engage in a long, detailed group handshake that pays homage to old bandmates and inside jokes acquired along the way. They get their bodies in sync, then they head toward the stage together to make some music and, hopefully, some magic.

Agency grew in Stephane's body when he saw Kele as a lead man on stage and when he studied the ways men like Michael Jackson, Prince, and James Brown used their entire bodies—Black bodies—as instruments. This is one reason crafting and sharing our body stories can be so powerful. While we grow freedom and agency in our own bodies, we can put pressure on our limiting master narratives to include varied paths and possibilities so that others might grow in freedom and agency too. Creating art with his body in public is Stephane's passion. He steps on stage embodied, having done his work to inhabit his body, and he shines in a way that connects to the humanity inside us all. In his freedom, he invites us to seek freedom through embodiment too.

> *Who is a person you looked up to when you were young, who was walking a path you were interested in? What is one way you can support representation in society?*

Uninhabited

"I just saw the mouse again," Dan reported, entering our bedroom wearing only his towel. He took a longer look at me, and his annoyance fell away. With a mischievous expression, he approached me from behind and cupped each breast lovingly in his hands. "Your breasts look gigantic."

I pondered my reflection in the mirror. "They do," I agreed. "Maybe I'm pregnant," I added playfully before walking away.

Once I said it, the possibility took up space. The sound bite kept repeating in my mind. In the shower, on the downtown A train, typing on my work computer—my womb resonated with the hypothesis each time. *Maybe I am.* I spent the morning smiling at my little secret. *Maybe.* Each trip to the bathroom confirmed what I was beginning to believe was true. No blood. A coy *maybe* evolved to a hopeful one. Dabbling became desire.

On my way home from work I swung into Duane Reade on 125th Street and Amsterdam and purchased a two-pack pregnancy test. As the man rang up the singular purchase, there was no trace of embarrassment or conflict in my demeanor. I wanted to be pregnant. I was eager to become a mother. I was a prepared student, ready to pass the test.

On my way to the bathroom I sped by Dan, who was preoccupied with scoring a loaf of bread. I knew I was supposed to wait for morning, but the urgency to name my new reality blurred my better judgment. I was nervous and awkward. I fumbled. I peed crooked. The test was inconclusive. I spent the night withdrawn.

Morning brought renewed wonder and butterflies in my stomach. I urinated with calm precision. Two minutes later, I gasped and then giggled. A perfect, undeniable blue cross. Waves of joy lapped over me, one after another. Something alive had taken root in my body. I was full of potential.

Dan was elated. He researched doctors in Harlem. I started taking prenatal vitamins. We meandered up Riverside Drive and talked about when we should share the news and imagined how people would react. We cheered on our little bundle of cells. I kept the pregnancy test on the sink, smiling at it multiple times a day, needing a mirror held up to my truth. Dan suggested taking a picture of it so we could throw the stick away. He played with the aperture on the camera long enough to validate my excitement, pulling the cross into focus against the vanity.

My fashionable girlfriend took me to Athleta to start my maternity wardrobe. I was reluctant to make such temporary investments.

She steered me toward items that would shrink and expand with me. I bought two stretchy shirts and a pair of loose, lightweight black pants with a wide and forgiving elastic waistband. They were delectable. I named them my butter pants and began wearing them regularly. I braced myself to gain weight.

Dan and I started a list of names. I eliminated alcohol and coffee, deli meat and shellfish, and then, when nausea set in, all food except saltines and broth. Busy preparing a home, my body collapsed onto the couch after each workday. Every nap was necessary. Sleep felt like mercy. I was repulsed by Dan's smell and covered my nose with a blanket when we sat on the couch together. When I entered our apartment after work each day, I walked through a wall of smells made up of the food Dan had eaten hours before.

Days were long and hard. I felt lucky.

We downloaded an app to my phone that updated us on the baby's progress. Dan talked to my belly according to its multiplying size. *Hello, my little lentil. Good morning, my lovely cashew. I'm your dad.* I was unrelentingly constipated. My body had been taken over. I tried to approach my misery with curiosity. I tried to get out of the way.

Then one morning, sitting on the toilet, I recoiled at what I was holding. Contrasting the bright white nest of toilet paper in my hand was an amorphous glob of tissue, midnight blue streaked with shiny crimson.

"Shit."

"What?" Dan called from the kitchen, alarmed.

"I'm bleeding," was all I said, but it already felt more conclusive.

The bleeding continued and the cramping began, both much more intense than my monthly menstruation. My uterus was being kneaded. The blood and tissue loss were steady. I shook with the intensity of not wanting what was happening to be happening.

Dan, desperate for something to do, called the doctor's office. I wilted on the couch and curled into the pain, breathing deeply. The nurse would not talk to him. I was the patient. He handed me the phone.

"Tell me what's happening," a woman said.

"I'm bleeding heavily and cramping. Should I come in?"

"No, there is nothing we can do. It sounds like you are miscarrying. I will have a nurse call you tomorrow."

"Okay," I said. "Thank you."

My body moved almost involuntarily to maintain my schedule. I took the subway to Columbus Circle to meet with my thesis advisor, stopping by Duane Reade for heavy-duty pads on the way. I grabbed a bag of gummy bears at the counter, a pathetic attempt at comfort. When my advisor asked if I'd been crying, I blamed it on the beauty of a Paul Monette essay I was reading. I wrote down what she said about my writing project so I could reference it later. I heard but could not listen. My body was seeping. We spoke of her work, her love life, my writing, my thesis, and my impending graduation. There was so much to feel so little about.

That evening, I sat down on the couch, took a deep breath, and picked up the phone to call my mom. After floating from above in denial all day, I dropped back into my body. I tucked my knees into my stomach and held them there. I heard my voice say, "I am losing the baby." I started sobbing huge, lurching sobs. Saying it aloud was confession. Saying it aloud made it real and true.

"Oh honey, oh, I'm so sorry," she said. "I wish this wasn't happening. I wish I could take this away from you. I wish I could be there to hold you. I remember."

She struggled to conceive. The doctors told her she could not have children and then, after a stillborn baby, she had five healthy kids. Her story was supposed to be hopeful. I felt depleted and hollow. She felt far away. I wandered into the bedroom and closed my swollen eyes.

I went to work the next day, not quite knowing what else to do. The cloud surrounding me was laced with shame. With a whispering voice, shaky through tears, I told my boss what was happening. She hugged me, then launched into her story. She had seven miscarriages before flying to Russia to adopt three children with disabilities. The sound of my own love loss drowned out her voice. Midday, I moved to the hallway to take a call from a nurse. "I'm bleeding a lot. It's like my period but heavier, thicker, more painful. It has been a full day now," I told her.

She scheduled an appointment at a lab down the street from my apartment to have blood drawn to check hormone levels and confirm the miscarriage. A handful of strangers walked past while I was on the phone. No one seemed to notice that my heart was exposed to the wind. My body was being evacuated. How could they not stare?

That night I had a primal urge to amble the streets of Manhattan. I imagined finding a loose square of sidewalk, ripping at it until my fingernails were raw, until I encountered dirt. My body wanted to squat and bleed into the earth directly. Instead, I stayed inside, leaving the couch only to change my pad every few hours.

Dan dealt with his disembodied loss by fixating on catching the mice in our apartment. He pulled the stove out and deep-cleaned the floor. He set new traps. He researched best practices and explored the apartment for clues.

I fixated on my blood, which was all I had left. One morning in the shower, a particularly large clump of tissue got stopped in our hair catcher. I bent down, picked it up, and rolled it around between my fingertips, searching for signs of life. I wanted to see my baby. I wanted proof. I put the clot in the toilet but could not bring myself to flush it down.

After several phone calls and an hour on hold, a lab tech iterated what I already knew.

"Hi. My name is Ellie Roscher. I'm calling back about my hormone levels from blood work. To confirm a miscarriage."

"Yes, you miscarried," was all the man said.

"Okay, thank you."

Something became nothing. I called my siblings and a few friends and told them that I had been pregnant and now was not. *This is totally normal. One in four women miscarry. Just keep trying.* There is such little vocabulary for this loss. It is grieving an idea, slowly reeling back in the path that had unrolled ahead of you, filled with potential moments of little hands and innocent laughter. It's wondering how the space created, dense with dreams, would ever be filled. It's looking at every pregnant belly and every baby through the lens of loss. It's longing for something unseen, untouched. Nature abhors a vacuum.

The next day, I called the clinic one last time to cancel my next baby wellness checkup.

"Do you need to reschedule?" a woman asked.

"No, I miscarried," I said.

"I'm sorry," she said.

I reintroduced coffee and alcohol, deli meat and shellfish. I went to work. I went to class. I worked on my thesis. I watched a beautiful little girl twirling circles on the subway platform to the guitar music of a street performer. I watched her parents watch her. Dan watched me watch them. I watched until I had to turn away.

Our best friends called to announce that they were pregnant, due a week before ours would have been. Dan and I passed the phone back and forth, sharing our excitement and encouragement with them. Once we hung up, Dan cried for the first time. He told me he could feel the loss. The absence resided in the possibility of raising our children together. He had yet to catch a mouse.

———◊———

Just three months after the miscarriage, with the pain still raw and consuming, I got pregnant again. Instead of joy I felt exhaustion and dread. It felt like betrayal. I hated my caution, my skepticism, my preparation for an inevitable death. It was too soon. The grief was too thick, too heavy. I was still getting to know the child I would never meet. I eliminated coffee and alcohol, deli meat and shellfish. I switched to a new clinic. When I told people, my mouth smiled, but my eyes did not. Nausea, bloating, and constipation set back in and took hold. I curled in on my enlarged breasts, guarded.

Dan was timidly happy. We paced ourselves. I turned in my thesis and took my last classes. I ate sleeves of crackers at my work desk. My graduation ceremony was outside, and the smell of grass made me sick. I focused on not puking while Vera Wang gave a lovely speech. Dan decided we needed a change of scenery and found cheap tickets to Puerto Rico for a long weekend.

The cobblestone streets of Old San Juan smelled of fermenting fruit. Vibrant pink hibiscus crawled up blue and yellow walls. We wandered through the heat. My body was either asleep or longing to be so. I watched Dan sip rum. The clouds, full of rain, held their breath. The mountains whispered ancient hymns. I did not know what language to speak. I did not belong in such a beautiful place.

The musty hotel we shared with artists and shamans was cluttered with chipped busts, spider plants, and nymphs spitting water. One night we climbed to the rooftop patio and sat. The wind off the Atlantic caught my breath and something inside me came unstuck. Grief spilled. *I do not want this baby.* I admitted silently to myself. *I want the dead one.*

The tangled ball of yarn in my chest took a slow, full breath. I sat there for a long time, watching a large ship leave the bay.

In the heat of late summer, I spent the morning packing for a short-term research trip to Kenya and a permanent move to Minnesota. I stayed pregnant. My feelings remained muted and conflicted, no trace of recapturing the joy of the first pregnancy. Yet each new day brought hints of curiosity and glimpses of hope. *Maybe.*

I left boxes and suitcases open, kissed Dan goodbye, and headed to my second baby wellness checkup. The nurse informed me that I had lost weight, but my vitals were strong. The doctor started the ultrasound. As the image came into focus, her demeanor changed.

"Oh. Oh, no. I'm sorry. The baby stopped developing four weeks ago. There's no heartbeat." I watched her reach down, grab the automatic image printout, and throw it in the trash. "We should get it out as soon as we can so it doesn't cause an infection. Let me go check my schedule."

She hurried out of the room, leaving me alone, undone. A nurse came in to turn over the room, surprised to see me. Desperate to escape the pain welling up inside of me, I offered to go to the waiting room. Maybe if I kept moving it wouldn't be true. I sat between two women bursting with life. Expansive and happy. One held the hand of a man next to her. The other rubbed her belly.

The nurse approached. "Are you free tomorrow?"

I was. We set up a procedure time, and I left.

I kept a date with my friend in Chelsea. Shame loomed. I coped by disconnecting. We sat in her garden sipping tea. She didn't know I was pregnant or not pregnant, a difference that felt like a chasm, like whiplash. In her gaze, I was simply a friend, graduate student, and writer. For an hour or two, I pretended. It was a kind respite.

"Hi," Dan called from his home office when I returned. Unassuming, he finished what he was doing. Eventually he joined me on the couch. "How was your appointment?"

I started to cry. "The baby stopped growing. I'm going in tomorrow to get it removed." I knew something was happening to him and to us, but I could not get out from under the thing that was happening to me. The aloneness startled me. *Was it because I didn't let myself attach? Was my body inhospitable? Why wouldn't my body let the baby go?*

Twice the role of being a mother presented itself. Twice the existence of a baby made itself known. A different life unfolded in front of me now, filled with bitterness and void. I saw myself sidelined by a heavy vacuousness. What if this is my story?

I sent a group text to my family and a group email to my friends. The responses felt anemic and added to the despair. *God has a plan. This will work out. The pain will go away once you have a baby.* Dan brought me white wine and M&Ms. I tried to offer whatever was inside of me affection, to sense it before it was taken away, but it remained an elusive idea.

"The mouse," I whispered to Dan as I watched it scamper across the kitchen floor.

The next morning, I pulled my black butter pants over my belly. My body, still thinking itself pregnant, had grown even while the baby hadn't. At the hospital I adjusted my gown so the doctor could sit by my knees. She was slender and graceful. Her long black hair looked disheveled. I wondered how long she had been awake.

"I'm sorry we're meeting under these circumstances," she said. "The procedure is simple. We will put you to sleep, dilate your cervix, and apply light suction. Do you have any questions?"

I did but didn't ask.

I woke to a nurse shouting my name and shaking my shoulder. She handed me a small plastic bowl of graham crackers and glass of apple juice. My teeth wouldn't stop chattering.

"It's time to go," she said. I rose gingerly, revealing a large pool of blood on the white bed linens.

"I'm sorry," I said.

For six weeks I lived in a state of limbo, believing that my womb was vacant, but having no verification. I had no body memory of the expulsion.

The doctor at my post-procedure checkup entered the room and reported enthusiastically, "Everything looks absolutely perfect!" By perfect she meant empty. "Just keep trying!"

I bled in the Amsterdam airport. I bled an hour before my friend's baby shower. I felt unfurnished and abandoned. I cried taking my nephews to the Children's Museum, as kids joyfully dodged my legs. I cried at a baptism of someone else's baby. I felt forsaken and barren. My uterus used to feel healthy, normal, and powerful. Now it felt deserted and raked bare. The hollowness was excruciatingly heavy.

We moved to Minneapolis and found an apartment with no mice. Grief wrapped itself around me. I walked through my days apart. My bones felt dehydrated. The silence started making a scraping sound. Somewhere I found the courage to ask for help. An intuitive healer listened and seemed to understand. "You need words to honor what happened," she said. She invited me to name the two babies. *Were they babies? Did they count? Am I a mother?* She invited me to light two candles, to talk to the babies, to thank them for making me more wise and more compassionate in my brokenness, in my invisible scars, in my ethereal wounds. "Or plant a tree," she suggested, "anything tangible and visible to witness the life and loss."

I put both babies' due dates on my Google calendar to repeat annually. I bought a necklace with two interlocking squares, one slightly bigger than the other. I touched the squares to my throat several times a day. I pulled up the picture of the blue cross on my sink and let myself weep. I grieved the babies and the anticipation of the babies. For a brief time, my body offered safety and warmth to something forming. For a few months, the sound of my heartbeat acted as a lullaby. I looked for them in the clouds and the cool wind.

I took my basal temperature each morning. Dan brought me the thermometer while I remained warm under the covers. I decreased alcohol and caffeine as my normal. I took prenatal vitamins to keep me strong in the waiting. In the wilderness. Some days I could convince myself that any hint of movement in my midsection was a baby leaping inside me. Other days I cynically named it gas and moved on. I lived in two-week cycles of ovulation and menstruation, hope and wanting.

Months later, in the middle of nothing in particular, I started crying and couldn't stop. I wandered into the bedroom and crumpled up in a fetal position on the bed. Dan gave me a few minutes and then cautiously approached me. He sat by my abdomen and gently caressed my upper back.

"What's wrong?" he whispered.

He should have known. Two lives took up residence in my body and then they vacated. A million moments would never come to be. My ache echoed in the expanse. The sadness felt like waves, not words, and I was just too tired to translate them.

"I don't know," I lied.

He made three more slow circles over my shoulder blades and then rose. "I'll make us some lunch," he offered and left.

My miscarriage season was lonely. I longed for connection with my spouse, my friends and family, and the babies. I felt deep isolation from society and people I loved. I felt othered, barren, defective, and marked. I felt disconnected from my body as I came face-to-face with my body's limitation. I wanted to grow a child and be a mother. Maybe my body couldn't comply. The world pressured me to carry on, and all I wanted to do was wilt and honor my loss. I had to claim the body and the story right in front of me.

Although miscarriages are common, I was struck by the silence around them. So many pregnant people don't tell others they are pregnant until they are a trimester into their pregnancy. So many miscarriages remain invisible to outsiders. There is a lack of ritual and societal reverence for the loss of a fetus. Almost immediately I felt a drive to talk about my miscarriages, and every time I did people came to me with their stories of love and loss, appreciative of a space to share. I found deep connection there.

I wanted to write a story about my miscarriages for me so that I could spend time in the memories, honor the babies, name the pain, and metabolize the hurt. I wanted to write the story to share with other people who had similar loss to expand the canon of stories of miscarriage and help them feel less alone. I also wanted to write and share my story with the society that has not included fertility issues in the master narrative.

I left two delightful, healthy boys with my spouse to attend a five-day writing workshop through the Collegeville Institute with Enuma Okoro called Identity and (Dis)Belonging. These months of identity fluctuation between being pregnant and not pregnant, a potential mother or a potential barren woman, was a time of intense dis-belonging. Upon reading my essay, Enuma asked me when the miscarriages had happened. When I said six years prior, she said, "Oh, so recent." Telling stories takes time. Healing cannot be rushed.

I needed temporal distance from the pain to write a true story about it. My two healthy children played a role as I went into the pain to craft my story. It was important to me, however, to not include them in the story. There is no happy ending. My pain did not end with the birth of my sons. I will always wonder after these two who I lost.

I move through the world aware that I could have had one arm, but I have two. My parenting story is similar. I could have had no children to raise, but I have two. What came out of the grief was forged meaning and expanded identity. My children, all four of them, are the loves of my life, and I do not take them for granted. I hold the two who are with me close, one in each arm, basking in the goodness of what is.

> *Think about a moment something was happening to your body that you did not want to be happening. How has your identity expanded in response to that moment? What is one way you can create more space for stories of fertility issues, miscarriage, and infancy loss?*

Obedience and the Inner Imperative

Linda was born in Texas at the beginning of World War II. She wore a cowgirl hat and boots as often as she could, toting fake guns, delightfully encased in her own imagination.

Her father, Clark, had joined the National Guard as a teenager with the other guys in town. He said it felt like the Boy Scouts. When Linda was two, he took a ship from San Francisco to Hawaii with the infantry. He left Hawaii for Burma days before the attack on Pearl Harbor. In Asia, Clark was captured. As he was being marched to a prison camp, priests came out of the local Catholic mission and offered blankets to the American soldiers. Their compassion and courage touched Clark, and he promised himself that if he lived through the war, he would become Catholic.

Meanwhile, back in Texas, Linda's mother, Leila, received a telegram from the US War Department that Clark was missing in action and presumed dead. The wife of another solider received a postcard from the Emperor of Japan saying that her husband was a prisoner and Clark was with him. Leila didn't know what to think, believe, or hope.

Linda lived a lonely childhood. After raising seven children of her own and while grieving her missing son, Leila's mother-in-law, Esther, moved in to help care for Linda and her brother, Clark Jr. She often sent them outside to play, locked the screen door, and watched them from the bedroom window. Linda watched Clark Jr. leave for school every morning a bit crestfallen. Lucky, Linda's dog and only remaining playdate, stood guard while Linda made mud pies.

A few years later, with no word from her husband, Leila started dating a man named Steve. He was Catholic, and when Linda was five, she was baptized along with her mother and brother. She remembers climbing up on a chair in the sacristy so Father Harrison could put oil on her forehead as a blessing and salt on her tongue as a reminder that the path would not always be sweet. She also received a medal, which was the big draw for her.

When World War II ended, after four grueling years as a prisoner, Linda's dad was liberated. Clark suffered from malaria and starvation, lost most of his teeth, and became legally blind. Not wanting to send him home rail-thin, Clark's superiors had him eat as much food and take as many vitamins as he could to bring his body back to life while he awaited his departure. He called his wife and said, "It's me. I'm coming home."

The day Clark arrived in Texas, Leila had a date planned with Steve. She called him to cancel, picked her husband up at the train station, and drove to school to pick up Linda from the first grade. When Linda came out of school, she could see the silhouette of her dad's officer hat in the car window.

"Linda, this is your daddy," her mother said.

Linda was bewildered.

When they got home, Linda and her father sat on her bed, and she introduced him to her dolls. They had no idea how to relate to each other. He did not like Lucky, Linda's confidant. It was hard for him to see a dog treated so well and served meat after what he had survived.

Father Harrison met with Steve, Leila, and Clark to counsel them. They had some big decisions to make. If Leila married Steve, she couldn't receive communion, which was very important to her. Clark told Steve, "If I had died, I would be happy for you to marry my wife and raise my kids. But I didn't die. I am here. I'm home. This is my family. I want them back."

Linda's daddy came home, they moved to a new city, and all decided to try life together.

Linda went to school in Waco, Texas. Her mom was sick a lot, depressed with the choice she had made, the life she had given up, and the life she had. Her dad became angry, struggled, yelled, and sometimes whacked Linda upside the head. When Linda was in the fourth grade, a group of Sisters of St. Joseph of Carondelet (CSJ) came from St. Louis to teach. They were happy, friendly, and loved children. "I watched them, and I knew I wanted to be a nun," Linda said. "I was devout. I wanted to be holy. I wanted to help people. My dream became clear."

When Linda was a teenager, Jim Crow laws ruled, and she hated them. The sisters had taught her to think of her body as an instrument of justice. Sometimes she drank from the wrong drinking fountain or sat at the back of the bus on purpose to show her disdain.

Linda graduated high school and prepared to enter the convent at age seventeen. She was thrilled. "I wanted to give myself completely to God. Nothing else would do." Her parents drove her to the train station and waited with her there. On the other side of the tracks, there was a circus in full swing. She looked intently at the performers for a few minutes, fascinated, then climbed onto the train for the long journey ahead.

Linda joined a group of fifty-three young women joining the order. They wore all black and did not talk except thirty minutes of recreation time in the evenings. They prepared to take vows of chastity, poverty, and obedience. There were curtains around each bed, which Linda thought was romantic. Some young ladies pined after the dances happening at the school next door. Some snuck away to smoke cigarettes and wondered aloud what they had done. Linda couldn't relate. She was a rule follower. Obedient above all else. She had no interest in boys or dancing or romance; she never imagined getting married and having children, so the sacrifices seemed easy. She lay in bed at night thinking, "I made it. I'm following my dream."

During her two-and-a-half years of preparation, Linda started feeling attracted to women. With no lesbian role models or language for her feelings, she didn't know what the attraction meant. She didn't know what she was giving up; she only knew she wasn't interested in a traditional marriage and family. Linda took her vows and became a Sister of St. Joseph.

With an undergraduate degree in English, Linda was sent to teach five-year-old kids in an elementary school. "I didn't know how to teach, and the kids knew it." She didn't want to teach and longed for a job she was passionate about. She longed for connection.

When Linda was twenty-eight, her mother died of leukemia. She was heartbroken. She loved her mother dearly and looked up to her for the hard choices she had made. Trips home became awkward. Her daddy told her, "You can come visit the house whenever you want," as if he knew she wouldn't be coming to see him. He was a good man; she loved him and felt sorry for him, but there was no relationship there. He drank heavily. She concluded solemnly, "It was not good." She reflected, "Mother kept us all to herself. Maybe we joined her in not being glad he was home."

In places like Minneapolis, the women's movement was in full force compared to Green Bay, Wisconsin, where Linda lived. With a longing to be where the action was, she went to Minneapolis to visit her friend Mary, who took her to a feminist bookstore and proceeded to mail Linda piles of books. They saw Cris Williamson, an outspoken lesbian musician and activist, in concert. Mary brought Linda to the Lake Street Bazaar, where at a booth they met Karen Clark, a lesbian running for the house of representatives in Minnesota. Blown away that Karen was an out lesbian running for office, Linda signed up to help with mailings and flyers.

Karen called Linda that night, asking her to door-knock with her, and Linda said, "Yes, of course." It was exciting to be asked. Karen's commitment was attractive. Through her work with Karen, Linda met lovely lesbian couples and thought, "Oh, I could have that." She felt a glimmer of hope in her body.

During her time in Minneapolis, Linda also heard peace activist Sister Rita Steinhagen give a homily, and Linda felt a deep resonance in her chest. She thought, "I am going to work with her someday."

Years later, a lot had changed. The sisters had stopped wearing habits. The mass was no longer in Latin. The sisters placed an emphasis on justice and were encouraged to do volunteer advocacy in their spare time. Linda called the St. Joseph House, a Catholic worker shelter for women and children. Sister Rita Steinhagen picked up. Linda asked if she could volunteer, and Rita said yes. "I don't have a car," Linda worried. "I will watch the donations and find you a bicycle," Rita promised.

Living with Rita Steinhagen, deepening her activism and advocacy, and working at the St. Joseph House, Linda fell in love with the simplicity of life and passion for justice of the Sisters of St. Joseph in Minneapolis. She knew Minneapolis was a place where she could tend to the questions rising inside of her. She was longing for a job that could use all her passion. She wanted closeness and a deeper conversation. When her superior told her to come home to Green Bay, she shocked herself by saying, "I have an inner imperative to stay here." And she did.

By this point, Linda was sure she was a lesbian and conflicted about what that meant in terms of her vocation as a sister. Linda went to an Al-Anon group for lesbians for years. There she was out as a lesbian, but not as a nun. She feared they would treat her differently, that they wouldn't understand, but it felt increasingly uncomfortable and restrictive to keep her identity as a nun secret. The women in the group were so sure of themselves. She hoped to be more like them, and yet she loved being a member of her community.

With her fellow nuns, she kept her sexuality secret. In her body, it felt like the secret took up more space and carried more weight over the years. She was protecting a part of her identity in these meaningful communities, bracing herself. The hiding was exhausting, which prodded her toward coming out. She felt fragmented and yearned for wholeness, but the wider Catholic landscape was daunting. For example, the archbishop had demanded that Dignity Twin Cities, a Catholic LGBTQ+ rights organization, meet at a non-Catholic site. If she came out, she thought the leadership in her community would ask her to leave.

She sought out a counselor and talked with a Jesuit friend in hopes of becoming clearer about her choice to stay or leave the sisters. They both said the same thing to Linda: The price you would pay for your sexual freedom may be too high. You love your community. If you can stay, stay.

She stayed and found closeness in her work as a graduate student in counseling. She got very good at writing grants and raised 8 million dollars in grant funding over eight years for justice organizations like the Phyllis Wheatley Community Center and Summit Academy OIC. She found closeness in her work as codirector of the Office of Consociates, recruiting, supporting, and discerning with people who wanted to live out the tenets of the Sisters of St. Joseph without taking vows. She found closeness in her community, with the nuns she lived with, and by showing up at court hearings, protests, and demonstrations with them to demand truth and justice. She got on a bus to the March on Washington, which, she said simply, was "so much fun." Where she showed up mattered. Her body itself was her voice of dissent. Protesting in community strengthened her on the inside. Her inner imperative took up more space. Finding relationships that offered mental, emotional, and spiritual closeness made Linda brave enough to consider coming out as a lesbian nun.

One day, Linda was recovering from surgery and reading a book about Harvey Milk. The sun was warm and bright, streaming in through the window. The thought came to her, "If you are living in the closet, why don't you pray in the closet?" She got up, entered her closet, closed the door, and stood with the hangers poking her in the back. It was dark, quiet, and a little lonely. She heard in her mind Rita, Mary, and her friends calling to her, *What are you doing in the closet, Linda? Come out into the sun.*

That day she committed to herself, "I am not going to die in the closet. I am going to find a way to come out."

Her chance came soon thereafter. The Sisters of St. Joseph were hosting an assembly on sexuality. They brought in a dynamic sister from the West Coast who was out. Linda signed up to be on a panel and prepared to tell her story. She feared getting in trouble and getting the leadership in her community in trouble. "For better or worse, I am the obedient daughter of a POW, and I love being in my community."

When I asked her what inspired her to sign up for the panel, she answered without hesitation, "The inner imperative." Over the years of placing herself in spaces of protest, her inner imperative had become embodied. It was physically painful to be closeted as a nun in her Al-Anon group and closeted as a lesbian with the Sisters of St. Joseph. She didn't feel integrity in the closet. She wanted to feel at home in LGBTQ+ spaces as a nun. She needed to be honest about who she was. It was time to claim her whole self publicly.

Linda sat on the panel and came out to her community as a lesbian. At the end of the session, a woman on the leadership team said to the group, "This is a holy day." Since then, Linda has never felt like they were ashamed of her or wanted her to leave. Her hope—to be who she is, be honest, and be welcome—has come true.

Linda got involved in the homophobia and heterosexism working group of the CSJ Justice Commission. They made a banner that read: CSJs Standing for Human and Civil Rights and walked in the Pride parade for years. Each time Linda was a little afraid they would get in trouble. Each time she was met with uproarious cheers from the crowd. Placing her body in that parade as a lesbian nun brought a moment of relief for her and for those gathered who had been harmed by the church. It felt dangerous and rich with healing. Ultimately, daily, Linda chooses to advocate from the inside, to fight for herself and the rights of people suffering from the prejudice of civil and church leaders while remaining a nun. There are moments, like when the archbishop fought fiercely to keep gay marriage illegal, that are heartbreaking. She said, "It's sad when you have to protect the community from the church." It feels like she is spanning a divide, required to hold herself together, reminding herself that she is loved. She does not want to participate in her own abuse. She lived halfway for too long. Yet she isn't walking alone, and the strength of the sisters buoys her.

Linda has been volunteering for Reclaim Mental Health Service, an organization offering mental health support to queer and trans youth, for fifteen years. Linda observes the youth and how beautiful they are together. They know just how to support each other. Watching a new generation of queer folks care for each other so well is healing and hopeful for her. She took part in a fashion show, where everyone brought random wardrobe gems from basements, garages, and attics. The youth created outfits for themselves and the nuns, who strutted their stuff in platform boots and boas.

The youth also named their bingo team The Twistahs and challenged The Sistahs to fiercely fun games. The Sistahs won the last bingo match before COVID-19 stopped the gathering. The trophy, which is not a trophy at all but rather a music box, stands in Linda's room, casting a rainbow on her wall.

When I talk about my Catholic upbringing, I say that bad-ass feminist nuns raised me. The nuns I am referring to are the Sisters of St. Joseph. They founded the school my mom and I went to, the school where I returned to teach. I have witnessed them protest The School of the Americas, war, poverty, and the death penalty. I watched them advocate for prison reform, immigration rights, and gender equity. They taught me to listen to the most vulnerable community members, believe them, and join them in the work at every turn. They did female community and transformative justice so well that as a young girl I pictured myself joining them. I have always been drawn to intentional community and collaboration. I was honored to sit with Sister Linda and listen to her story. She pulled a Lady of Guadalupe mug out of her walker for me. She wanted to know all about my work and my books and thanked me profusely for listening well when all I could do was thank her for who she is and for gifting me her time and her story.

> *What groups have you worked to change from the inside? Where is one place you can put your body on purpose to advocate for human rights?*

The Expansive Silence

Andrew was the first deaf person I interviewed for one of my books. We met up on Zoom at the height of the COVID-19 surge. We tried to maintain eye contact as much as possible while communicating through an ASL interpreter off-screen. Even mediated by a screen, I was struck by how much passion and compassion Andrew exuded. For someone who doesn't speak with his voice, he is refreshingly loud. As you read his story, notice how you picture him when I quote him. Give him the courtesy of imagining his animated face and his body creating a whole world with his words.

Andrew does a quick scan of every room he walks into. Is anyone signing? Is there an interpreter? Almost always, unless he has planned to be there ahead of time, the answer to both questions is no. Eventually, someone will try to talk to him. He'll point to his ear, signaling that he is deaf. It gives him a moment of power. The room shifts.

Then folks generally have one of three reactions. Some people pull away awkwardly, feeling like they don't have tools to proceed. Some will try to connect by telling him what they imagine it must be like to be deaf. Or some will pity him and treat him like he is helpless. He doesn't want their pity. So he helps them. He does the work, offering the tools. He suggests a piece of paper and pen, or texting, or text-to-voice software. He reminds them of the myriad ways humans can communicate.

When people see Andrew signing, they think first about what he can't do. "So many people think that because I am deaf, I'm done. My life is nothing. They push me aside and move on." He doesn't hear and speak in the same way I do. But he is quick to remind me that doesn't mean he can't listen and speak. In fact, he argues animatedly he does both better than most hearing people. He's patient in listening and speaking.

"My hands are my life," Andrew says clearly. "I have the privilege of having hands. I use my hands to show emotion and engage in the power of language." Andrew's hands are the heart of his language, but when he speaks, he uses his whole body. And because he uses his whole body to speak, he watches people's whole bodies as they speak too. "Signing is natural. A projected voice is so limited. Hearing people too often rely on words and underutilize their bodies. They don't take up enough space. We use our whole body in ASL to show what we mean. The way you choose to sign a word has power. We say things with our bodies that you can't hear."

Andrew honed his emotional intelligence by watching body language and reading the room. There are words he might be missing, but the bodies are telling the truth. He is a professional code-switcher. He can talk to hearing people who do and don't sign, and to deaf people who do and don't sign. He works so that the hearing people aren't confused or frustrated. The world of the hearing requires him to figure out how to fit in.

As a kid, one of six people in his house, Andrew was the only one who didn't hear. He often felt left out. He used his body to get people's attention. "I got frustrated, feeling outside of the conversation, and I lashed out in anger. I vocalized and stomped and grabbed onto my dad until he stopped and listened to me." He tried hearing aids, but they were painful and caused ringing in his ears. Without them he felt freer. He figured out how to communicate through signing and with his body. He appreciates his family for reacting and listening to him.

"I'm a loud person. My family taught me that being loud was good. So I shout. I scream if need be. With deaf people, I sign big and take up space with my hands, but I am calm because I trust I will be heard. With hearing people, my hands sign smaller and more contained, but I use other things like vocalizing or stomping to be loud enough to be heard. I get bigger with my emotions. I'll repeat the sign for *What are you talking about?* until they stop and include me."

Andrew has two parents and three siblings who are hearing. One of his hearing siblings is his twin, Ben. Ben is not fluent in sign language like his two sisters. He never had to be. From a young age, Ben and Andrew communicated with their own language. Deeply connected as twins, they understood each other's body language and noises, like the way an older sibling translates baby talk for a younger sibling. As they grew, their connection grew, and their language grew. They communicate with a combination of finger spelling and signs, and to this day, they are the only two who can understand it.

Andrew watched Ben grow up as a hearing person who looked just like him. Ben doesn't sign with his friends. He doesn't have to work as hard to be heard or included. When Andrew was twelve, thirteen, and fourteen, he had moments of jealousy. He had moments he wished he could hear. "I thought Ben had everything. I wanted to be more like him, and knew he would never want to be more like me. I only saw what I didn't have." Those feelings didn't last forever. "If we switched, we wouldn't be us. If we could both hear, we would have the same experience of the world. We'd be too much alike, and it would be boring. Ben is there and I am here. Now I'm glad I'm me."

Andrew feels very lucky to live in a hearing family that cares, that took the time to learn how to sign and support him. Not all deaf people have that. Not all deaf people are taught to sign, and then they get blamed for being lazy. "How do you learn if no one is talking to you? If you can't afford college? I am deaf, but I am a White and able-bodied deaf person who had the wealth to go to college. I have a lot of privilege."

Minnesota has a strong deaf community. There are Facebook groups, walking groups, and beer-drinking groups. Andrew says, "I love our deaf community, but we have our problems. A lot of deaf people identify so strongly with being deaf that they cannot see their other privileges. Within the community, there is a hierarchy. White-body supremacy puts the idea in our heads that my deafness is more important than other forms of oppression, but it's not. My first experience in the world is as a White person, then a deaf person. I walk into a room and know I am safe. Some people who use ASL will judge others and say, 'That's not ASL enough,' when really what they mean is, 'That's not White enough.' White deaf people, including myself, still have a lot of work to do around oppression. I don't understand what it's like to be a person of color who is deaf.

"So many people in our community are deaf plus. Deaf plus Native. Deaf plus blind. I can see. I can use my hands. My family signs, so I know how to communicate, and I know I deserve to be heard. That all matters. That's privilege."

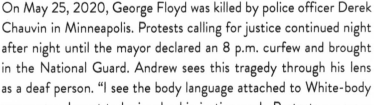

On May 25, 2020, George Floyd was killed by police officer Derek Chauvin in Minneapolis. Protests calling for justice continued night after night until the mayor declared an 8 p.m. curfew and brought in the National Guard. Andrew sees this tragedy through his lens as a deaf person. "I see the body language attached to White-body supremacy. I want to be involved in justice work. Protests are scary for our deaf community, though, because we can't always protect ourselves. There are rarely translators there. If we can't hear a siren or verbal warnings, it's confusing. It's hard to navigate chaotic situations. If someone grabs my arms, my communication tool has been taken away from me. It's like someone covering your mouth. If a cop approaches me and doesn't sign, and the situation escalates, I might not be able to defend myself properly. That's very scary. But our cycle as White people is: We look. We get mad. We move on. We need to stay and fight this time."

Even and maybe especially in moments of extreme conflict, Andrew is convinced the hearing community can learn from the deaf community. He has come a long way from when he was a child, internalizing the lie that hearing is better. Now he realizes it shouldn't be him trying to fit in all the time, but other folks working to shift their communities to include him for their own good. Our words fall short. We need more than words. We need to talk about, look at, and really listen to bodies. Take, for example, the word *violence*. It is one word, and when it is said, two people might think two different things. But ASL offers several signs for the word *violence*, depending on the context. The signs look different and convey much different emotion. One sign depicts violence happening *around* you versus another that shows violence happening *to* you, and responsibility is placed differently depending on the sign. One sign for violence points the index finger of one hand up while the index and middle fingers of the other hand swing and hit it. In this case, the victim of violence is passive, implying innocence. So which sign you choose to talk about the violence in George Floyd's murder will communicate a lot about what you are choosing to convey.

As people sign, they make micro-decisions that are then discussed, like which sign for violence is most appropriate for the context. What is happening with the eyes, face, and body of the signer adds layers and texture. The language is a dynamic, alive, relational dance that is up for discussion. The word *racism* is too big to just be a word. Andrew appreciates how the sign for the word requires emotion and body expression to do it justice. All people see the same visual representation and not just a set of letters that stimulate a different visual in our minds. Andrew and many in his deaf community use the phrase, "What I mean to say is . . . ." all the time to check in and make sure their messages are being properly conveyed. Imagine if the hearing community took cues from the deaf community about the integrity of word choice and body language as valued elements in compassionate communication. Imagine if we were as committed as Andrew to hearing and being heard. Imagine if, like Andrew, our imaginations were alive and our creativity engaged when we spoke, if we could see a vivid picture of every word, if we used our whole body on purpose to articulate and connect.

Imagine a world where the hearing community turned toward the deaf community to learn how to listen and speak.

Speaking with Andrew reminded me of how rigid and lazy we can get around language and connection. I think about living in Uruguay, and how tired I was at the end of the day after speaking in my second language. My mind was so active, and I used tools beyond my words every single day to get my ideas across. It took effort on my part and on the part of the folks with whom I was communicating. I think about writing an essay, spending a day wandering around in my mind to find the right word to convey an image or emotion on the page. I think about my young kids, and how clever they are at communicating when the right word isn't available. I loved the feeling of being so deeply in tune with them, communicating clearly even before they had words.

I do not need to code-switch or work hard at my language often because I am in the dominant culture. Andrew reminded me how much I lose by not taking the time to listen to people who speak differently. It is so often the people outside the dominant culture who can see the limits of the dominant systems and how they perpetuate barriers to connection. What if we asked them what they see and took the time, with hearts wide open, to listen?

When was a time your words were misunderstood? How can you better use your tools beyond your words to communicate?

Claiming our bodies as a means of connection opens us up to intentionally embracing pleasure. Our bodies can identify six unique, vivid flavors in a single sip of complex red wine. They can take in the grandeur of a mountain range, causing an internal, hushed sense of awe. Our shoulders relax at the first breath of spring, thawing our hearts and turning our chins back up to the sky in hope. Our bodies experience pure ecstasy in lovemaking where we cease to be able to identify where one person ends and the other begins. Our ears process the intricate harmony created by an orchestra; a sound powerful enough to transform our thoughts. Actively noticing the pleasure our bodies can change our mindset, and dare I say worldview, harboring a gratitude for our bodies and their ability to connect, expanding our sense of abundance in the world.

Bodies are brilliant tools of connection, often smarter than we give them credit for. Consider athletes and actors who work to suspend thought to clear up room for purer, unencumbered physical genius. Consider the communication that happens between a baby's body and a birthing parent's body during pregnancy and breastfeeding. Or the body's ability to warn us of danger, maintain homeostasis, and stay alive with numerous involuntary and continuous actions. Bodies are nothing short of astounding. How can you approach your body with reverence, curiosity, and honesty, and reflect awe in your body story?

Reflection Questions

* What did your body experience while reading these stories? Did any of them resonate with you and your body's story?
* What is your body doing when you feel a deep connection to a person or to an activity?
* Talk about a moment when music communicated something to you.
* Which of your senses do you underutilize?
* Has your community ever asked you to hide a part of who you are? Are there two parts of your identity that are in conflict? How do you work toward wholeness?
* Do you use your body to speak? Do you choose your words carefully? What is your body language communicating right now?
* When in your life has your body served another person or the community?

* How does your body connect with other bodies on social media? How do tools of technology enhance connection? How is it limiting?
* Talk about a time you used your body to connect with others.
* With whom in your life would you like to build a deeper connection?
* What narratives exist in your birth family, found family, place of work, communities, and society at large that came to mind while reading these stories about connection and communication? Do you have counter-stories that could expand the perception of the dominant culture?

Writing Prompts

Set a timer for five minutes. Start with the phrase "What I meant to say is . . ." and finish the sentence. Write a litany of sentences that all begin with that phrase or write stream of consciousness without pausing or overthinking it.

Write about a time when words fell short of your communication needs. Write about a time you were able to connect and communicate beautifully without using words.

Your 80-year-old self meets . . .
    . . . your 20-year-old self
    . . . you right now
    . . . you in 5 years
    What does the 80-year-old say to all the versions of you? (Feel free to pick different ages.)

Breath Practice

Find a comfortable seated posture with a tall spine. Gently seal your lips and breathe through your nostrils. Tuck the index and middle fingers of your right hand down to touch your palm, keeping your thumb and ring finger elevated.

Close the left nostril with your ring finger and inhale through the right nostril.

Release the left nostril, close the right nostril with your thumb, and exhale through the left nostril.

Inhale through the left nostril.

Release the right nostril, seal the left, and exhale through the right.

Inhale right.

Switch. Exhale left.

Inhale left.

Switch. Exhale right.

Continue for about ten breath cycles, ending on an exhale through your right nostril, and then return to your natural breath.

This may be difficult during allergy season or when you have a cold. In that case, you can place your attention on alternate nostrils without closing the nostril off with your hand.

Body Practices

Dance. Turn on some music or not. Grab a person you trust or not. Move your body intuitively without overthinking it. Drop into your body and move how it wants to move with a variety of movements.

If dancing makes you self-conscious, when did that self-consciousness start? Did your ancestors give up dancing? Did you? When did you lose the suppleness and inhibition of a child? How can you reclaim it?

Sit down on the floor close to a wall, facing it. Lie down on the floor and situate your rear end flush up against the wall with your legs up the wall. If this is difficult, try the posture against a couch with your knees bent. Place your arms straight out in a T shape or along the sides of your body if it is more comfortable. Allow the top of your body to melt toward the back of your body and the floor. Let the earth hold you up. With every few exhales, relax your skin and muscles deeper. Release any gripping in your body, then your mind, then your breath. Stay here for several moments and notice if anything comes up. Notice sensations in your body. Notice if your mind wants to wander. Notice any shift that comes with the change of perspective. It can often be more restful when we rest consciously. Create stillness and dwell there. You are worth your time.

(Do not do this practice if you are pregnant.)

Three

Bodies Persevere
Choosing Our Story

The wound is the place where the Light enters you.

—Rumi,
Suffering and Hope in the Enchanting Garb of Poetry

When I work with teenagers, I have them brainstorm and categorize the myriad messages they receive from the outside world, asking, "What words would your parents or guardians use to describe you? How about your siblings and extended family? How might your teachers describe you? Or your coaches? What words would your friends use? What role do you play in your friend group? Who would your teammates say that you are? Your classmates? How might a stranger looking at your social media profiles describe you?"

I have them look at the list and notice who sees them clearly, who may have a limited or misguided view, and which messages if any might be untrue and downright harmful. They notice which messages resonate. They make intentional choices as to which messages to accept, which to revise, and which to dismiss. I ask them, "Who do you say that you are?" They write a series of "I am" statements that reflect their true self.

The messages we receive from other people can be powerful when we internalize them, influencing us to live small. We can get used to and get comfortable in the boxes others make for us even if they are restricting. Minnie Bruce Pratt writes that every time our limited being expands, we experience it as an "upheaval, not catastrophe, more like a snake shedding its skin than like death. The old constriction is sloughed off with difficulty, but there is an expansion: not a change in basic shape, but an expansion, some growth, some reward for struggle and curiosity." The change, the growth, and the expansion can feel like a loss. We are letting go of lies and habitual ways of living that were familiar and comfortable. Even if they were limited, they were ours. Pratt wonders, "Our fear of the losses can keep us from changing. What is it, exactly, we are afraid to lose?"

The stories in this chapter are body stories of people who recognized how other people's stories about them were not serving them. They were brave enough to deny the constricting messages from other people and write their own expansive stories. They sloughed off the old skin, sustained the loss, and embraced the growing pains. In so doing, they grew their sense of freedom and agency in their bodies. In so doing, they became more embodied, more in touch with their true selves, and are living toward deeper healing and wholeness.

Claiming Autonomy

Cameron was born into a family of hockey players and coaches. Even though they come from five generations of lawyers too, skating was the real family profession. Their grandfather, born in 1924, played hockey. He got polio on the way home from World War II, which ended his skating, but he went on to coach. Cameron's dad has never missed a year of making a rink in the backyard. On the ice by age two, Cameron played hockey in kindergarten and first grade.

Cameron has always been small, shorter than their friends. Family and strangers alike turned "So tiny, so cute!" into a refrain. They internalized that their goodness was somehow tied to their tiny cuteness. Buttoning up their uniform shirt before heading off to first grade, Cameron has their first memory of frowning at their tummy, thinking of themself as fat.

In the second grade, Cameron switched from hockey to ice skating. It wasn't a school sport; it was a world unto itself. Cameron had school friends and skating friends. By fourth grade, they had a private coach and competed in seven or eight competitions a year. Permanent calluses formed on their fingers from lacing up their skates. At age eleven, they got their axel. By the end of middle school, Cameron got their double salchow and started competing in synchronized skating too.

In high school, Cameron missed a lot of school to travel to competitions. They were not allowed to sled or ski for fun; they were only allowed to be injured while skating. Skating was their job. Both their parents worked full-time jobs, in part to pay over $1,000 a month for synchronized skating lessons, ice time, and coaching. One of Cameron's coaches played mind games and had favorites. She'd tell a girl through the loudspeaker that she was sticking her butt out. She'd scream at a girl, blaming her for "ruining everything" if she fell, resulting in a lower score. Every finger had to be placed in the right position. Girls wore SPANX and dyed their hair to please her. Tiny and cute were expected and awarded points. Cameron's purpose was to be gazed upon, to be pleasing to the judges, who doled out value in increments of tenths of a point.

In synchronized skating, teams compete in a short and a long program. There are twenty skaters on a roster and sixteen compete. Picture a gaggle of girls, in matching sparkling dresses with short, flowy skirts, their faces covered with thick makeup and their hair pulled back in shiny, secure, and matching buns. Junior year in high school, Cameron was an alternate in the short program, sharing a spot with their best friend. Two weeks before nationals, Cameron's team was in Milan, Italy, competing in the Spring Cup. From the sidelines, Cameron watched a girl on their friend's line fall during the short program. The line didn't recover in time to perform the following element, which dropped their score significantly. Coach replaced Cameron's friend with Cameron in the short program for nationals.

Over the next two weeks, Cameron bit the insides of their cheeks raw. They could barely sleep from nerves. At nationals, during the warmup, Cameron thought, "*I'm not going to be able to do this.*" But they did. They have no memory of the short program skate, but it went well, and Cameron skated off the ice right into a huge hug from their coach. The team won nationals.

At the junior worlds in Sweden, Cameron skated well in the short program yet again and the team place fourth. Cameron solidified their place in the short program.

They continued to skate well under pressure, helping their team to a second-place finish at nationals and a third-place finish at junior worlds in Switzerland the following year. After receiving a medal at junior worlds, Cameron untied their skates and took off their dress. Slaphappy and beaming, the achievement had fully sunk in. It was a moment that permanently changed them, a moment no one could ever take away. Then and only then did Cameron finally allow themself to think, "*I earned this. I am a part of this. I belong.*"

On the last weekend of April in Cameron's senior year of high school, they tried out for the hockey cheer team at the University of Minnesota. They went straight from tryouts in Mariucci Arena to their club, where they skated with the team from nationals and worlds for the last time in their spring ice show. On the drive home, they listened to a voicemail telling them they made the U of M hockey cheer team.

By college, Cameron had lost twenty-five pounds. They lost baby weight in their face and with their bone structure visible, they looked older. At five feet, two inches, even five pounds heavier or lighter was highly noticeable. A coach commented, "You look good." It was a new, more mature phase of tiny and cute. Their competition dress felt looser, which felt good. They were eighteen, toned, and strong. They started getting a lot of attention. Strangers greeted them, opened doors for them, and gave them free stuff. U of M teammates commented that they looked different from at tryouts. It took a while for Cameron to consciously realize they were restricting their diet, and then they started doing it on purpose. They were better at restricting when they weren't trying to restrict than when they noticed and tried. "I'm not even good at having an eating disorder," Cameron bemoaned.

Cheering was different from synchronized skating competitions. They learned how to sit. They weren't supposed to touch their face or hair or adjust their uniforms. If someone was rude, they replied, "Go Gophers." If someone took a picture up their skirt, they kept skating. "I know how to yawn while smiling," Cameron said. "The rules, expectations, and culture communicated to us that you are not a person. You are part of the venue."

Being on the hockey cheer team earned Cameron a $250 book scholarship and the ability to skate at Mariucci Arena for free. They also got access to trainers and tutors. Cameron and the hockey cheer team got letter jackets and matching practice uniforms. They performed at home games and invitationals at the Excel Center where the Minnesota Wild play hockey. In Excel's arena, they had their own locker room, leaving them starstruck. Cameron's first and third year, the U of M hockey team made the Frozen Four tournament, and Cameron skated in front of 20,000 people. They loved it—the cheering, skating, signing autographs, and posing for pictures. "It was the Minnesota equivalent of being a Disney princess," Cameron laughed. They admitted to thinking that hockey was boring, except for high-stakes third period play when a big game was on the line. "But when you start a cheer and an entire stadium full of people follow? That feels incredible."

Cameron and their high school boyfriend kept dating for the first year of college. When they broke up, Cameron enjoyed being single. Then Cameron started dating a guy named Max. He drank a lot, was very protective, and wanted to be with them all the time. He knew their schedule to the minute. Cameron wrote his papers for him, picked him up from the bar, and saved him when he started choking on his own vomit in his sleep. They hung out with Max's friends and family significantly more than Cameron's. Eventually, Cameron had to ask Max's permission to hang out with friends. They existed for his pleasure, adjusting to please. It was a role they knew well.

Max never hit Cameron, but he slammed doors and punched walls around them, and dispensed odd punishments like taking a pile of Cameron's clothes and pouring pop on them. He was a charmer, always talking himself out of outbursts and talking himself into the good graces of people to suit his agenda.

Over New Year's, a young woman on Cameron's dorm floor went to Chicago for the weekend with friends. Cameron stayed in Minnesota. By the river in Chicago, a guy dropped his phone in the water and Cameron's floormate went in to retrieve it and drowned. When Cameron received the news, Max laughed, "Well, she was being stupid."

Cameron was horrified. "*That's not a human reaction,*" they thought. They looked in Max's eyes and saw something missing behind them, less light. They said to Max, "She was a good person."

That snapped him out of it, and he backpedaled, but it was too late. Cameron saw something in him they couldn't unsee. Cameron tried to leave Max, and there were consequences, so they stayed. Cameron started lying to their friends about him, downplaying fights and defending him when friends encouraged them to try to leave again. Cameron shut down and went into survival mode.

Max often used sexual coercion as a mode of control. On one occasion, Cameron mustered, "I really didn't want to," and Max simply replied, "I could tell." A few months into therapy, Cameron realized what Max did to them in the context of a seemingly mutual dating relationship was indeed rape.

That June, Cameron left Max right before traveling to Spain to study abroad, hoping the geographical distance would support their safety and healing. When they arrived back home, tanned and full of stories, Max was right there to greet them. The time and distance did hone Cameron's clarity and courage, however. They saw Max as a scared little boy, and Cameron's fight-or-flight mode kicked in. "My body told me I had to get out of there. My legs had to move. It was the first time I listened to my body in his presence."

The last time Cameron left Max, he stalked them, which in some ways was worse than being with him. It's easy for Cameron to feel shame about how long it took to leave for good, but each time they left, it was closer to a permanent fissure. Cameron disclosed the abusive relationship and filed a restraining order against Max to a woman named Lauren at the U of M's Aurora Center, which serves survivors of sexual assault and harassment on campus. Max had forty-five days to contest it but never did. "I never married him or had kids with him," Cameron proudly claimed. "I got out without ties." They haven't heard from him since.

In 2015, Cameron spoke publicly as a survivor of sexual assault through the Break the Silence organization. Their post read:

> My name is [deadname], and I am a survivor of sexual abuse.
> I break my silence because it wasn't my fault.
> I invited an abuser into my life, but I did not invite the abuse.
> I break my silence because my body is mine, my life is mine, my future is mine.
> I am not defined by my tragedy.
> I break my silence because he did not break me.

Five years later, they named Max publicly saying he abused them for 18 months and raped them multiple times.

Around this time, Cameron's brother was home for Christmas and commented, "You are really skinny."

Cameron changed the subject immediately and realized, "I would rather talk about being raped than about skipping meals."

They had done a lot of work to be able to talk about being a survivor of sexual assault. That had been the priority. They had not yet turned toward their restricted eating and body image and were not ready to hear concerned comments about their weight.

Cameron restricts their eating more when there is a lot of change in their life. Even good change can encourage less eating, like years after leaving Max when they started dating again or when their skating jumps are going well. They said, "Life is easier when I'm skinny, and being better at my jumps is a side effect of that." Being a strong athlete helped hide the problem. Cameron names their thin privilege, pretty privilege, and able-bodied privilege, being naturally slight and building muscle easily. They have visible abs that others pine for. When they were working the fitting rooms at a clothing store, for example, grabbing different sizes of clothes for people, customers would project their own self-loathing onto Cameron's body. In professional skating, tiny and cute can be advantageous. Their body is their income.

In their late twenties, Cameron came out as gender-fluid nonbinary and changed their name. Their goal is to work in skating shows. They never imagined being in the Olympics, yet they are beginning to see that they have what it takes to make it as a professional skater. They always had what it takes to make it.

Most of Cameron's skating friends quit after high school. Others quit after college. Some think Cameron is not moving on from childhood, but they are following their dream—coaching and skating—and finally feel like they are behind the wheel. They are claiming freedom and agency in their body. Finally, it is not about points, but about art. It is not about perfection, but about emotion. They are better than ever, skating not to please others but to please themself.

Cameron has met some amazing adults who skate professionally. Garrett has skated for several companies, including the Ice Theatre of New York and Holiday on Ice, and is now the co-CEO of American Ice Theatre (AIT). Garrett pushed Cameron to contend with limiting beliefs. Cameron's early career trained them to be clean, to get the trick, to pass the skills test, to blend with the team, and get the job done. No flair. No play. Their coaches got the skaters to conform with the other fifteen girls in matching buns or the other cheerleaders with matching pom-poms. Now, Cameron is training the flair and the fun. They are identifying as a talented, emotional, and unique performer. The power does not reside in the external gaze, but the internal one.

Garrett, a collector of people and true artistic collaborator, invited Cameron to join the Minnesota chapter of AIT. Kate, the other co-CEO, is helping Cameron skate authentically and see that skating is their life work. "I finally see how much I was holding myself back. There is no ceiling. My life will be divided into before and after AIT. I realized I was good when I realized how much more I had to learn. Feeling while I skate is a new kind of freedom. When I put more in, I receive in a new way. Now that I am out as nonbinary, when I put more in, it feels like I am putting more of the real me in. I get so much more out of it. When my artistry grew, my technique got better too. I started choreographing and things come out of me so differently when it's not for the viewer." The toe point and the finger placement used to be for the pleasure of the audience. Now it is in service to the art.

Right before COVID-19 shut everything down, Cameron performed with AIT and got paid to skate for the first time. They restricted food before the show, and they can see it in the pictures. They hope feeling their body and listening to it more will help them be brave enough to live into a new season of healing.

Decades into skating, finally believing in themself, Cameron is having fun. During COVID-19, when rinks shut down, Cameron loved skating on the lakes with the sun in their eyes and the wind in their face, their mind wandering back to childhood memories of skating for hours outdoors. They are part of a supportive, talented, and artistic community. They can take a day off jumping without feeling lazy. They can have a hard practice without punishing themself and without feeling like a bad person, without feeling unlovable. Cameron skates knowing they are good at the art, and art entertains.

Cameron used to feel like life was happening to them. Like they were being pushed and batted around through a current. They tried to keep from drowning, barely staying afloat. Cameron went to the U of M for skating and fell into a major. Then fell into a relationship with Max. Cameron often felt like a shadow, doing what people told them to do, desperate to appease. That has all shifted. Now, Cameron is curating their days, making choices that serve them.

Building a life. They care about the why. They choose to spend time around life-giving people, people who see them and support them. Cameron remembers and enjoys their performances. In short, Cameron is living in their body.

"I know I am an artist. I finally see how good I can get and believe I will get there. Failure is possible because the opportunity to fail is possible. It's a risk, and when the immobilizing voice whispers that I can't do it, I listen to the voice that knows I can."

Working through edits in the story, Cameron reflected on how seeing *they* pronouns and the name *Cameron* in writing resonated. They said, "My whole childhood, I was looking so hard for who I was. I was so lost, barking up the wrong tree. Which tree is the right tree? I asked everyone I found to tell me who I am. Who will tell me? It's hard to reflect on because now I know I was looking in places I would never find the answer. When I finally stopped, I realized it's me. No one else can tell me. When I look inside of me, I know.

"First, I had to get out of the burning house. The fire right in front of me was all I could see. I was dying to get out." Now, out of the burning house, they explained, they've leveled up. They can see farther. This season of life feels like the scene from *Alice in Wonderland* when Alice rapidly outgrows the house she is in, sending the white rabbit running. "I am growing too big for the cage others put me in."

Cameron's story is a counter-story for so many reasons. One is that our master narrative still claims that sexual assault happens to women in short skirts by violent male strangers in a dark alley. Assault can also happen between two people who are dating. Consent is ongoing, enthusiastic, and informed. It took time for Cameron to realize they were an abuse survivor in part because the master narratives around rape and sexual assault are so strong, persistent, and pervasive that survivors check to see if they match the extensive criteria. If it's worth saying aloud. If it's safe to report. Cameron has gone public as a survivor in part to vary the stories and encourage our society to expand to support people's safety and believe survivors.

> *When was a time you did something to please someone else at the expense of yourself? Today, what is one thing you can do that you enjoy, that brings you pleasure, that helps you live embodied?*

Running toward Herself

A few years back, I developed a yoga and writing workshop that pairs yoga with writing prompts. It's a way to get unstuck, to get stories you carry in your body out of your body where you can see them, contend with them, and craft them. It's also a way honor the story of your body. About halfway through my very first yoga and journaling workshop, I gave this writing prompt:

Pick a part of your body and write three snapshots that center around that body part from three different seasons of your life. I think about my relationship to my hair, hips, uterus, or teeth at age six versus eighteen versus thirty-seven.

I walked around the yoga studio slowly, keeping time and watching the group write. The quiet in the room had a weight and charge to it. I invited them to form groups of three and share. Initial timidity shifted to warmth and connection. I heard laughter and saw tears.

Eventually, we shifted back to the large group, and I asked if anyone wanted to share. There was a long, pregnant, vulnerable pause. My mother, of all people, raised her hand and said she picked her breasts, writing about when they budded as a teenager, breastfeeding her five children as an adult, and having cancer removed from them a few years prior.

Then Melissa, a yoga student of mine, said, "I wrote about my hair. I used to wear it long to please people. Then I wore it short to piss those people off. Now I wear it exactly how I want to please myself."

There was a longer version of that story that I desperately wanted to hear.

de·fi·ance
/dəˈfīəns/
noun
noun: **defiance**
open resistance; bold disobedience.

Melissa is the youngest of four children. Her two brothers and sister are ten, eleven, and twelve years older than she. Her parents hoped her birth would help save their marriage. It didn't.

Melissa's dad was the type of man who believes girls don't need to learn how to drive because boys can drive them where they need to go. He was also the type of man who was abusive to his wife and children. He never physically hurt Melissa. She could do no wrong. She was daddy's little girl.

Melissa's dad thought his daughter's hair should be long, and he always got his way. Even though Melissa's mother preferred a simple cut for her daughter, Melissa let her hair grow long to please her dad. As a small girl, she stood between her mother's knees while her mother brushed Melissa's blonde hair, which stretched to her lower back. Sometimes it took so long, Melissa fell asleep.

When Melissa was five, her mom got fed up with tending to her hair. While her dad was away hunting, her mom cut it off from her lower back up to just under her ears. Melissa's father was livid. Melissa was scared for her mom and for herself. She wasn't sure if she had done anything wrong or not. Melissa watched her mom level eyes with her father. Her father's eyes were filled with rage. In her mother's eyes she saw defiance.

Defiance runs through Melissa's female bloodline. Her maternal grandmother was a full German who married a full Pole in a small town where such marriages just did not happen. Melissa's mother entered the first grade at age four. She pitched a fit on her older brother's first day of school so fierce, they sent her along too. She excelled and graduated high school at age sixteen. All through school, she punched boys who picked on her older brother. She was the alpha.

When Melissa's parents got a divorce, she stayed with her dad. He worked hard to make sure Melissa hated her mom as much as he did. It took. She remained his perfect little princess. She grew her hair long.

Melissa pushed the limits, and her father never said no. Then, she did the one thing that he found unforgivable. She started dating a Black man. Melissa slowly started moving things to her mom's house, knowing the end was inevitable. She left a picture of her boyfriend out in her room on purpose. Her dad found it and blew up. Melissa locked her door, petrified of his rage. She moved out the next morning and never went back.

Melissa, then a senior in high school, shifted from pleasing her dad to pleasing her boyfriend. Like her father, he was controlling. Unlike her father, he wanted her to have short hair, so she cut it and dyed it black. In their six years together, Melissa gave birth to a daughter with a full head of thick, black hair. Holding her baby girl in her arms, Melissa felt a primal connection. She was meant to be her momma. This little girl was her soul descendent.

Melissa left her boyfriend. Later, when she met the man who would become her husband, she still had short black hair. He preferred her hair long and blonde, so she grew it out. By the time she was pregnant with their first son, her hair was down to her lower back, just as it was when she was five. It remained long through the fourteen years they were together, through having and raising their second son, through her husband cheating on her and having children with other women, through his abuse, and through his asking her for a divorce.

Melissa's ex-husband kept her sons, and like her father did with her, worked very hard to make sure the kids hated her. She realized she had always been someone's daughter, girlfriend, wife, or mother. She always belonged to someone else. Melissa felt alone without her husband, home, or access to her sons. She fell into a deep depression and struggled with suicidal thoughts.

Melissa survived for her daughter. She loved and encouraged her daughter's confidence and adventurousness. She put her daughter in gymnastics and let her climb as high as she wanted on the playground equipment while other parents judged her as rash and neglectful. She taught her daughter how to care for her curls with mousse, gel, and oils. Although her daughter's defiance complicated life for Melissa, she recognized it as inheritance and strength.

Needing to learn quickly how to be alone, Melissa started running. She let her hair flow natural and free at her shoulders. She ran to breathe. She ran to feel strong. She ran from her dad and her ex-boyfriend and her ex-husband. When she finished her first half-marathon, she thought, "*I got through a divorce and a half-marathon; I can do anything.*"

Bored of her perpetual ponytail, Melissa cut her hair in an undercut six months after her divorce was finalized. The bottom of her head was shaved, and she kept the top short. It was, in her mind, a courageous act of defiance. Her ex-husband wanted her hair long, so she cut it short. He called her a lesbian, which she took as a comforting compliment. She associated that haircut with strength. With giving him the middle finger. With her freedom from him. It set her apart from other women. She showed up to soccer games in the suburbs straight from the law firm in a fancy dress and fresh undercut. Among the other moms, she felt like an oddball, which is exactly what she wanted. She could have the underside of her hair shaved and the top of her hair longer—severe and soft, brave and kind. Both sides of her. We are never just one thing.

Healing has been gradual. She started therapy. She joined a yoga community. In small-group work, she allows other people to hold space for her to grieve and fall apart. She lets other people take care of her. She feels her feelings without judgment. She journals, meditates, and practices yoga on her mat daily.

Melissa's daughter shows her great grandmother's, grandmother's, and mother's defiance. At age nineteen, she moved to New York City on her own. Knowing she couldn't stop her, Melissa helped her move and then visited fourteen times in the first year to make sure she was okay. They remain extremely close and talk every day. Melissa talks to her own mom every day too.

Single for five years now, Melissa is learning how to be her own person, how to be a person alone. She doesn't belong to anyone. Slowly, a shift has happened in her. She doesn't run to escape people or problems. She runs because she loves it. No longer having to cook in bulk to please other people, she makes meals for herself because they meet her needs. Now, she doesn't cut her hair as an act of defiance, but because that is how she wants it. She thinks it looks beautiful.

Recently she saw her father at a family wedding, and he didn't recognize her.

Melissa is just now starting to think about dating again. To be willing to love someone and be loved back. She is ready for a new beginning. A clean slate. She stands in front of the mirror, looks deep into her own eyes, and smiles. She lifts the clippers and begins to shave her head.

> What is a character trait you have inherited? Are you running away, running toward, or both?

The Lump in My Throat

Over the course of fifteen years, every time a yoga teacher called for camel pose, I whispered *fuck* in my head. To create camel, I kneel on my shins and put my hands, fingers facing up, on my lower back. I lengthen my torso, walk my gaze across the ceiling toward the wall behind me, and grab my heels. Opening through my throat, I would feel claustrophobia and panic. I heard white noise. My breath got short. I wanted to flee, to climb up out of my skin and run from my body. I hated it until it was over.

Then one day, I got tired of resisting. I turned toward the lump in my throat with resignation and a desire to unravel.

I noticed I chronically duck my chin as if to protect my throat. I actively press my tongue against the roof of my mouth by default and clench my teeth in my I sleep, grinding what feels like fear down into dormancy. Yet it remains, lurking.

My voice falters when I have a cold or for days after a loud party or concert. I get laryngitis a handful of times a year, and when I do, I get light-headed trying to force air out to speak. It feels like a layer of gray gunk takes up residence, lining my throat. My instinct is to raise my voice above the barrier, pulling breath from my upper chest, but dropping down below it and breathing from my gut works better. I want my voice to matter.

While massaging my throat, neck, and jaw, a healer asked me if I suppress my truth when confronted. She asked me if I feel restricted in my life, and if I was allowed to complete my sentences as a child. She said tightness in my throat may be a sign that I grew up too fast. She asked me if I have poor personal boundaries. Then she asked me, "Which words are you sick of repressing?" And, also, "What do you still need to say?"

When I was very young, my neighbor asked my older sister and me if we wanted a homemade chocolate chip cookie. "No thank you," my sister answered for both of us. I looked at her, confused. I held my tongue, but I did want one.

My mom drove by my school when I was in kindergarten and started to cry. I was at recess, standing on the playground staring at the ground, alone. As a kid I was afraid of breaking the rules, making a mess, getting yelled at, or taking up too much space. I was afraid of being fat. I was afraid of not being wanted or loved. I didn't know when to speak and when not to. At gymnastics, I feared my body acting out in the middle of a twisting flip. The practice was to override the fear, but it loomed. My mask looked like toughness, excellence, and intensity.

A man once told me he didn't want me anymore, but he didn't want anyone else to have me either, so he stayed. I was afraid of him, so I stayed. It was easier that way. While with him, my throat got so sore it that would wake me from sleep. They knew me by name at the clinic where I went to for strep tests, hoping for an easy diagnosis and medicine to soothe me. It was never strep. When he did leave, I moved four states away. He arrived unannounced and waited outside my new place of employment, one I hadn't told him about, to prove he could always find me.

Fresh out of college, I lived in a big house with ten strangers. One night, a friend of my new roommate came into town. He mixed us all drinks. After my second drink, I lay down on the couch and couldn't get up. My body was cement. The room was blurry. Later, words like *please* and *stop* and *no* got caught in my throat. Later still, canker sores formed on my tonsils. It hurt to swallow for weeks. For years afterward, I blamed myself for what I let happen to me.

When I was a young adult, the man to whom I reported workplace sexual harassment told me to change my wardrobe. He joked to the man next to him, "How come no one ever tells me I'm sexy?"

Men give me unsolicited advice to temper my passionate voice. They mean well. They are also the men who interrupt me the most.

While launching my second book and facing imposter syndrome, my faltering voice became a hindrance. I returned to a healer, and she told me that a blocked throat chakra can lead to fear, resisting love, and longing to be in control.

In her mind's eye, she saw the gray coating in my throat that I felt. While she massaged my neck, an image of a bird emerged. The bird spastically picked apart a nest gathered at the base of my skull. A little girl, clearly me, emerged and watched attentively. With the nest disassembled, a clear path between my mind and my body appeared. I felt unstuck. I didn't walk down the path; it was enough to know it was there. I pictured my throat gently held with flowers and light, a weightless suppleness, a peace that made movement possible.

The healer recommended I get a throat chakra stone and sent me to a store called The Enchanted Garden in a strip mall. The woman there instructed me to choose any blue stone I was drawn to. I chose a chrysocolla stone, and at home researching, learned it was a teaching stone that stirs curiosity and allows teachers to let go of self-doubt and share their truth with others more clearly and easefully.

The healer told me she sees abandonment on both sides of my lineage going back for generations. She told me that fear can be passed down to my body. The fear that lives in my throat feels new and raw. It also feels inherited and old. The healer told me, "You are good at loving. Maybe your love can break the cycle of fear. Maybe, if you are brave, you can pass on something new."

It sounded easy, but I knew better. When my second child was born, a doctor cut me open and pulled him from my body. I heard him cry and my soul recognized him, lunged desperately for him, yearned to hold him to my chest. We belonged to each other.

I brought him home from the hospital. My firstborn had a winter cold and my newborn caught it. Crackly breathing prompted a trip to the pediatrician. The doctor took one look at his chest and called an ambulance. Time in the emergency room brought in respiratory specialists, a nasal cannula, and several monitors. I held him and a nurse wheeled us to a room where he quickly became inconsolable. He squirmed and squirmed, slipping out of three tiny IVs. He stopped breastfeeding, then stopped taking a bottle, then stopped taking a pacifier. I sang and snuggled and bounced him to no avail. No one slept. We were transferred to the pediatric intensive care unit, where he had his own nurse, serious sedation, and more tubes attached. They asked us to read about several invasive procedures before signing a consent form for all of them in case they had to act quickly. In case he stopped breathing and started dying fast.

Within a day, he needed a breathing tube inserted, which required a feeding tube and a central line. Only then did they realize how sick he was. They purposely paralyzed him until the ventilator was working more than his lungs. They tweaked endlessly. Fluids in, forced air in, Foley catheter in, sedation in, antibiotics in, breast milk in. Tubes everywhere. He was so tiny. They worried about his heart in addition to his lungs. Every morning at 4 a.m., a stranger threw a lead apron on me while she took x-rays of his chest. Beeping, watching the monitors, tweaking. He crashed. They bagged him. He responded. Twice.

At some point the free fall ended. He settled into the expansive plateau between getting worse and getting better. The official diagnosis was bronchiolitis caused by respiratory syncytial virus (RSV). That same virus can present as laryngitis in adults. The machines kept him alive. The virus ran its course. His tiny lungs fought to heal. Time in the wilderness continued. My heart shut down so I could do the work of waiting. I wanted to hear him cry. I wanted to hold him.

I became one of those people you never think you will become. I walked into the Ronald McDonald House without shoes, unshowered, looking for a meal. I acclimated to the fluorescent lights, the incessant beeping of machines, and the hush of the unknown. I gathered up prayers like bread, accepting offers from friends and family to shovel and deliver groceries so I could focus on my joyful two-year-old at home and my sick two-week-old in the hospital. I pumped breast milk every two hours and touched unswaddled baby skin during blood gas labs drawn every four hours. I received glances laced with pity. I sat in silence. I was too scared to speak.

There was no room on his face to touch between the tape and the tubes, so I stroked his newborn hair. "Oh, my sweet baby love. Momma's here. Momma's here." His eyes opened now and again, tracking my voice. It was painfully inadequate. I had no control. I was unclear how to love him enough to keep him alive. I feared passing my fear on to my son.

At some point in the expansive waiting, a resident suggested introducing a steroid. His numbers shifted a bit, and then a lot. He got better as fast as he got worse. The tubes came out, he started breastfeeding, and after three weeks in the hospital, when he was four weeks old, he was discharged. On our way out, the doctor said, "Don't treat him like the sick kid. The best thing you can do for him is to parent him without fear."

Several months later, at the end of yoga class, the teacher invited us to drop our right ear toward our right shoulder. The bird's nest was there, built back up. I created the shape, and the nest unraveled a bit. Tears, welling from deep in the abyss, spilled and spilled out. Instead of forcing the wave back down, I opened. I let myself be a vulnerable, snotty mess. I offered myself loving, tender affection. I got out of my own way. What came out of me could not go back in. It could not be controlled, and I no longer wanted it to be.

Healing is hard, but so is not healing. I was so tired of being afraid.

Then one day about a year later, when camel was called, I tried saying *yes* in my head instead of *fuck*. I said it aloud by accident. The teacher smiled and came closer, witnessing my opening. And just like that, the resistance to the pose faded away.

Lately, I try to stay open as long and often as I can. I tend to move slower and notice deeper. My breath anchors me in my body and in the present moment. When fear clings, I more often choose to turn toward it with curiosity. I relax my tongue, unclench my jaw, and untuck my chin. I open my awareness to include my ancestors and descendants and what rushes in is a love that has the potential to gently dissolve the fear. I tap into courage. I begin again. I say yes to the word *no*. Then it becomes clearer what I still need to say.

> *Where do you sense restriction, resistance, or fear in your body?*
> *Who or what supports your opening?*

Herbs of Healing

Elizabeth is one of my former students who stays in touch. She is brilliant, and I see to it that our paths cross, so I can hear what she's thinking about and up to in the world. As an adult, she shares with me things about her high school years that I didn't know at the time. It's a chance to circle back, create space to re-craft our stories, deepen our relationship, offer our younger selves care, and heal. When Elizabeth heard about this book and the process of sharing body narratives, she expressed interest right away. There were three things she wanted to create a story around, and in her mind they were disparate and unrelated. I encouraged her to start and trust the process. Late into our first session together, she paused and smiled. Indeed, all three themes had woven themselves together in her narrative as they did in her body. Sometimes our stories coexist, and sometimes they mingle. Our bodies house them and allow them to inform each other.

When Elizabeth was nine, her family moved to Minnesota. To make friends, she joined a basketball team. The girls all picked boy nicknames. Elizabeth picked the name Bob, and it stuck. It suited her.

Elizabeth liked introducing herself as Bob because it played with gender, was a bit unexpected, and because she presents as feminine, it landed with a certain quirky cuteness. She was uncomfortable with her female body in high school. She didn't like her legs, was embarrassed by her arm hair, and detested the changes that were happening to her during puberty. Elizabeth created an alter ego in Bob that distanced her from her fraught feelings. Looking back now as an adult, she can see how Bob was a response to boys oversexualizing her in ways she didn't feel comfortable with and didn't fully understand.

In high school, bodies get pegged. According to Elizabeth, she got pegged as a "manic pixie dream girl." She was admired in a Zooey Deschanel sort of way. Boys let her know it was sexy that she went by Bob and that she was hot, but not hot enough. They wanted to fool around with her but weren't interested in dating her. They liked joking with her but wouldn't take her seriously. They rewarded her for being cute and docile. She found it all very confusing and kept becoming who she thought they wanted her to be, but it was never enough. Going by Bob was controlling her own narrative while offering fodder for boys to add to their narrative of her; it added to her attractiveness while keeping her hostage in the painfully small box. She didn't like being sexualized by other people. She believed back then that the urges of other people, including boys and men who harassed her, were her fault.

Ultimately, Elizabeth struggled with self-doubt. She didn't think she was good enough or smart enough. Her first standard was set by her dad. Elizabeth's dad is a brilliant cardiologist. He heals people's hearts. In her childhood, his work made him physically distant and then emotionally distant. In high school she struggled with bouts of anxiety and depression. Instead of supporting her, her dad would say things like, "You are overreacting" and "Stop acting crazy."

Elizabeth took on the belief that, because she struggled with math and numbers, she was not intelligent. She played up the flighty persona as a protection mechanism. I remember one day in my class, she answered a question with a remarkably astute response. She also answered in an overly squeaky voice laced with apologetic body language. I saw it as a coping strategy. She was on a journey. My male colleague, however, instead of building her up based on her insight, publicly shamed her for her demeanor. "Say it in a normal voice," he said. "You should want people to take you seriously." She went further under cover.

In college, Elizabeth realized her brand of intelligence. She earned a degree in social work and fully claimed her humor not as a byproduct of her cute quirkiness, but an expression of her wit. She continues to look younger than her age and is verifiably cute, and she is not to be underestimated. She's damn smart too.

In 2019, Elizabeth took a job with Refugee Youth Service and moved to France. She lived and worked in a refugee camp. Many of the refugees were from the Middle East, Sudan, and Ethiopia, on their way to Great Britain via France. As a female American employee, she got a lot of unwanted male attention on the border. She has an ethnically ambiguous look, so men couldn't always place her. Teenage boys asked other staff if she was a new refugee and if she was single. Folks thought she was an Arab from Iraq or Iran and called her a bad Muslim.

Elizabeth worked mainly with boys under eighteen. Tensions ran high. The French riot police were rough with the young men, who in turn took their frustrations out on women like Elizabeth. The police were blunt with her. French employees, once hearing her speak and placing her as an American, refused to talk to her. Meanwhile, others flocked. Pegged yet again:

> "If you were in Eritrea with me, you'd be the perfect bride."
> "You're so sexy."
> "Take me to America with you!"
> "You're so beautiful."
> "You must be so rich."

Refugees found camaraderie with Elizabeth because she had darker skin than White European and American workers. Yet they also considered paler skinned White female volunteers the gold standard for beauty. They'd want to learn English slang from America, the global media empire, while directing their anger at the US government policies toward her. Many refugees have an understandable preoccupation with looking their best. Male and female refugees, then, fixated on Elizabeth's most miniscule indiscretions like a pimple, body hair, or lack of makeup. This all left her feeling jarred, objectified, and sexualized. It registered in her body, the layers building.

Back in the United States, Elizabeth unraveled and healed by spending time in her body. She got into weightlifting. While practicing yoga, she couldn't help but think, "My body can do amazing things." Piercings and tattoos helped her reclaim her body and her identity when she felt the male gaze stealing it away.

Her body is her own. Her sexuality is her own. She wants her body to look like she wants it to look. She goes by both Bob and Elizabeth equally and now does not experience fragmentation between the persona and the person.

Elizabeth's favorite tattoos are a grouping of three on her right forearm, large stalks of garlic, oregano, and rosemary. Italian healing herbs. They hold the story of her reconciliation with her dad.

When Elizabeth was twenty-two, her father called to tell her he had cancer in his chest. She was shocked. By then they had no relationship at all. Her dominant memories of him centered around his control. He had surgery and started chemo, showing signs of vulnerability and mortality. Other more loving memories surfaced. Memories of him growing things and making food from them. While sick with chemo and missing food, Elizabeth's dad talked with her about recipes, and they connected in the kitchen. She helped him tend his garden and cooked with him. "Go out back and grab me some oregano," he'd direct. Over growing herbs and cooking meals, they slowly rebuilt trust. The herb tattoos represent where she comes from. Repair. Wellness. Feeding one another. They are on her forearm so she can see them, so they are front and center while she is cooking. She likes to have them close.

Elizabeth's dad is in remission from cancer, and their relationship is also mended. She can see and appreciate that they look alike. They have a similar sense of humor and a similar sense of outrage. They both work with people in serious trauma. Elizabeth recently got certified as a clinical social worker and feels like she is an expert in something important. She smiles, "I'm like my dad. I fix hearts too."

How were you pegged in high school? How are you pegged at work? In your family? In the world?

Other people will project their ideas and stories onto us continuously. Getting quiet, dropping into our bodies, hearing our truth, and telling our own stories can strengthen our resolve and clarify which stories we will integrate and which we will let go. Working through the reflection questions, breath work, and body practices while writing our stories can give us soothing tools to stay on the vulnerable and sometimes painful embodied path inward. In the work, being around toxic people and absorbing their lies will become less and less tolerable. As we live from our increasingly healed and whole sense of self, we will naturally gravitate to and attract people who empower and encourage us, holding a mirror up to gently remind us of who we are. We know, and we know that we know. The practice is a remembering. A returning home.

Reflection Questions

* What did your body experience while reading these stories? Did any of them resonate with you and your body's story?

* Who are you trying to please? How? What narratives have other people told about you that you have had to let go of to live into who you really are? Talk about a time when other people wanted you to be someone you did not want to be.

* Who and what has helped you remember who you are and place your attention on the traits you want to grow?

* What is your body doing when you feel powerful?

* What messages did you receive about your body as a child?

* What does your hair say about you?

* What are you an expert in? Where does your intelligence shine?

* Take a multiple intelligences test and talk about your findings.

* Has there ever been an activity, like cooking, that helped heal a relationship in your life?

* Which words are you sick of repressing? What do you still need to say?

* What master narratives get told or not told about eating disorders, domestic abuse, sexual assault, and harassment? How might your body story shift and expand our lexicon for the better?

Writing Prompts

Set a timer for five minutes and for that time write messages you have received about who you are and who you should be from other people and society. They may come as sound bites or more subtle messages. Cross out all the messages that you do not want to take on. Set a timer for five minutes and fill the time writing "I am" statements. Who do you say that you are?

Pick a body part and write three snapshots of that body part from three different seasons of your life. Repeat the prompt later with other body parts or other snapshots.

Write the story of a time you lived through adversity. How did it affect your body? Your thoughts? Your identity? Did your identity shift by surviving the hardship? How do you choose to apply meaning now looking back? Take some time to honor the resilience in your body and being.

Breath Practice

Taking a slightly slower inhale than exhale is energizing. Taking a slightly longer exhale than inhale is calming. Take a few moments to check in with your body and decide if you'd like to increase your energy or increase your calm.

Increase your energy:
Find a comfortable seated posture with a tall spine. Gently take a full inhale through your nostrils then take a slow, open-mouthed exhale. Repeat this breath three times, letting your exhale be audible and textured. Let your day go. Then seal your lips and take a gentle six-count inhale and a gentle four-count exhale for about seven rounds of breaths before letting your breath return to normal.

Increase your calm:

Find a comfortable seated posture with a tall spine. Gently take a full inhale through your nostrils then take a slow, open-mouthed exhale. Repeat this breath three times, letting your exhale be audible and textured. Let your day go. Then seal your lips and take a gentle four-count inhale and a gentle six-count exhale for about seven rounds of breaths before letting your breath return to normal.

Body Practices

Before you get too far into your day, step outside and look around. Lie down on the ground and look up at the sky. Stand barefoot, touch a tree, or pick up a fallen branch. Notice what happens to your body when you encounter nature. What childhood memories surface when you think about outdoor spaces that bring you joy?

Cook mindfully, maybe with someone you care about, maybe using a recipe from one of your family members or ancestors. Or use Elizabeth and her dad's tomato sauce recipe:

TOMATO SAUCE RECIPE

* Heat pan with garlic and olive oil.
* Toss in mushrooms, saute 2 minutes.
* Add chopped tomatoes (preferably peeled, but that's a pain in the ass, so go with cherry tomatoes).
* Cook 2 to 4 minutes.
* Add oregano and rosemary to taste.
* Add pepper and a ½ cup of cheap sparkling wine.

Four

Bodies Transform
Embracing Our Ever-Unfolding Identity

Once you start approaching your body with curiosity rather than fear, everything shifts.

—BESSEL VAN DER KOLK,
The Body Keeps the Score

At my child's six-year-old checkup, he weighed in at around fifty pounds. I gained and lost that much weight with each full-term pregnancy. I looked at his long, growing body and imagined carrying him around all day and sleeping with him attached to my body all night without a break. And I marveled at my own strength. I pause on my sporadic gray hairs, my cesarean section scar, my smile lines, my crooked pinky toe, and the scar on the roof of my mouth, all laced with stories. My tight jaw, an emerging bunion, and rounded shoulders are all signs of my daily patterns and posturing in the world. Layers of stress pile up over time, and it takes time, then, to unravel and unlearn too.

My affection toward my body shifts as my understanding of what it has been through and what it is capable of expands. I become. As I age, I care more about what I think about my body than what the world thinks. I am the best person to care for me. My edges soften with growing reverence, compassion, and respect for my body and its story.

Can you remember inhabiting your child body? Do you remember what it looked like and felt like, not from pictures but from your own vantage point? Our bodies change over time, as do our stories about our bodies, and with those transformations our identities shift. Our bodies have been through so much over time, and it shows in how we transform.

The stories in this chapter are beautiful articulations of body transformation. The participants are forging meaning and expanding identity as they tell the story of their bodies. They honor how their bodies changed and are changing in joyful, painful, complicated, and incredible ways. They are living examples of the fluidity of bodies and identity. They are bravely and counter-culturally becoming, accepting change as an opportunity to not stay small or bounce back or hide but to expand in unexpected and powerful ways.

Befriending Yourself

Laura and Franco got married when she was twenty-five. They thought they'd wait a while to have children, but one night, in a tent on the shore of Lake Superior, they surprised themselves and each other by sharing feelings of excitement and anxiousness about growing their family. Laura was one of five kids and Franco was one of four. They wanted a big family, and they wanted to start the adventure straight away.

Two years later, Laura was still childless. The myth they had been sold of being young, healthy, and in control of their story died a slow, painful death. The birth control pills she took since she was seventeen masked hormonal imbalances. Struggling with infertility, frustration toward her body consumed her. *Why won't you do this good thing I want you to do?*

Laura did get pregnant eventually, and she became acutely aware of the space she took up in the world. Her belly entered the room first. She was overwhelmed by how much her stomach was the topic of conversation. Her body was open to public consumption like never before. Her husband, conversely, lived through his professional day without being ogled or asked how he was feeling. Laura contended with her relationship with her body as well as the world's relationship with her body.

While pregnant with her first child, Laura went to an orchestra concert. During a swelling section of the symphony, she felt the baby kick for the first time. She sat marveling at the feeling of life inside of her. She wondered if the baby would be musical. Maybe it would like the drums.

Looking back on herself—twenty-seven years old and pregnant for the first time—she is filled with tenderness. That version of herself had no idea yet how motherhood would break her heart and how much her body would endure.

Laura loved nursing her baby boy. It helped her heal and connect. Nursing was beautiful and powerful. It felt like her body was doing what it was made to do.

To Laura's surprise, she got pregnant easily the second time. She held her oldest on her lap as her belly grew and thought, *I have all my kids right here.* Her second son was born two years after her first. His birth mirrored his personality—fast and furious. The nurses met Laura at the entrance of the emergency room, and she birthed him twenty minutes later. She was filled with the natural rush of an unmedicated birth. She felt strong, like she could do anything.

Laura got pregnant the third time easily again, and all thoughts of infertility evaporated. She took pregnancy tests repeatedly just to bask in the joy. The line on the stick got fainter and fainter. Feeling alone, Laura told people she miscarried, and she was warmly welcomed into the sisterhood. No one tells you how brutal a miscarriage can be, that it can be physically painful, like a birth. She assumed she front-loaded her mothering pain during her two years of infertility. Laura was desperate with loss, never getting to hold this baby. We just haven't found words for carrying death inside of you.

Merely three months after her miscarriage, Laura got pregnant again. Fear accompanied her for the entire pregnancy. She couldn't trust anymore. She and Franco found out they were having a boy but didn't tell anyone until he was born. It was a long, sweet secret. Laura fell in love with the idea of having three boys. Her third is now the son that repeatedly asks her to tell him birth stories, delighting in the details and differences.

With a house full of little boys, Laura got pregnant unexpectedly. And then she found out it was twins. Identical twin girls. She was elated to raise two girls. The doctors mentioned a rare disease called twin-to-twin transfusion syndrome that can surface with identical twins in which they share a placenta and network of connected blood vessels. They told her repeatedly not to worry, so she didn't. When they got diagnosed with twin-to-twin transfusion syndrome, Laura girded herself for the challenge.

At twenty-four weeks, just past the threshold of when fetal twins are considered viable, Laura went in for a laser surgery to sever the connected blood vessels in the placenta. The surgery didn't work, and severe bleeding in one sac led to an emergency cesarean section on the same day. Because Laura has a very high metabolism, the anesthesia wore off during the first laparoscopic surgery, causing severe physical pain.

Abby lived for one day and Maggie lived for two. Laura was left to heal from two surgeries and mourn the deaths of her two girls. Looking back now, she has no idea how she weathered the layers of pain. She had three kids at home, a child she never met, and two she only knew for hours after birth.

Deep grief took hold. In the depth of that grief, to her great surprise, Laura felt acute desire for another child. She did not want Abby's and Maggie's deaths to be the end of her birthing story. She waited. She healed. She knew the risk. And she tried again.

With eyes wide open and her vulnerable heart exposed, Laura got pregnant a sixth time. The pregnancy was challenging. She struggled with anxiety the whole time. As the baby filled her body, the fullness of sorrow filled her being. Convinced it would end badly, Laura wrote publicly throughout the pregnancy.

Laura felt her bones hold onto trauma. Her muscles remembered. Swelling and shrinking. Her body became a text she could go on retreat to study. She marveled at how different being pregnant felt in her late thirties as opposed to her late twenties. She had a huge belly, huge breasts, and wrinkles. At almost forty, she felt why bodies want to be pregnant at sixteen. It was tiring carrying the extra weight. Her pregnancy clothes were threadbare and had lost their bounce. She also had an old, worn-in confidence in her later pregnancies. Nothing was new. The deep knowing felt empowering in a way that simply wasn't possible with her early pregnancies. She knew when she needed help, when it was time to see a therapist, and when it was time to care for herself better.

Like always, Laura got very big. Strangers said, "Oh, you must be having twins."

"Nope," she'd answer with a pang of longing for her daughters. She rarely talked about them, though. People tended to reference her three happy and healthy boys to minimize her pain and loss. She didn't want to give people the power to do that. Secretly, she'd pray, "God, you owe me a girl."

It was not to be.

Her fourth son was born, and three years after, her fifth.

With her last two boys, Laura wanted to deliver vaginally. Recovery was so much different between vaginal birth and a major abdominal surgery. And there was an unspoken reason too. She did not want two scars. She wanted her cesarean section scar to belong only to Maggie and Abby. That scar tells their story. When she is old and decrepit, she wants her nursing home caregivers to see that c-section scar and know something about her story. The scar is a tangible reminder of the daughters she lost. It makes the pain visible.

She had to fight hard to keep this agreement with her girls. With her fifth son, she got preeclampsia and had a hard induction. The baby wouldn't come. Deep into labor, she took a deep breath, turned on the *Hamilton* soundtrack, and synced with her body to progress her labor. One contraction at a time. She midwifed herself through fear and pain and birthed her fifth and final son naturally.

Laura's youngest was born days before stay-at-home orders came out in an attempt to keep the COVID-19 pandemic from spreading. With her other children, Laura pumped and left breast milk in bottles for the caregivers while she was at work. With her youngest, she quit her job to focus on her writing. The time did not go toward writing, however, but instead toward facilitating online learning and keeping her family afloat. Stuck at home with five boys during a pandemic, she was filled with gratitude and overwhelm.

Almost forty, with no work clothes to put on, no social functions to diversify her time, no childcare support, no grandparents in town, and a spouse who bakes as a coping strategy, Laura was frustrated with her body. The baby weight wouldn't come off. She didn't feel like herself. She was convinced the world did not need to hear from one more White lady momma writer. Deep insecurity bubbled up around her personal and professional identity. She offered tender compassion to others but withheld the same kindness from herself. She had never taken the time to befriend herself.

Laura did not hear good stories about women's bodies. Older women loathed their bodies and felt guilty for eating dessert. Society's master narratives proclaim again and again that women's bodies are available for consumption. Nursing again brought healing, this time with her youngest son. It brought healing to Laura's relationship to her body. Bearing children invited her to see that her body was capable of expansiveness and creation. Being part of the holy, ordinary work of feeding a child brought dignity and agency. Nursing did not feel like giving her body up for her child. It felt like a way she and her babies chose each other, chose to share life with each other.

Knowing her fifth son was the finale, Laura reflected on her childbearing season ending. She missed the insatiable hunger that comes with pregnancy and breastfeeding. She missed easily digesting huge, heaping plates of bountiful food, that she jokingly called The Nursing Mother's Special. She missed feeling little feet kicking her from the inside, rolling to change position, a feeling she hopes to never forget. She missed her toned arms, muscular from carrying a child.

Over time, the voice wondering

Was it my fault?
Could have I done more to save them?
But what if?

quieted just a bit. Birthing, nursing, and raising her last two sons after Maggie and Abby died ushered in healing. Laura is slowly learning to forgive her body.

The bearing and birthing season, which lasted over a decade for Laura, looked nothing like she imagined. Her story is filled with more loss and more children than her plan entailed. She is the mother of five boys and the mother of seven children and also the mother of eight. The girls and the miscarriage show up all the time, often in the most ordinary moments. Sometimes at night, when Laura is getting plates out for dinner she pauses and thinks, "How many of us are there?" Laura and Franco talk to the boys about Maggie and Abby. There are pictures of them up around the house and a garden in the yard for them with their names in mosaics on stones. They continue to be a part of the family's story.

Laura is cognizant of the stunning work she has taken part in. She identifies motherhood as being a cocreator with God. Being pregnant and raising children is the clearest example of that for her. She is grateful for her body. She believes God loves bodies and embraces them. She feels it to be true when she bears and nurses a child. It is good and beautiful.

With her bearing and birthing season passed, perhaps now is the time for Laura to befriend herself. Perhaps now, facing layers of joy and sorrow in her body, she can explore what it means to mother herself.

I recall the image of Laura at the orchestra concert, pregnant with her first child, again and again. Her body had already lived through two years of trying to get pregnant. The stories she told herself in those two years had to shift, as did her identity. And in that moment, she could never imagine what her body and being would go through in the decade to come.

All the stories in this book are, of course, highly condensed and curated versions of what happened. Laura's story is expansive in its breadth and has a protective speed to manage the layers of trauma. She could slow down, go deeper, and write a memoir-length body story about each pregnancy and birth, which would require unearthing and unraveling layers of embodied memories. Now that her youngest is no longer an infant, she is just beginning to look back, to lift the top layer and peek under the corners. There is a lot to unpack, and rarely ample time, quiet, or psychic space to process.

Not long ago she said to her therapist, "One of these days, I should take a closer look at my last birth."

Her therapist, knowing how traumatic it was and how much more she is processing in other areas of her story replied, "Not just yet. All in good time."

The response surprised Laura and validated the weight of it all. She senses she may be carving out time to forge meaning and heal from her season of bearing and birthing for decades to come. Her body has lived through so much transformation. Mothering herself, she reminds herself daily to be patient in the practice and be astounded at her own ability to hold grief and gratitude together.

Part of our work to become more embodied is to be willing to parent ourselves. We can care for the child self, offering tenderness and affection that can lead to healing. We can love ourselves the way we deserve to be loved and maybe the ways we needed to be loved but weren't. The child self is the self that has been with us the longest, and in that way may be the wisest. If we tend to that child self, nurturing ourselves retroactively, befriending every version of ourselves, we can find a deeper sense of home in our bodies. The work of crafting our body stories, as we mine through memories, is part of this healing through parenting ourselves.

> *What version of yourself may benefit from some tender compassion? What is one tiny way you can befriend yourself more deeply today?*

Inhabiting the New Normal

When Molly was nineteen, she tried yoga to spend some time in her body. Strong and graceful, she felt her identity as a chubby kid and her struggles with body image ease a bit. Yoga gave her a connection to her breath, a hiatus from the world, and a path into her body.

At age twenty-five, Molly had an isolating job and a controlling boyfriend. Wanting to expand her tools, she took her first pole-dancing class and loved it immediately. In Philadelphia at the time, pole-dancing was still considered taboo. Its naughty reputation added to its allure. Yoga and pole-dancing became escape tactics that brought Molly relief. As someone who believes every woman should be able to parallel park and do a pull-up, she felt like she had arrived. Her bodily strength overflowed to her mind and her life.

Molly's pole-dancing friends had a different way of being in the world, and they tended not to care one lick about what other people thought. When Molly danced, she felt like herself. Her body was strong and beautiful. She stopped dating jerks and proclaimed dancing as her significant relationship. Her pole became her dance partner. It never talked back, stepped on her toes, or abandoned her. So Molly danced, and she got good.

Then, Molly got diagnosed with Stage 2 cancer in her left breast. It felt like betrayal. Her body, the place she went for safety, was trying to kill her. She had nowhere left to escape.

Molly's body ceased to be her own. Treatment made her too sick to do yoga or dance. The long mermaid hair covering her breasts sizzled and fell out. Newly bald, there was no hiding. Yet hair grows back. Breasts do not.

After studying the list of horrifying options, Molly opted for a double mastectomy. The surgery was hard, and she thought the scars were ugly. It is an amputation that comes with all sorts of stereotypes. When she tells people that she is a breast cancer survivor, most people look at her breasts instinctively. She came to despise pink ribbons. Pink ribbons are cute. There is nothing cute about breast cancer. Cancer is grotesque.

Losing her hair and her breasts felt like a direct attack on the strong and graceful femininity Molly had earned and claimed as hers. She spent more time applying makeup and shifted her nail polish color from black to pastels to add a sense of femininity to her bald head and flat chest. She didn't want to look sick. She listened to podcasts and TED Talks during her treatment to make sure she had something more interesting than her health to talk about when someone asked in a sad, puckered voice, "How are you doing?"

She didn't want anyone's pity.

Molly believed that after her cancer treatment, things could go back to normal. Sure, she'd have short hair and fake breasts, but hair grows back, and porn tits are exciting. She wanted to get to the other side of cancer and resume the life she knew.

Then, in one of her reconstruction appointments, the plastic surgeon told Molly her skin was too thin for nipple reconstruction. In that moment of all moments, the bottom fell out. She imagined her body without nipples, and she felt like a circus freak. It was this piece of information that made her fully realize she would never again line her hands up with her nipples in low plank during yoga. She would never breastfeed a child. She would never have a partner suck on her nipples to arouse her. In fighting for her life, her body shifted irrevocably. There would be no return to normal. There was no going back.

When Molly looked in the mirror, she couldn't see herself in her reflection. She had gained weight. She was pale. Her eyes looked scared. Molly sifted through her options. She could go nippleless. She could get a 3D nipple tattoo. She could implant objects in her breasts that looked like nipples. She found a lab growing nipples not yet approved by the FDA.

Then she remembered a friend who had recommended a tattoo artist who specializes in botanical tattoos that cover mastectomy scars. She didn't want to see her scars anymore. As soon as she googled his work, she knew her chosen way forward was no nipple reconstruction and instead, a gorgeous, sprawling chest tattoo.

Molly texted back and forth with David, the tattoo artist, for six months. She told him she wanted to look like she walked into an enchanted forest and came out wearing flowers. And, she added, she didn't want it to look like she was hiding. He showed her three mock-ups, the first of which was perfect. Sweet smelling peonies burst forth in the dynamic, asymmetrical design. She put a deposit down and traveled to Chicago for her eight-hour session.

Molly's tattoo was a pivot toward recovery. She bought shirts that show off her tattoo. It helped her live into her new reality and find home in this version of her body. Her new normal. A marker for the next phase of life.

There are days when she still feels deformed and chubby. There are days her eyes still look scared. However, that's not every single moment of every single day, and she considers that an improvement. She considers that being human. Molly has been cancer-free for two-and-a-half years. Her hair grew back wildly curly, and she feels comfortable in her skin.

Her chest remains a very charged area of her body. The body remembers. Once on vacation in the Dominican Republic, she got a massage. When the woman touched the muscles just below her collar bones, she burst into tears. Another time, a man she was dating texted her that he was going to hop in the shower, and that she should come join him. She responded with sheer panic, sobbing. She used to love showering with people, but nippleless, it felt too vulnerable, too soon and too scary. When she told him about her hesitation, he responded brilliantly and with great understanding, then offered to suck her nippleless breast whenever she wanted.

Molly went to graduate school to become a physical therapist specializing in the pelvic floor. Her body has endured so many dings, like a young cancer diagnosis, and she wants to hold space for people when they are uncomfortable. Physical therapists are supposed to optimize movement in daily living and well, sex is part of daily living. So many women, because the pelvic floor is so private, live with discomfort they assume is normal but really can be improved. Molly doesn't want to do physical therapy for cancer patients because it could activate her trauma, but she does think the discomfort her body has been through helps her be able to support healing for someone in a different vulnerable and often feminine context.

For a long while, Molly didn't return to yoga or pole-dancing. Her chest felt tight and restricted, and she didn't want to explore how those two activities might now be harder and different. She didn't want her peers in those communities to expect the old her to be the one coming back.

It was the global pandemic of all things that invited her return. She has a pole and a yoga mat in her apartment, and she explores the activities in privacy. She streams online yoga classes and joins her pole-dancing friends on Google Hangouts every Friday night. She bought a bike and started an anti-inflammatory diet. She finished grad school and is helping her patients learn about their bodies and live into healing. She loves her tattoos, which helps her be tender to the story living and breathing in her chest.

Slowly, she is building trust with her ever-unfolding body.

I do not take my left arm for granted, but listening to Molly, I realized I do take my nipples for granted. Hearing her body story opened my own relationship with my body. Molly told me her body story via Zoom during the pandemic while she was living in Philadelphia and I was living in Minneapolis. Molly showed me pictures of herself at different stages so I could see the transformation of her body. I saw her chest and hair before cancer, and during and after her tattoo sessions. It struck me while listening to her how present she is in her body. She inhabits it in a way that honors her transformation.

At different points during the conversation, she got up to grab a snack, she took a break to go to the bathroom, she told me part of her story while standing, and she grabbed a therapeutic cane to tend to muscle knots in her shoulders and back while she was talking.

After we signed off, I stood up for the first time in a few hours and realized I should have taken care of my own body in all the ways she took care of hers during the conversation. I claim to be an embodied person, and yet at times I struggle to listen to my body and address its needs. Molly affected me with her story and with her embodied life. It struck me that she allowed her body and its needs to take up space in the world. It's inspiring and invites me to do the same.

> Is there a part of your body that makes you feel different or marked that you are ashamed of? Will telling the story of that body part soften something for you?

His

Sawyer was born in St. Paul, Minnesota, to twenty-three-year-old newlyweds. They were delighted with their first-born, but they didn't know him as Sawyer yet. They chose a different, more feminine name that meant "pure one, gift from God." They thought they had a baby girl.

They belonged to the Community of Christ the Redeemer, where members have "joined their lives together to actively pursue holiness, love one another as brothers and sisters in Christ, and work together for the spread of the Gospel and building up of Christian life in today's world." Sunday mornings included a Catholic mass and a multi-hour prayer meeting with lively praise songs and fervent biblical teaching. Leaders were men. Families lived near one another in "clusters" and vacationed together.

At daycare, when Sawyer was four, he and a boy named Adam showed each other their bodies during a bathroom break. "Boys have penises and girls have vaginas," Adam stated. It sounded definitive. Sawyer thought it would be cooler to have a penis, but he didn't, so he must be a girl.

Sawyer felt like a boy. He was drawn to the boyish version of clothes, shoes, toys, and characters. But he also internalized that there were some boundaries you just can't cross. He could put on his dad's running shoes and shorts, but he was playing dress-up. He could run through the sprinkler bare-chested, but he had to wear a girl's swimsuit to the public pool. His hair could be unkempt most of the time, but he had to comb it and wear a dress for weddings and holidays. His parents allowed him to play outside shirtless, but only until age seven. He went along. It felt unfair but inevitable. At his first communion, he wore a white dress and veil. His mom stuck pink flowers in his french braid. When Father Mike offered him a wafer as the body of Christ he said, "Amen." *I agree.*

In Sawyer's imagination, however, gendered rules didn't apply. He pretended to be an explorer, pioneer, priest, and pro wrestler. The characters were often biblical and always male. He idolized Nitro from *American Gladiators*. When Sawyer and his three-year-old brother Greg acted out the Christmas story, Sawyer was Joseph. "I'm taller," he reasoned, as he helped Greg into a frilly blue robe from Grandma Loraine. At her house, Sawyer dug for worms and fished off the dock, pretending to be Tom Sawyer. As Alec from *The Black Stallion*, he imagined riding on the beach without a saddle or a care in the world.

With kindergarten at a private Catholic school came a plaid uniform jumper. At recess, Sawyer often played by himself, throwing a tennis ball against the wall and fielding it with his baseball glove. He grinned when the gym teacher said he would be the first girl shortstop in the major leagues, but he felt queasy and ashamed when kids asked why he had boys' shoes. When called a tomboy, he asked what it meant. "You know, a girl who acts like a boy." A girl who doesn't act right. The wrong kind of girl.

Sawyer's family left the Community of Christ the Redeemer when he was ten. Word got out that Father Mike had been sexually abusing teenage girls and young adult women, while community leaders covered it up. Sawyer's parents felt betrayed, but they changed churches and remained steadfast in their Christian faith. Sawyer's dad found a spiritual father in Dr. James Dobson, the founder of Focus on the Family, a ministry dedicated to "building healthy marriages that reflect God's design," and providing resources for parents to raise children according to biblical principles.

When Sawyer was eleven, his mom took him on an overnight retreat, just the two of them, where they listened to Dr. Dobson's six-part series, *Preparing for Adolescence*, on cassette tapes. These tapes formed the basis of Sawyer's knowledge about puberty, peer pressure, dating, and sex. They said boys will become interested in girls' bodies while girls will become interested in the way boys talk, walk, and think. When Sawyer's parents bought him a subscription to *Brio*, Focus on the Family's magazine for teen girls, Sawyer was curious about *Breakaway* for boys, but knew it wasn't for him.

After being unconcerned with social dynamics among his peers in elementary school, Sawyer started paying attention in middle school. He wanted friends. He wanted to fit in. And he was painfully aware that tomboy girls and effeminate boys were perceived as gay. He was terrified of people thinking he was a lesbian. Not only was that morally wrong in his mind, but it also just wasn't true. He had crushes on boys. He wanted a boyfriend, but boys only seemed interested in girls who wore makeup.

Sawyer started experimenting with earrings and lip gloss. He switched lunch tables. He started passing notes, talking back to teachers, and skipping class. He tried not to notice and tried not to think about the ways his body was changing. Finding a place to belong was more important than how he felt inside.

------------◊------------

Years later, Sawyer headed to the University of Wisconsin–La Crosse for college with a yearning to belong. He had been warned about the dangers of the college party scene and felt both intrigued and intimidated by it. The first weekend of college, his new friend Emilie invited him to Campus Crusade for Christ's weekly meeting, nicknamed *Real Life*. The auditorium was packed with people greeting each other while a student band played. The group became Sawyer's entire social circle. He went to bible study on Wednesday nights, retreats every semester, and Campus Crusade root-beer keg parties.

Their teachings were based firmly in purity culture. Girls should be modest. Boys should initiate and lead. God designed sex for marriage between one man and one woman. Any sexual activity out-side of that context, even lustful thoughts, was a sin. Sawyer didn't agree with all of it, but it was theoretical. He wasn't dating. Sawyer and Emilie became inseparable roommates. Late-night talks led to falling asleep together. They cuddled and said, "I love you." None of this registered as romantic or sexual.

It was 1999. Sawyer was restless, searching, and uneasy. He and Emilie got their eyebrows pierced. Next came tattoos. Sawyer chose a cross with a Jesus fish intersecting an anchor. The needle was thrilling on Sawyer's shoulder. Before he left the shop, he paged through a booklet and saw a blue and purple design that spelled "His."

"You know, for God," the tattoo artist explained. "Like you belong to God."

Within a week, "His" was tattooed on Sawyer's lower back.

Sawyer sought new sensations. He started smoking ciga-rettes. He went to a house party and got drunk for the first time. The warm, giddy fearlessness that took hold of his body was enticing. Throwing up was embarrassing, and Emilie's disappoint-ment didn't feel good. But those moments of drunken euphoria unleashed a craving within Sawyer that he would seek to satisfy again and again.

Two years later, a lot had changed. Sawyer had taken a semester off to volunteer in Guatemala and had a falling out with Emilie and the Campus Crusaders upon his return. Then he met a guy named Jon. Jon's plans to become a high school English teacher were identi-cal to Sawyer's. A Korean adoptee from the Milwaukee area, Jon was handsome, warm, and easy to talk to. They became fast friends. Jon had a girlfriend, but late-night study sessions, ping-pong battles, and lingering hugs made Sawyer wonder if Jon's feelings went beyond friendship. His own certainly did.

That summer, Jon broke up with Amy. Over the phone a few months later, he explained to Sawyer, "Knowing that there was someone out there like you, made me want to see other people."

Sawyer said, "Do you mean you're interested in me? Or other people?"

"I mean you," Jon clarified.

Sawyer was ecstatic. The connection was genuine. They exchanged "I love yous" during their first weekend together. After attending a family wedding, Jon told Sawyer he hoped they'd spend the rest of their lives together. Sawyer tearfully responded, "Me too."

Early that summer, when Sawyer realized that Jon was about to propose, his first thought was, *It's too soon!* He had no idea why. They had frequently talked about a future together, and he had no doubt about his love for Jon. The thought left quickly, and Sawyer responded with a firm embrace, passionate kiss, joyful tears, and a genuine yes.

Sawyer returned to campus before Jon that fall for RA training. He connected with Leah, an aspiring high school science teacher, basketball player, and liberal-minded free spirit. They stayed up late talking about their families, relationships, and sex. They fell asleep drunk in Leah's bed. They flirted in a way that raised eyebrows among fellow RAs.

Leah and Jon became friends too. One night when the three were at the bar, Sawyer took hold of Leah's shoulders and said, "Did you know that if I wasn't marrying Jon, I'd marry you?" And then, "I love you." Leah mentioned it the next day, they both laughed it off. Sawyer apologized. She responded, "It's okay. It wasn't a big deal."

In February of 2005, Sawyer had graduated, and Jon was student teaching. They lived at Sawyer's grandparents' house and returned to La Crosse often to visit friends, including Leah. One night, while the three of them watched a movie, Jon fell asleep, but Sawyer and Leah were wide awake. Leah's hand brushed Sawyer's and stayed there. Sawyer's eyes welled up with tears. "I don't know why I'm crying," he said. It wasn't sadness, fear, or guilt. It was recognition. And when they kissed, the thrill was like being reunited with a long-lost love he didn't know he'd been estranged from. *Oh, there you are.* During breakfast the next morning, the momentary touch of her hand on his knee sent a jolt of pleasure through his body. A switch had been flipped, and he couldn't pretend it didn't happen. He recognized within himself the capacity to be attracted to people of any gender, and to be in love with more than one person at a time.

Two weeks and several drinks later, Sawyer told Jon, "I think I'm bisexual."

"It's Leah, isn't it?"

"This doesn't change my feelings about you," Sawyer insisted. "I love you. I'm attracted to you. I still want to be with you. My feelings for Leah don't mean I have less love for you."

Sawyer would have loved to stay with Jon and be with Leah, but neither Jon nor Leah seemed open to that arrangement. Jon was upset, but accepted Sawyer's bisexual identity and listened lovingly as Sawyer explained what it meant to him. Meanwhile, Leah became emotionally distant. There was so much Sawyer wanted to say. Uncovering this dimension of his sexuality was a gift, a missing puzzle piece. But it came at a cost. His relationship with Leah was never the same, and his wedding was six months away. He didn't feel ready to get married but was relieved that Jon wanted to stay together.

On July 30, 2005, Jon and Sawyer got married. Sawyer was twenty-five and Jon was twenty-three. Sawyer's sisters were his bridesmaids. At the reception, they laughed and danced and celebrated. Jon wore a tuxedo and Sawyer a white dress.

In 2012, the Minnesota state legislature proposed a constitutional amendment to define marriage as between one man and one woman. Sawyer joined the campaign opposing the amendment at the age of thirty-two, while five months pregnant. He felt alive, full of hope that his baby would grow up in a world with fewer barriers to love.

Sawyer gave birth to Anthony Justice Plotz in August. Two months later, on National Coming Out Day, Sawyer came out to his parents and siblings as bisexual. He told them he wasn't volunteering with the Vote No campaign simply because it was the right thing to do. It was personal. He was deeply in love with Jon and grateful for the bond of marriage, and he was also attracted to women. It felt important to claim his place in the LGBTQ+ community. "I don't believe I deserve rights that others are denied simply because my life partner happens to be a man." As Sawyer spoke, Jon, a calm and steady presence at Sawyer's side, held baby Anthony.

———◊———

At age thirty-five, Sawyer was working at a LGBTQ+ equity organization. He attended a trans ally training led by his co-worker, Eli.

"Since the audience includes both trans people and aspiring allies, we're going to start by splitting up into two groups," Eli explained. "If you're a trans person, you can go to the room next door, and if you're cisgender—not trans—you can stay here."

Sawyer's stomach dropped. He flashed back to when he first heard the term *genderqueer* a few years prior, referring to a person whose gender identity is between or outside the binary categories of male and female.

At the time, Sawyer thought, *Huh, that's me.* He even mentioned it to Jon, but in a lighthearted, off-handed way. Genderqueer was a label that fit better, but he had never thought of himself as transgender before. Sawyer didn't move, but when Eli asked them to journal about what it was like to have their gender align with the sex they were assigned at birth, Sawyer couldn't do it because his didn't. His mind raced. He wrote about how excruciating it felt not to join the trans people in the next room. He felt hot. His mouth was dry. There were tears behind his eyes.

"Does anyone want to share?" asked the facilitator.

Sawyer said, "I do. I've never said this out loud before, but I think I might be transgender."

He was met with nods and warm smiles. Sawyer left the training exhilarated and overwhelmed. He didn't say anything to Jon. Something had been uncovered, and there was no going back. But it felt like too much.

Whenever people referred to Sawyer as "she" after that, it felt wrong. He realized it had always felt wrong and worked up the courage to tell his coworkers that he wanted to go by they/them pronouns. Later that week, after Jon had gone to bed, he googled "chest binder." He pulled out a soft tape measure and placed an order.

The next day, Jon asked, "What were you measuring?"

"Nothing." Sawyer mumbled.

"Come on, what's going on?" Jon prodded.

"My chest. A binder is basically a really tight tank top," Sawyer explained. "It makes a person's chest look and feel flatter."

He then told Jon about what had happened at the training. As soon as Sawyer mentioned the word "transgender," Jon said, "Wait, are you saying that you're a man?"

Sawyer heard fear in his voice. "That's not what I'm saying! And you can't just ask me that question!" He felt angry, sorry, confused, and afraid. What if this was the end of his marriage?

He did his best to answer Jon's questions. Jon admitted he was scared. They promised to be loving and honest while taking one step at a time. Jon started using they/them pronouns and taught three-year-old Anthony how to do it as well. Anthony made the switch easily and started calling Sawyer "Papi." Mama no longer fit.

Sawyer wanted to change his name too. One day in a coffee shop, while he was going through the alphabet one letter at a time, he heard someone call out the name "Sawyer."

Sawyer, he thought. He remembered his childhood love for Tom Sawyer, and knew he'd found the one. It took him three months to tell anyone. Asking people to call him by a name he chose himself felt like the boldest thing he had ever done.

"I like it," Jon said when Sawyer finally told him. "It fits you."

A month later, Sawyer decided it was time to tell his parents and siblings. Sawyer invited his parents and two sisters who lived at home over for dinner. Rose, the youngest, couldn't come, but Sawyer decided to proceed. After tucking Anthony into bed, Sawyer walked into the living room, sat down next to Jon, and announced that he had a life update. His mom's face lit up. She sensed another grand-child on the way. Sawyer said, "I've decided to change my name to Sawyer.

"I've been thinking about this for a long time. Jon and I have talked about it. I've been going by Sawyer at work for a month."

Sawyer searched their faces and saw shock and fear.

"It's because I'm transgender. But before you make any assump-tions about what that means, I want to explain." Heart still pounding, Sawyer went into educator mode.

"Gender is dynamic. Transgender can refer to anyone whose gender is different from what was assumed about them at birth. Many trans people experience dysphoria or distress because their body feels disconnected from or not aligned with the gender they identify as. I've never felt like a girl or a woman," Sawyer explained.

"So, are you saying you're a man?" asked his mom.

"All I'm saying is that I'm changing my name to Sawyer."

"Are you going to get surgery? What about Anthony? What about Jon?"

Jon reassured them that Anthony already knew. His and Sawyer's relationship was strong. They were still a family.

This seemed to ease anxiety in the room, but Mom's furrowed brows, Dad's persistent frown, and Rebekah's watery eyes said it all. They each hugged him on the way out but left without a sense of understanding.

Sawyer had planned to take Rose out for breakfast the next morning. He was about to leave the house when his dad called. "Mom is here too," he said. "We're asking you not to come. Mom has been crying so hard she can't breathe. We've hardly slept. We want to talk about this more before you tell your siblings. Please tell Rose you can't get together today. You can say the roads are too slippery to drive."

Sawyer stared out the window.

"I mean this with love," Sawyer's dad said. "You are mistaken. We know you. We know the essence of you."

Sawyer said, "Fine. I won't tell Rose today. But I'm not going to lie. I'll be there in twenty minutes to pick her up."

Several months later, Sawyer told the rest of his siblings, who responded with cautious support. On July 3, he posted on Facebook, "Today is my birthday. It's also the day I announce that I'm changing my name to Sawyer. I'm genderqueer and transmasculine, and I want and need a name that feels like me."

Sawyer's post was met with hundreds of positive reactions and comments. Being called Sawyer brought relief, a settled sense of recognition. It was like scanning a crowded restaurant and seeing the person he'd been waiting for. *Oh, there you are.*

Whenever Sawyer started to think about transitioning further, he stopped himself. He couldn't imagine bringing up top surgery and hormone therapy with Jon. Instead, he took smaller steps to align his body with how he felt. He searched "queer masculine haircut" and got a fresh, clean fade. He stopped shaving his legs and armpits and shopped in the men's clothing department. But his body was still the wrong shape for the clothes he wanted to wear and his gender dysphoria was intensifying. He and Jon also wanted a second child. It's possible for trans men on testosterone to stop taking it and get pregnant, but he didn't want to make decisions about surgery or hormones until after he was done having kids. In August of 2017, Sawyer and Jon agreed to stop using birth control. A few months passed with no pregnancy. Sawyer's typically reliable sex drive decreased. Wondering if his antidepressants were the cause, he stopped taking his medication.

On a Friday in December, Sawyer gave a presentation on gender and sexual orientation at a local high school. Students asked him, "Why are people transgender?" and "If someone is in an opposite-sex relationship, but one person comes out as transgender, does that make their partner gay?" Sawyer answered as calmly and professionally as he could. The lump in his throat had to wait until the bell rang.

The following Monday, Sawyer decided to get drunk rather than go to work. He'd been sober for over three years and knew this was a bad idea, but convinced himself it would be a one-day slip. On the way to the bar, he stopped at the liquor store, bought a bottle of vodka, and hid it in the trunk. He hadn't even had a sip of alcohol yet, but addiction had already highjacked his brain. Once he started drinking, he'd keep drinking like he needed it to survive.

Four days later, Sawyer checked into Pride Institute, an LGBTQ+ treatment center. It was his second time there, but his first as Sawyer. He started taking his antidepressants again, exercised every day, and recommitted himself to staying sober one day at a time. He shared about his experience of gender dysphoria and started introducing himself as "Sawyer, alcoholic, he/him." No one outside read him as "he" yet, but at Pride he felt brave enough to give it a try.

Surrounded by LGBTQ+ people in recovery, Sawyer felt supported, validated, and popular. Pride had the sexually-charged atmosphere of a queer summer camp. For the first time in his life, gay men and bisexual women flirted with Sawyer and treated him like a man. A new resident named Hailey with blonde highlights and pink nail polish caught his eye. She was thirty-six, divorced with three kids, bisexual, funny, and smart. He felt like a fifteen-year-old boy with a crush.

One night, Hailey made a self-deprecating comment and Sawyer countered, "Are you kidding? You're hot. And if you want to make out, you know where to find me."

Hailey laughed, but later that night sat next to him and rubbed his back in a way that showed him the crush was mutual.

"Can I walk you home?" Sawyer asked. It was 9:55 p.m. and everyone had to be in their rooms by 10 p.m.

"I was hoping you would," Hailey replied with a smile.

When they reached her room, Sawyer asked if he could come in. She laughed again. They weren't allowed in each other's rooms. He walked in anyway, shut the door and kissed her. For the next two weeks, Sawyer and Hailey stole every opportunity to do it again.

Somehow, they never got caught. On January 24, 2018, Sawyer completed the program at Pride Institute, after a six-week stay. "Come to my house on February 3," Hailey said. "I'll be home by then, and we'll have the place to ourselves."

Sawyer hadn't told Jon about Hailey, his new pronouns, or the likelihood that he would need to medically transition to stay healthy and sober. Jon had been such a loving, supportive, accepting, and patient partner. At what point would it be too much? When Jon said "I do" at the altar in 2005, he thought he was marrying a cisgender woman. Jon was straight. How could it possibly be fair to expect him to stay?

Sex with Hailey on February 3 would be wrong, Sawyer thought. *But if Jon and I don't make it, at least it would be because I did this wrong thing, not because I am this wrong thing.*

So, he did the thing that the fifteen-year-boy in him wanted to do so badly. A week later, the terrified trans adult in him told Jon. The conversation was volatile. Sawyer was radically honest, desperate for Jon to know both how sorry he was, and how much he hoped the relationship with Hailey could continue.

In therapy, Sawyer and Jon discussed identity, transition, polyamory, and trust. There were tears and incredible love. They renewed their commitment to be as honest and as loving as they could be, and to turn toward each other when things got hard.

———————◊———————

While he and Hailey were seeing each other with Jon's consent, Sawyer found out that he was pregnant. He had given birth to Anthony five years earlier, before he knew that he was trans. This pregnancy felt different.

He waited until his thirty-eighth birthday to share the news on social media. The previous birthday he had announced on Facebook that he was changing his name because he was not a woman. Now, he was announcing he was pregnant. He wrote, "Many things can be true. I can be a transgender person named Sawyer who prefers they/them or he/him pronouns and give birth to a child. Pregnancy is something my body is capable of, not because I'm a woman in the cisgender sense, but because I've been given a gift that allows me to experience the world in a unique way. Kind of like a superpower. Or like a seahorse. In all thirty-two species of seahorses, males carry and give birth to the babies."

Sawyer knew from experience that pregnancy and childbirth are feats of strength. His body's ability to protect and deliver life did not negate his masculinity. Yet, most people did not see it that way. As the pregnancy progressed, Sawyer was referred to as a woman and "a mom-to-be" regularly by strangers, acquaintances, and most healthcare providers. He didn't correct them often. Gender-related concerns were on hold again.

Zachary was born in October, one month early. Sawyer pumped milk six times a day and bottle fed, like with Anthony. But this time, the dysphoria it caused became too much. Sawyer switched to formula feeding and went back to work full time. Life was hectic. He buried his needs.

Eight months later, Sawyer's boys were sleeping, and he was scrolling Facebook before bed when he came across a link posted by someone he'd met a few times at queer events. The author wrote about recognizing himself as a trans man in his mid-thirties, and his decision to go on hormones and get top surgery. Sawyer thought, *Good for him*, then started to fold laundry. Jon came looking for Sawyer and found him standing next to the washing machine, dazed.

Jon asked, "What's wrong?"

Sawyer burst into tears. Jon tried to hug him, but Sawyer backed away. "Can you just leave me alone? I need ten minutes and then I'll come upstairs."

Sawyer curled up in a ball on the floor, crying as hard as he'd ever cried. *This is what I was afraid of,* Sawyer kept thinking.

Sawyer stood up and started hitting a freestanding punching bag as hard as he could. He felt an overwhelming urge to drink. Instead, he said the first three steps of Alcoholics Anonymous out loud. Step three says, "We made a decision to turn our will and our lives over to the care of God as we understood God." Sawyer felt like he understood nothing. He felt out of control. He grabbed the punching bag to keep from bolting to the liquor store, and silently screamed, "God, help me understand what the fuck is wrong with me!"

Hugging the punching bag, he imagined he was hugging himself as a child. Then, lyrics from "Sigh No More" by Mumford and Sons came into his head: "Love, it will not betray you, dismay, or enslave you. It will set you free. Be more like the man you were made to be."

He had heard the song a week ago and hadn't been thinking about it at all. But the words were there, right when he needed them. A feeling of calm swept over him. "Okay," he said out loud. He smiled then chuckled. "Okay." He closed his eyes and pictured himself at four years old. That child was a boy. A boy who was sad and felt invisible. If that little boy had been allowed to grow up, he would be a man now. At age thirty-nine, Sawyer could go on testosterone and get top surgery for that boy. Decisions that had felt confusing and impossible suddenly felt obvious and doable.

———◊———

Two months later, Sawyer's sisters organized a girls' weekend and invited him. He wasn't a girl but didn't want to be left out. Sawyer decided this was the perfect opportunity to tell his family of origin that he was finally ready to be more like the man he was made to be. On Saturday night, Sawyer sat with his heart in his throat. It was getting late. Someone yawned. This was his chance.

His mom asked, "Does anyone have anything interesting coming up?"

"I do," said Sawyer. He imagined four-year-old Sawyer sitting in his lap. "Remember when I announced that I was changing my name to Sawyer? And that it's because I'm transgender?" He looked around the room. "I have some updates about that."

Sawyer told them his plans to start testosterone and get top surgery. Crying, he told them about the blog, the song lyrics, and the sense of clarity he'd felt since. Sawyer's mom got up, walked across the room, sat down next to him, put her arm around him, and said, "I bet you think I'm totally freaked out. But I'm okay. I love you. God loves you. I can't say I totally understand this, but I'm willing to try." It felt like a miracle.

Sawyer was nervous to tell his dad. He started writing a letter but kept getting stuck. Weeks went by. In late October, Sawyer's mom texted, "I told Dad about your plans. I couldn't hold it any longer, and not have anyone to talk to about it. He has some concerns like mine," she said, but ended with, "love to you and your beautiful family." He wondered if they'd ever see him as their son.

Sawyer and his dad didn't talk for a month. During that time, he started hormone therapy. In the parking lot of a gender affirming medicine clinic in Minneapolis, he recorded a video of his voice "pre-T." Then he met his new primary care doctor who talked him through his first testosterone injection. Sawyer was nervous to give himself a shot. But when the short, thin needle pierced the skin of his belly, guided by his own hand, he felt relieved, and very alive.

Sawyer wanted to be seen and heard in a whole new way during his transition. He created an Instagram account called @Sawyer_a_boy_story to document. His mom and siblings followed, and he kept them in mind as he posted, hoping it would help them understand. It did. Sawyer's mom was also talking to Sawyer's dad, and he was starting to come around.

Sawyer had his mom and dad over for dinner again. As Sawyer described how he'd felt as a child—not a tomboy but a *boy*—something clicked for his dad. He looked at his four-year old child in his memories and saw a boy. The next morning, his mom texted, "Thank you for a wonderful evening. Dad is a totally different person. He woke up and said, 'This is the lightest I've felt in weeks.' Watch, he'll end up being your biggest supporter!"

That Christmas, Jon gave Sawyer a custom-made ornament reading: "Love, it will not betray you, dismay, or enslave you. It will set you free. Be more like the man you were made to be." Sawyer spent years assuming that being his true self would make his life fall apart, but those fears were replaced by acceptance and love.

The physical changes on testosterone were subtle at first, but increasingly evident. He worked out regularly with a personal trainer, lost weight, and gained muscle. Facial hair appeared. Shaving his face for the first time brought back memories of borrowing his dad's razor at age six. It brought a sense of gender euphoria, a term often used by trans people to describe the thrill of expressing their authentic gender. Sawyer's body began to take on a more masculine look, but he still wore a chest binder every day when he wasn't sleeping or showering. He felt burdened by the restrictions it placed on him, both physically and mentally. He couldn't wait for top surgery in July. But in March, COVID-19 changed everything. Elective surgeries were canceled. He understood, but his mental health suffered. It was hard to wait.

On July 3, 2020, Sawyer turned forty. For the previous three years, he had written a long Facebook post on his birthday about his journey. This year, it was Sawyer's mom who wrote a brave birthday Facebook post. "Many of you reading this might be confused," she wrote. "I was too at first, but I've learned a lot." She explained that "being transgender is not a trend, a fad, a political statement, or a rejection of God. The decision to transition is often arrived at because a person's very life depends on it. Sawyer and Jon are together, in love, and spectacular parents to Anthony and Zachary. This little family is magical. They embody unconditional love." She urged her friends to listen to LGBTQ+ people and ended by writing, "When an issue becomes a person, it changes everything."

It was the best birthday present he could have asked for. The next present was a phone call reporting his top surgery had been rescheduled for August 24.

On the morning of the surgery, Sawyer's mom took care of Anthony and Zachary. Jon and Sawyer listened to "Sigh No More" on the way to the hospital. All went well. By 8 p.m., Sawyer was at home, asleep in a recliner, with an ACE bandage around his chest. Jon helped manage Sawyer's pain medication so he wouldn't be tempted to take too much.

When the wrap came off and the drains came out, he got to finally see his chest. He'd been waiting for this moment for so long, but he tried to keep his expectations low. He reminded himself that it was major surgery, and it's ok if it doesn't look good yet. His chest was completely flat. His nipples had been removed, resized, and grafted back onto his body in a wider, more masculine position. A thick, fresh scar began under one arm and stretched all the way to the other side. Sawyer had never seen his chest like this, but still had the "*Oh* there *you are!*" sensation when he looked in the mirror. His new look was not everything he'd dreamed of. He wanted to be leaner and stronger, but thought, "Ok. This is good. We can work with this." He felt relieved, relaxed, and grateful. He couldn't wait to heal so he could run through the sprinkler bare-chested like he did when he was six.

At a year-and-a-half, little Zachary will only remember Sawyer as a transgender man. He loved the song "Baby Shark." When it got to the "Momma Shark" part, Anthony encouraged Zachary to say "Papi Shark" instead.

"It's okay, Anthony." Sawyer told him. "Zachary can know that families have mommas."

"I know, but for this family we have you, our Papi."

On August 17, 2021, Sawyer was coming up on his one-year anniversary of top surgery. He had no complications during the healing process. He started lifting weights in the winter and progressed to six workouts a week by spring. But a flare-up of pain in his neck and shoulders had been lingering since June. Hoping for relief, he made an appointment with a massage therapist. Reading him as a cisgender man, she casually said, "Just take your shirt off, and we'll get started."

Sawyer's mind raced. *Wait, should I? Can I? Am I allowed to? What will she think of my scars? Will it change the way she treats me?*

He tried his best to appear casual while taking off his shirt. Unfazed, the massage therapist asked him to lie on his back and began applying gentle pressure to his chest. Sawyer settled into a deep state of relaxation, knowing that he deserved healing and the wholeness that comes with integrating his body, mind, and spirit.

Before putting his shirt back on, Sawyer caught a glimpse of his lower back in the mirror. The blue and purple design was still there, but the tattoo's meaning had transformed. He still belongs to God, but also to himself. His identity and his body are his own. He, him, his.

I went to high school with Sawyer. We played softball and traveled to Guatemala together. He was kind, quiet, and studious. He was a great outfielder. I reconnected with him after college when we were on the same anti-war committee. I met Jon there and liked him right away. I followed Sawyer on social media and asked him if he was interested in being part of this project. We met on Zoom during the pandemic every few weeks, plodding through his memories. It was heavy and good.

So often the media shows trans folks as failed men or women or restricts a trans identity to something like "being a man trapped in a woman's body." He heard transgender folks say they knew their bodies didn't quite fit at an early age. Sawyer felt self-conscious about, what seemed to him, the slow realization and the seemingly late transition. His story is not simple, and it is not a neat, linear arc. Sawyer's crafting and telling his trans story continues to shape our view of gender in meaningful ways. It makes him the author of his narrative.

What if we all became more fluent in the language of gender, sex, and sexuality, recognizing the limitation of binaries, and worked toward attaching words to our messy humanity? What may have been different if polyamorous, genderqueer, and transgender were well-known words and concepts of his childhood, with endless nuance and variation? We agreed we need more people telling their stories so our paths can be as varied as we are.

Collaborating on this project brought Sawyer and me close. Our boys love climbing trees together. He is a fantastic parent. He makes a delectable chocolate-covered cherry. It has been a delight to witness his continued unfolding and hold space for him to craft his story.

> What is something your body can do that may be gendered by society but feels like your own superpower? What is one choice you can make to express your gender in a way that feels in line with the person you really are?

Symbols as Story

When I was twenty-five, I moved to rural Uruguay for a year. Right before I left, my friend Courtney died of cancer. I was heartbroken, and Uruguay proved to be a good place for my broken heart to be exposed to the elements. The plethora of butterflies got my attention, and then, because I was looking for them, I saw them everywhere. I took them on as my companions.

The butterflies reminded me of Courtney because she had a butterfly tattoo on her left foot. When butterflies hovered and fluttered around me, I was filled with a sense of wonder and thin space between here and not here, recalling her laughter and fierce love.

Toward the end of my time in Uruguay, I went to Iguazu Falls with my friends. At the Devil's Throat lookout, I squealed with delight into the roar of the water, the mist from its power drenching me. I hummed with aliveness. Butterflies of all colors and sizes danced around my face. It was Courtney's birthday.

My Uruguayan town had few streetlights and no large buildings. I had time to sit and watch the spectacular sunrise and sunset in their entirety, a daily orchestra performance of vibrant colors. When I returned home, I got a tattoo of the sun from the Uruguayan flag on my foot to match Courtney's butterfly. Each summer, when it finally gets warm enough in Minnesota to peel off my wool socks and let my bare feet breathe, I think about Courtney, the dancing butterflies, and our journey around the sun.

A decade later, I got my second tattoo on my inner left wrist. It's a strong, balanced, graceful Gaelic symbol that means *new beginnings*. It marks the season of my life losing, growing, birthing, and caring for babies. They were the most intense, holy, and mystifying years of my life thus far. After my two miscarriages, I had two hard, full-term pregnancies filled with nausea, depression, shingles, constipation, and an SI joint dislocation. I gained and lost and gained and lost fifty pounds. I did not enjoy what I was told to enjoy, the serious physical restriction and temporary disability. I did not appreciate having my body objectified and commented on by friends and strangers alike.

My first birth consisted of 58 hours of labor ending in an emergency caesarean section. My second child got very sick one week after we got home from the hospital, and he spent three weeks in the pediatric ICU unconscious and intubated. This first hospital stay led to a tumultuous relationship with breastfeeding and several subsequent hospitalizations.

I love being a mom. It is my very favorite thing. I made up a catchy song about it that I sing to my kids now and again. I cry watching them eat cereal because it is all so beautiful, and love is so gut-wrenching, and time is so fleeting. My experience of caring for infants—with serious sleep deprivation, a tectonic plate shift in identity, and sharp primal feelings of the fiercest love I have ever known—was magical and messy. Holy and overwhelming. A hormone rollercoaster. A lonely, isolating reminder of the patriarchy. A sacred adventure. A humbling process of letting go. The tender trenches.

As I emerged from the six-year fog of losing, carrying, birthing, and sustaining babies, I felt disembodied, numb, puffy, tired, and a little stunned. I shut down part of myself to get through what my body went through. I wanted to integrate my body, mind, and spirit again. Bouncing back struck me as the wrong verb and the wrong direction. I wanted to grow forward, to expand outward, to get to know and fall in love with my new, aging, extraordinary, rearranged body. I went to see my friend Tina Green who does body alignment and integration work called Rolfing. We did ten sessions together, once a month, and it was as if she gently peeled away the layers of self-protection one by one. She facilitated the release of pain housed in my body. She held space for me to cry and process while breaking up scar tissue and loosening the clinging, guarding fascia.

I told her about my body loathing, how there was not enough laughter in my days. I told her I felt stuck at times, and at other moments like I was crawling out of my skin. When Tina did an energy scan during the first appointment, it felt like she was brushing my hair—luscious and relaxing—like magnets were aligning with her hand. She placed a finger on my womb and another on my chest and it felt like feathers of energy were floating up out of my torso.

I was fascinated.

During our second session, after working on my left foot, she asked me to look at my feet. The left was warm, supple, and straight. The right was cold, crooked, and curled. At the end of the session, the floor felt different under my soles. In the month between sessions, I explored how I hold stress in my feet, scrunching them, grabbing onto the carpet, clinging.

During our fifth session, I talked about losing a part of myself in my love for my babies. I wanted to emerge from the infancy trenches. I wanted to be a mom and a stable woman who brings her own things to the table. My kids were no longer breastfeeding. They slept through the night. One of them could even go to the bathroom and put on his shoes without assistance. I wanted to embrace this new stage of parenting and unfold as a mother and a whole human who celebrates my other identities too.

Tina moved to my C-section scar, and at her touch, a wave of energy flowed up my chest and welled in my eyes as tears. My body was a deep pond and her touch sent ripples, a swell of energy up to my head and down to my feet. Something was breaking free. I saw my scar as a line in the dirt, with roots shooting down into me from the seeds. She was tending the soil, breaking up the rock, preparing my body to be fertile ground again. Growing babies is not the only creation my body is built for.

It felt like Tina was breaking apart the fear that invited me to hold back and stay small. While Tina tended to the built-up scar tissue underneath the surface, I turned toward the layered fear and explored. What was I holding on to? Why was it difficult to release the stored-up pain?

I didn't want to let go of the pain because I loved the affection I got from my mother when I was sick or hurt as a child. I associated pain with love. I didn't want to let go because it felt like my pain honored my miscarriages and I was afraid of forgetting them in my healing. I didn't want to move on from them. And I didn't want to let go of the pain because I was afraid to admit that I was done having kids. The door to having children was closing. A stage I loved was over. I was afraid that doing this healing meant my babies would become boys and eventually leave me. When my children left, what would be left? Would I be enough?

Tina asked what belief system was wrapped up in my fear and I said, "I don't believe that life is supposed to be easy." I felt at home in the struggle, in the hard. The hecticness of raising infants kept my fear of ease at bay. I was busy doing something important. Someone needed me. I had a purpose, keeping the baby right in front of me alive. I did not have to sit in the quiet and stillness of ease and face myself stripped down in non-doing. I recoiled from ease, worried that I wasn't pushing hard enough. I equated ease with laziness, taking my privilege for granted, and not earning my keep. My work was to rewire those beliefs so that I could live into ease and embrace the peace and calm that comes with healing and growth.

The following day, my body was tired. I cried all morning, but there was no weight to it. It felt like a detoxing as natural as sweating. I was emerging.

By our eighth session, the heavy lifting had passed. My body remembered Tina's touch and released easily. We talked about how I felt fragmented. My life as a mother and my life as a writer felt totally separate. The integration work created space in my body for me to be more than one thing simultaneously. I brought my whole self to more moments, not dramatically swinging from one extreme to the other but gently flowing and inhabiting it all.

Tina talked with me about the quadrants of our bodies. The quadrants of order and grounding in me were stronger than the quadrants of activation and flow. I experienced having babies as grounding, which was a gift, until it became unbalanced, and the grounding felt like being stuck. I bring order to our family, which is beautiful until it became unbalanced and felt like rigidity. We talked about balance between groundedness and flow, work and rest, my public and private self. She invited me to continue to honor the grounding and order while also turning toward activation and flow. To turn toward my public and professional life and to tend to my inner work as a writer. As an artist. As a healer.

By my ninth session, my body and heart felt warm, soft, and open. I showed Tina my idea for a tattoo, a constant reminder to create ease and balance. I told her I wanted to write about bodies, the stories of bodies, and what we carry, what we let go of, and who we become.

Little by little, I found more alignment in my body and in my life. I marveled at my new body and self. I took my seat as a woman who sleeps through the night, delights in her kids, loves her job, practices yoga, appears on podcasts, loves snuggles the most, and gets to dry her hair a few times a week. I am not who I was. I have transformed. I have the worn-in beauty of a survivor who continues to grow, who is open to the opening. I poked around at the new lay of the land, exploring who I am now as a layered and strong woman, mother, and writer. Ordered and activated. Grounded and flowing.

As Tina massaged the tissue underneath my left shoulder blade, I cried softly. My body affectionally said to me, "You've done well, now rest. I give you permission to rest." In my womb I felt the old book of survival had been sent away and replaced by a new book of knowledge telling the story of healing that leads to balance, ease, thriving, and wholeness. The drive in me let up just a bit. I felt present and happy.

My tattoo has all of this wrapped up in it and more. I see a new beginning, where I am a mom who does not hide behind my kids, who loves them fiercely while committing to my own growth. I prioritize their needs and let them see me prioritize my own as well. In the tattoo I see the babies who stopped growing inside me, about whom I will always wonder. I see my two children, who are the loves of my life. I see my spouse, my foundation and strength. I see my Irish bloodline. I see a call to live in the tension between death and life, between logic and art, between now and forever. It acknowledges the baby-birthing stage of my life and invites me to birth new things.

I love my tattoos. My tattoos are tangible symbols of my story, excuses to talk about my body. My body and its story are sacred and they're mine. My experiences leave marks on my being, and the tattoos make that visible to me and the world. They remind me that my body is temporary. My body will die. I am not my feeling body, but the one who tells the story of it. My body is my vehicle for the ride.

One of my tattoos is from my twenties, and one is from my thirties. I imagine getting a new symbol each decade to honor my body as it transforms and make visible my ever-unfolding story, my ever-expanding identity.

How does your body experience connection to others across time and space? What is one thing you can do today to celebrate a part of who you are that rarely gets prioritized?

Our society is not big on change, or aging. We can pine for the past and categorize bodies in harmful and limiting ways. What if, instead of policing bodies, our master narratives allowed space and grace for our bodies to change, expand, and become? What if instead of bouncing back after birthing a child our bodies could unfold and expand? What if instead of blaming people for their difference in ability we create a society that is accessible to all bodies? What if we allowed our gender, sex, and sexuality to be complex, dynamic, and alive instead of static, singular, and binary, using a constellation instead of a spectrum for our becoming, a rhizome instead of a tree? What if we embraced wrinkles as signs of wisdom instead of desperately trying to erase them? What if we engaged in the work of more fully inhabiting our ever-transforming bodies and identities as the work of our lives?

Master narratives tend to tell linear, individual hero stories that privilege and center bodies that are young, strong, productive, cis-hetero, White, and male. We can craft counter-stories that challenge and diversify those master narratives so that one day we may live in a society that widens what is normal, accepted, and celebrated and values our bodies as we transform into deeper, wiser, more embodied selves.

Reflection Questions

* What did your body experience while reading these stories? Did any of them resonate with you and your body's story?
* Talk about a time in your life when your body went through a major transition or transformation. How did your identity shift? Did your sense of freedom and agency grow, shrink, or stay the same?
* Do you more often escape your body by dwelling in your mind or escape your mind by dwelling in your body?
* Have you ever been ashamed of a part of your body because you felt it was different from the norm?
* How did you express gender as a small child? What messages did you receive through puberty about your gender that you have internalized?
* How does your sense of self transform as your context changes?
* When was a time you did not feel at home in your body?
* What are some ways you like receiving physical affection? Giving physical affection?

✳   What master narratives are told around major body transformations like pregnancy, gender confirmation, or reconstructive surgery? Do the narratives that exist in your birth family, found family, place of work, communities, and society at large allow space for major body transformations?

Writing Prompts

Create a T chart on your page. On the left side of the paper, write down lies you tell yourself, lies other people have told you, or those society tells you about your body. On the right side, write the truth. Recognize which lie or lies on the left side carry the most weight or have the most charge to them. This may be one of your core lies. Spend some time here. What experiences contributed to creating that lie? Choose the phrase on the right side of that core lie and take it on as a daily mantra, a refrain you can repeat to yourself throughout the day.

Set a timer for seven minutes. Write a litany of sentences that all start with the phrase "I remember . . ." Don't overthink it. Don't stop writing. Just see what comes up without trying to control it. You will end up with a list of memories that will not be chronological but do correlate. When the time goes off, stop writing. Take a look at your list. Choose a memory that carries a lot of charge for you and go back to that memory. Walk around in the memory, noticing. Journal about what comes up and notice how the memory feels in your body. Repeat this activity often, shifting how much time you put on your timer. It is a good way to get memories out on paper where you can look at them and craft them into a story and do the work of meaning-making while respecting the stories that live in your body.

Write a memory from travel and what you learned about yourself outside your more regular context. Where are you when you take your body for granted? Where are you when you are very aware of your body and how it is being perceived?

Write about how your body and your relationship to your body have shifted over time.

Breath Practice

Find a comfortable seated posture with a tall spine. Gently seal your lips and breathe through your nostrils. Notice air entering and leaving your nostrils without altering your breath. Simply notice that you are breathing. After a few breath cycles, empty out your lungs and create a square breath:

Four-count inhale

Four-count hold

Four-count exhale

Four-count hold

Continue for about ten breath cycles and then return to your natural breath.

Body Practices

Sing. Sing from your diaphragm and feel the resonance in your whole body. Sing a lullaby. Sing a pop song from your youth. Sing a spiritual. Sing an ancient chant. Send your note out into the world and notice the resonance in your chest. It's okay to make noise.

Find a quiet place free of distractions. Choose a seated or reclined body posture that is both alert and calm. Look around you, even behind you, taking stock of your surroundings. Notice the exit and windows. Notice the smells and ambient sounds in the room. When you are ready, blink your eyes closed and invite your attention away from your environment and toward your body. Notice the air temperature and your clothes touching your skin. Notice any tingling or sensation on your skin.

Go deeper to your fascia, a complex matrix of connective tissue holding your joints in place.

Slowly bring your attention to your muscles from the crown of your head down to the soles of your feet. Notice any sensations of expansion, constriction, fatigue, or soreness without judgment.

Go deeper, noticing your bones. Bring your awareness to your joints, where your bones meet and move, more of an event than a place. Notice what emotions and memories live there.

Then go deeper, below the skin, tissues, and bones to your vital organs. Notice your heart beating and your lungs and diaphragm expanding and contracting.

Now bring your awareness to your breath. No need to alter your breath, simply notice that you are breathing. When your mind starts to wander, gently bring your attention back to the sound and rhythm of your breath. The one who notices your body, your breath, and your thoughts is your true self. You are not your thoughts or your feelings. You are the one who witnesses them.

When you are ready, slowly bring your attention back from your breath to your organs, to your bones, muscles, fascia, and then skin. Allow your attention to arrive back on the surface and all the sensations and stimuli there. Take one additional full, cleansing breath before blinking your eyes open and coming back to your room.

Throughout the day, come back to your breath and allow it to anchor you in your body and in the present moment as it arrives. Remember that you are not your body expression, but the one choosing how to express yourself in the world, moment to moment. Spending time as the witness observer of your body, thoughts, and feelings can lessen any clinging to a certain aspect of your identity and deepen your sense of alignment in your inner and outer life.

Five

Bodies Overcome
Surviving Oppressive Systems

Counterstories take up an oppressive but shared moral understanding and attempt to shift it, rejecting its assumption that
people with a particular group identity are to be subordinated
to others or denied access to personal and social goods. They
are, then, narrative acts of insubordination.

—HILDE LINDEMANN NELSON,
Damaged Identities: Narrative Repair

In high school I absent-mindedly scheduled a meeting in a room
that a group member couldn't get to in his wheelchair. When I
got married, I invited friends to attend who could not yet legally
marry due to their sexuality. A few months after George Floyd was
murdered in my town, I got pulled over for speeding with my kids in
the car. A White-bodied female officer gave me a ticket and sent
me on my way. I was aware that I was not afraid. In December, I
am attuned to my Christian identity watching our media culture.
Chanequa Walker-Barnes writes, "In any society, the most marginalized people best understand the rules of the system, because

they need to know the politics and dynamics in order to avoid being crushed by them."

Apart from being a woman, my body is supported by the structures of my country. As someone not being crushed by the system, I can locate and implicate myself in the systems that do crush others. I can see where I have long-held privilege without being paralyzed and broken by shame. I can see the action and attitudes of individuals *and* see the patterns, policies, cultures, and systems advantaging certain bodies, often bodies like mine, over others. I can move past passive empathy to action. It is the work of feeling in my body and knowing in my bones that systemic oppression constricts the psyche of the oppressed and wounds the soul of the oppressor. It is the work of unlearning innocence and learned helplessness.

The master narratives favor my body over others and lead to attitudes, policies, and practices that dismiss, limit, and attempt to erase some bodies more than others. The body stories in this chapter address the fatigue and vigilance it takes to stay safe in a body marked as other and less than by the dominant culture. The stories in this chapter are not buying that some bodies are subordinate to others. They are narrative acts of insubordination, actively countering the limiting narratives coming at them from the systems level. As bell hooks writes, "My writing was an act of resistance not simply in relation to outer structures of domination like race, sex, and class; I was writing to resist all the socialization I had received in a religious, southern, working-class, patriarchal home that tried to teach me silence as the most desirable trait of womanliness." These stories speak into the silence. They are asserting truth that is always already there, truth remembered. And they are working to shift our master narratives so we can all deconstruct oppressive systems together and build communities where all bodies can be safe and belong.

Pride and Fear

Whether we realize it fully or not, we make a plethora of daily decisions about how to express ourselves in the world. We decide what clothes and accessories to wear, how to do our hair, what tone of voice and words to use, what pictures to post on social media, how much literal and figurative space to take up in the world with our bodies and beings. The motivation behind these decisions varies from wanting ease to wanting to make a statement, from habit to experiment. What looks similar from the outside from one day to the next may feel vastly different internally as the meaning behind the expression changes. We put ourselves out into the world and do not have control over how other people respond to our choices. There may be a disconnect between how we see ourselves and how others see us. The feedback loop between our being and our environment molds our sense of agency and freedom. We do not choose the oppression tied to the choices we make about how to express ourselves. There are social consequences for our choices, affecting our safety and our sense of belonging, placing us inside or outside the dominant culture's master narrative. Take, for example, Fardosa's choice to wear a hijab.

Fardosa started wearing her hijab when she was in the fifth grade. She wore it on and off at first, unclear of her own motivation. Her mom taught her to be proud of being Somali, Muslim, and Black. She lived in a Somali Muslim neighborhood and felt supported, even sheltered.

Then, when Fardosa was in the sixth grade, terrorists flew planes into the twin towers. Her world changed drastically. At a gas station soon after, Fardosa's uncle asked her to take her hijab off, but she refused. Saying no shifted something in her. Choosing to wear her hijab had an added layer of pride. She understood differently how it was a sign of solidarity and a sign of her heritage. She is Somali, Muslim, Black, and proud. Her hijab is an extension of her, a cultural and religious choice. Since that day, she has worn her hijab daily.

Fardosa went to a high school with students from all sorts of different cultures. Some of her closest friends were Hmong, African American, and Mexican. She was not supposed to date as a Muslim girl, but instead of seeing prom as an obstacle, Fardosa gathered a group to go as friends. One of her White friends had the group over for a barbeque before the dance. Fardosa reminded the host that she couldn't eat pork, so her friend made steaks. At the barbecue, Fardosa's Hindu Indian friend whispered to her, "Don't tell anyone, but I can't eat meat." Her friend was embarrassed, and didn't want to draw attention to herself, so Fardosa ate double steak and gave her friend her sides. Fardosa realized she had a pride and comfort in her identity that her friend had not yet found. Some of Fardosa's friends took their hijabs off for prom and school pictures. Fardosa kept hers on. She was not afraid to speak up for herself and navigated the world confidently. She made barbeques, prom, and school picture day work for her. Her rules and her choices mattered. After prom, she asked her friend to tell her more about her Hindu culture so she could be a better advocate.

Fardosa situates herself in a wave of Muslim women in North America who claim the hijab and lean on it. It unites them. Early Muslim lawmakers in the United States did not wear the hijab. Then Ilhan Omar gained visibility by wearing it with pride. Several Muslims competed for the United States in the 2016 Olympics, but fencer Ibtihaj Muhammad was celebrated as a highly visible Muslim because she competed in her hijab. Halima Aden, a Muslim woman from St. Cloud, Minnesota, also gained visibility by competing in the Miss Minnesota competition wearing her hijab and burkini.

As anti-Muslim sentiment flared following the 2016 election, some who may have once seen the hijab as a sign of oppression reframed the hijab as a sign of empowerment and freedom. If a person in a hijab got harassed for being Muslim, a person *not* wearing a hijab might start wearing one as a visible sign of support.

In Fardosa's family, women take their hijabs off when they are together at family functions like weddings. They complimented Fardosa's curls and encouraged her to show them off, but Fardosa liked to wear her hijab all the time. When Fardosa told the women in her family she was going to wear her hijab for her own wedding, they revolted. "It's at night! It's with family! Don't wear it," they pleaded.

She explained to me, "It's a woman-to-woman thing. A mother-to-daughter thing. The hijab is part of my mother's identity that she passed on to me. Men don't get to talk about my body or my choice to wear the hijab." Eventually the women in her family supported her decision. "My hijab is a symbol of my connection to God. I made a promise to God, and I am wearing it for me. It's a representation of my culture and religion. When I put it on, I am representing all of Islam. It is a responsibility that makes me proud."

Moving from her strong foundation as a proud Black Somali Muslim, Fardosa's courage in the face of discrimination grew. She recounted, "One day I was crossing the street, and a man shouted at me from his car, 'Go home!' I shouted back, 'You go home!' We both should probably go home. This land doesn't belong to either of us." She paused. Reflecting back on the moment she added in a more serious tone, "I realize now that yelling things like that put my life at risk. But I can't walk away. I was raised to speak up for myself."

In 2016, Fardosa and her sister spoke in a church in small-town Minnesota. The event was lovely. People were hospitable and asked interesting questions. On the way home from the event, however, young guys in a red pickup truck followed her. They tried to force her off the road. They yelled, "Terrorist!" out their open windows.

"Let's take our hijabs off," her sister begged.

Without turning her gaze from the road, Fardosa responded, "We're still Black."

Fardosa tried to remain calm and stay on the road. Her sister took pictures of the truck's license plate and called the police. The police headed toward them and kept them on the line. The driver of the truck slowed and turned before the police arrived. Fardosa and her sister drove home in silence, fear a passenger in the seat between them.

"The police officer called me that night to make sure I got home safely. That meant a lot," Fardosa said. "But it was the first time I feared for my life. It changed everything."

She used to run by herself regularly to clear her head. That alone time was so important to her. Now she's cautious. Even though she loves being quiet in nature, she doesn't go wandering or running alone anymore. She's afraid. She thinks before she speaks to strangers.

"Before 2016, I was clueless. Now I see the hate prevailing. It comes from the top, and that's terrifying. I'm not sure how to live to the other side of this fear."

In 2017, Fardosa and her friend stopped in a diner on their way home from a girls' weekend at Bay Lake Camp. When they walked in, the staff and patrons stared at them like exotic animals. It was the type of stare that didn't let up, that made her feel unsafe. She stood her ground and stayed. She asked that her meat be prepared on a pork-free grill, but when the food came, she didn't trust it. She asked for ketchup with her fries, and the server brought a small bowl of ketchup with bacon bits in it. She ate her fries with no ketchup, paid, and left for home.

Fardosa misses the confident and proud girl who went running by herself and talked back to strangers on the street. Now, when she is outside her neighborhood, she is hyperaware of her surroundings. Discomfort and paranoia loom.

"When I am with a group of my people in a safe space, we talk loudly. We joke. In public, I feel pressure to keep it down. To be quiet. To behave so I don't make a bad name for Somalis, for Muslims, for Black folks." She sighed, "It's exhausting."

Yet she persists. "My hijab is a symbol of liberation. I don't have to live up to society's standards. It's a symbol of resistance. It is a symbol of Islam. It's a constant act of worship." After a moment she added, "And it's mine."

Fardosa's family and community supported her building a strong foundation of pride as a Black Somali Muslim when she was young so she could engage in what feminists call *coming to voice* and bell hooks calls *talking back*. That talking back looks like her retort to the man who yelled at her on the street, and it also looks like her decision to speak publicly, participate in this book project, and wear her hijab day in and day out. Her truth-telling reveals the powers working to tear her down. Talking back is an act of defiance that heals and creates space for new growth so she can remember herself rightly despite the oppressive systems working to constrict her sense of freedom. She is engaging in her work of liberation and healing in a way that hopefully inspires people with racial and religious power to engage in the connected work of repentance.

> *Think about the choices you make and the ways you outwardly express your identity. Do you think about social consequences, or do you factor in your physical safety when making these choices?*

Over the Rainbow

As a small child, Justin loved to dress up. His favorite item was his mother's shirt slip. On him, it looked like a dress. He put panty-hose on his head for braids, grab a lunch box for a picnic basket, and became Dorothy from *The Wizard of Oz*. The parents in the neighborhood, including Justin's, relished his innocent, limitless creativity and allowed him to run around naked or in his favorite dress. When he was three, the neighbors brought him to Home Depot for a quick errand in his slip. He liked the way the silk felt on his skin.

Justin's mom worried about him and wondered with her friends how long she should encourage his dress up in public spaces. It did not take long, however, for his peers to regulate him. Justin told his preschool friends he wanted to dress up like Nala from *The Lion King* for Halloween.

"You can't be Nala," one boy said. "Nala's a girl."

Justin asked his mom about the interaction. She told him it was fine to dress up as Nala, but the seed had been planted. His body had an assigned sex and gender, and with that came rules. Soon after, Justin's best friend Sophie told him they weren't supposed to run around the neighborhood together naked anymore because she was a girl and he was a boy.

Justin brought his dress inside his house. He played Dorothy and made his mom play all the other parts. Spirited and bossy, he directed his mom around the living room and told her when she was doing it wrong.

By middle school, Justin was hyperaware of his body and gender rules. To avoid presenting as femme, he embraced an unkept, aloof look instead. He didn't realize at the time the cost of putting away his queerness.

By high school, Justin was very tall and extremely petite. He excelled at cross-country running, swimming, and track. He spent significant time naked, in Speedos and short shorts with other boys. He shivered constantly on the pool deck. He was never bullied, but teammates called him Twigs as an affectionate nickname. Afraid of his femininity, he deflected with laughter and made fun of himself. His three sports teams became safe communities for him to own his body.

The summer between his junior and senior year in high school, Justin traveled to El Salvador with a group of students and teachers. He noticed strong binary gender norms in the culture. In the boys' room, his attraction to boys surfaced. When he got home, he went shopping with his best friend Kathleen. He bought his first pair of skinny jeans and hasn't taken them off since. He came out as gay to his inner circle.

Justin also dropped his sports and joined the theater. Finally, he got to dress up again. Theater allowed him to try on different bodies and personas for a time and then put them back. He was supposed to wear makeup. He could mess around with gender without having to claim that fluidity as part of his actual identity. It remained a costume and a role, contained and safe. Justin got cast as the King of Hearts in *Alice in Wonderland* and created a queer, larger-than-life persona with striking makeup and a flashy outfit. Absolutely mesmerizing, he stole the show.

By the time Justin arrived at Augsburg College in Minneapolis, Minnesota, he expressed his queerness through his body daily and on purpose in public. He feared confrontation without the safety of the stage, but took on a "Fuck you, get out of my way" mentality. Meanwhile, alone in his dorm room, Justin experimented with full drag, watching YouTube videos and perfecting his makeup. He bought his first wig and dressed up with his close friends.

Split Britches, a lesbian group in New York City, reimagined *A Streetcar Named Desire* in the 1980s. Augsburg theater took it on, and Justin played Blanch in full drag. He loved it. His naturally slender shape translated well to a normalized cis-presenting female form of drag. He felt cautiously at home as a gay, queer, gender-bending man.

Then everything changed.

Sophomore year in college, late at night on the weekend, Justin went outside his dorm to smoke a cigarette. He was drunk. A group of guys walked by and asked each other, loudly enough for him to hear, why he was wearing high heels.

"Fuck you!" he shouted.

They kept walking, but soon came back in a car. They got out of the car, and as they approached him, one of the guys called him a faggot.

Justin got in his face. "Define that word for me. Give me a definition!"

It escalated quickly and the guys physically assaulted both Justin and Justin's friend.

Justin's biggest fear—expressing his queerness and getting hurt for it—became reality. It confirmed his fear was warranted. It heightened his fear of physical harm. To this day, he is consciously aware of that fear living in his body. Part of him, years later, has not let the incident go. It fueled the other part of him to go back into the world expressing himself even more passionately. Being assaulted made one thing abundantly clear: This was not a role anymore. It was not a costumed theater character he was trying on that got attacked. It was him.

"I got assaulted. I am queer," he said. "This is not something I can put on and take off. It's who I am."

The assailant was not an Augsburg student. Tyler, Justin's friend who came out as trans soon after, used Facebook to organize a weeklong rally to support him. Students wore red on Monday, orange on Tuesday, yellow on Wednesday, green on Thursday, blue on Friday, and purple on Saturday. At the rally and march, Justin was a little uncomfortable. He didn't want it to be about him. Yet the campus-wide response ignited in him a drive to give back. It focused his desire for justice beyond his body. It birthed in him a motivation to organize and bring his personal involvement to the issue of queer rights. Justin acutely felt the presence of and the importance of his queer chosen family in the larger LGBTQIA+ community.

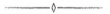

Justin applied for and was awarded a research grant during his senior year of college. He was the only artist among a group of scientists. He used the funding to research, write, direct, produce, and star in a one-person show. *Utopiacopia* has two female characters, both played by Justin. Marcy is a wound-up, controlling, single, conservative cat lady in her 40s, with a strong Minnesotan accent. She is the flight attendant on a spaceship headed for planet Utopiacopia. The audience members are the passengers. Dorothy, based on *The Wizard of Oz* character, symbolizes innocence, youth, and idealism. She sneaks onto the ship with Toto (a stuffed cat dressed as a dog) thinking it's an airplane headed for San Francisco.

At the beginning of the performance, Justin's character and prop transitions between Marcy and Dorothy are clean. As the performance continues, chaos ensues, and the transitions become intentionally clunky until one half of Justin's body is Dorothy, and the other half is Marcy. The two women must work together to get into the one remaining spacesuit. In Justin's singular body, the audience clearly sees Marcy on one side and Dorothy on the other, struggling simultaneously. He externally portrays the internal fragmentation that comes from society halving us, limiting us to one thing, one expression. It's stunning and invites relief.

The show ends with Marcy/Dorothy taking her mask off and singing "Somewhere Over the Rainbow." Justin, in partial drag, exits the theater onto the busy Minneapolis Lake Street.

Being the only body filling two characters on stage was intense. Justin loved the high risk and high reward. It felt like the two characters and Justin were all fighting inside his body at the same time. During a dress rehearsal, when Justin walked out onto Lake Street, a motorcycle gang drove by and one of the riders catcalled him. He said it was both hilarious and terrifying. A spike of fear shot through his body then and each night when that moment of the show came up. He was not drinking or dancing. The sun was still out. On Lake Street in drag, no longer Dorothy or Marcy but Justin, he felt vulnerable and bare.

In Minneapolis, the drag scene consisted of female impersonators singing at bars like The Gay 90s. Justin loved it and he wanted more, so he moved to New York City to fully immerse in the drag scene there.

Justin strutted down the streets of Manhattan late at night in a thong and flowy shirt. He felt free. He felt like he was contributing to keeping New York City one place where you can do whatever you want, be whoever you want. He tried on the name Eggz Benedict, a nod to his grandpa's favorite dish, and it stuck. His friends called him Legs Benedict because he'd often go out without pants.

Justin worked parties in drag. He posted where he was going on social media to draw a crowd. At his peak, he bartended brunch at The Standard Hotel on Saturday and Sunday from nine in the morning until four in the afternoon, went home, took four hours to apply makeup, left home at 12:30 a.m., and worked parties at Webster Hall from 1:00 to 4:30 a.m. He worked three parties a week. It was excessive, and it was exactly what he wanted.

While working parties, Justin got very interested in the hospitality business and rose to manager at a corporate hotel bar in the East Village. He slowly, proudly turned it into a gay bar.

After years deep in the scene, Justin grew weary. He could keep going, but he started to ask if he wanted to. Queer life happens in the club, but the drinking, drugs, and late nights were slowly taking their toll. He wondered how he could celebrate his queerness in the world while caring for his body. You can be sober as a drag queen, but Justin didn't trust himself. He liked to drink a lot.

Turning toward his 30s, Justin has less of an urgent need to express his queerness. He put Eggz Benedict to rest. He misses his old life but does not want to return there. Justin runs the bar in a wildly popular Manhattan restaurant and dreams of starting a small farm in Upstate New York where he could open a retreat center for queer activists who need respite and renewal. He integrates his queerness into his daily life in simple, ordinary ways.

Away from the drag scene, Justin's fear of confrontation looms, subtle and ever-present. He says that it's easier for him to succumb to fear when his gender-bending is less dramatic in presentation. When Justin is in drag, he feels invincible. In more mundane clothes, like cutoff shorts and a sleeveless flannel, for example, he fears getting blindsided by violence. It's not always clear who the enemy is.

I was one of the teachers in the story who went to El Salvador with Justin. I was part of his inner circle that he came out to soon after on National Coming Out Day. I joined the efforts to support him after his assault and watched *Alice in Wonderland* and *Utopiacopia* in awe. Justin shared his unfolding body story with me over the years. When we sat down to do a series of interviews for this book project, I asked him about his pronouns. I wanted to call him what he wanted to be called. What followed was a rich, fascinating conversation about gender, language, and labels. He does consider himself gender non-binary, gender fluid, and genderqueer, and yet he likes and uses he/him pronouns. In his teen and young adult years, he did so much work to define what he/him means to him. His maleness is expansive enough to house Blanch, Dorothy, Marcy, Eggz Benedict, and Justin. The work he did to come to peace with his gender carries weight and comes with consequences. He admittedly feels pressure to use they/them pronouns to be in solidarity with other queer folks and put pressure on the limiting binaries, but he also wants his queer community to stay curious about his story and keep breaking language open. In this way, his body story is a counter-story that widens his sense of agency and freedom while calling us all to stay attentive to ever-shifting language as it pertains to our ever-shifting body expression and identities.

> *What choices do you make on purpose and not on purpose to express your gender? How might you choose to express your gender if there were no social consequences?*

I Am

Sage is a talented athlete whose Division I gymnastics career ended abruptly when she tore her ACL. She wanted to process the story around that injury with me. The day before our scheduled interview, she called me and said, "I want to keep our session, but can I change topics?"

"Of course. What are you thinking?"

"I want to tell the story of my skin. It's time. I'm ready."

"Then so am I."

She knew I was working on this book and wanted to share her story broadly. She was struggling with White folks in her life being oblivious and dismissive of her experience in the world as a person of color. She married into a White, Catholic family, and often felt othered at family functions. After George Floyd's murder, such atrocious things were said aloud in front of her that she could no longer keep silent and carry on. When her in-laws and coworkers claimed to not see color or called BLM a terrorist organization, she spoke up. Telling stories created space for her to process and claim an identity in repair. She doubled down on her equity work, rising to DEI leadership at the national level in the gymnastics judge's association, as a board member of Brown Girls Do Gymnastics, and at her place of employment.

After a few hours of story-sharing together, when it was time to take a break, I told her she may have unlocked something inside of her body. Often memories tucked away more deeply will surface after someone begins to craft a story. That is exactly what happened for Sage. Over the course of the next several months, she sent me more images, memories, and stories as they bubbled up. We wove, revised, reworded, and rearranged until the story resonated in her chest.

White supremacy attacks the intelligence, character, beauty, and ability of Sage. Sage's story is an intentional recognition of how the master narratives we tell around race can dismiss, break, and limit people of color. It is a story about how master narratives limit freedom and agency in folks who deserve better. Sage is telling a counter-story that not only creates a greater sense of agency in her body and shifts her self-perception, expanding what she believes and knows is possible, but also challenges the master narratives in powerful ways. It decolonizes in her unlearning the undesirability placed on her by the oppressive system.

Her story, in that she is learning to love herself without mediating herself through the lens of White cultural ideals, breathes hope for her healing and wholeness, which predicates the possibility of reconciliation necessary for all to build and belong to a more humane society. Replacing the tree, branch, and root metaphor with the rhizome is helpful here. Sage's sense of belonging and interconnectedness thrives in a system that is nonlinear and nonhierarchical. You will see folks struggling to place her because the tree system is too singular and limiting. She belongs to her parents, her ancestors, her partner, her descents, her teammates, the world, and to herself.

One day at the gymnastics gym, before her coaches came out of the office to start practice, Sage's teammates circled around her. One of her teammates told her to sit down and then asked, "What are you?"

"I don't understand," Sage said.

"Are you Mexican or Italian or" then in a whisper added, "African American?"

"My mom is White, and my dad is Black," she replied.

Now, as an adult, Sage wishes she could go back and answer differently. She can also appreciate that in the moment, she was a child in survival mode. She longed to belong and didn't fully understand the dis-ease of her White teammates. Little did she know back then that "What are you?" would be a hurtful refrain throughout her life.

From a very young age, Sage felt outside the group. Her skin was not the same color as her dad's or her mom's. She was an only child. All her relatives on one side were blacker than her, and all her relatives on the other side were whiter than her. She felt like the *other*. The odd one out.

Sage's dad has an intense way of making his points. To teach her not to burn food, he burned food. To teach her how serious her peanut allergy was, he convinced her the yellow bag of M&Ms candy was poison. When Sage was four, he decided it was time to talk to Sage about race. He told her Santa Claus isn't real so she wouldn't trust strange White men at the mall. Around that time, he told Sage about the KKK. He wanted her to understand that regardless of the actual tone of her skin, the world considered her Black. He said, "If the KKK shows up at our door, you and I need to run away, but your mother doesn't. We are not White. We are Black. You come with me. You are Black *because* you are not White."

She imagined the scene vividly. The KKK were on horses. Her dogs tried to protect her, but the horses got past them. She imagined her father running away faster than the horses even with her little body on his back. Although they escaped in her imagination, they were running away from her mom. That was Sage's first lesson in racism.

In Sage's grade school, there were students of color in her class, but there was no helpful conversation or identity formation around race or being biracial. Three boys picked on Sage incessantly. They followed her around, taunting her. They took her lunch and school supplies. When she got older, they pulled her bra strap. They told her, "You don't belong," and she felt it. She wasn't White, so she must be Black, but she wasn't Black enough. The undertone of their taunts whispered, "What are you?"

The teachers categorized the harassment as immature boys paying her attention. Having been pulled away from his corporate job on a weekly basis to defend Sage while the parents of the White students were not called in, her dad told Sage the best path was for her to stand up for herself. While learning that she would be bullied for her skin color, she was also learning she'd have to navigate the harassment on her own. The teachers and principal said Sage needed to be mature and deal with her own problems. Her dad asked the teachers if it was about her gender or her race, and they didn't know how to answer.

The harassment didn't stop. The anger didn't stop.

The parents of the boys were never summoned. The boys received no consequence. So Sage's parents pulled her from the school at the end of fifth grade, worried that the harassment of the boys and the apathy of the adults would hinder her ability to learn.

In middle school, the taunting continued. One day, she poured an entire bottle of ketchup on a boy in the lunchroom, fed up with his ridicule. When the teacher in charge did not reprimand the harassment and instead tried to give her detention, she came up with an alternative punishment during the school day so she could get a needed break from the White students and so she could get to the gymnastics gym right after school.

Recently, Sage's elementary school principal walked into her mom's aerobics class. After class, the woman approached Sage's mom and asked how Sage was doing, adding, "She never left my mind. I am sorry for how I treated her. She was a good student. I can see now that I was biased against her, and I have never forgotten her."

Sage's mom replied, "Well, she is incredibly successful, and it is despite you, not because of you. I hope you never treat another kid like that again. My daughter is stronger than you, and for her sake, I do not forgive you."

She told Sage later that she channeled her love for her husband and Sage to say the thing that needed to be said.

Sage realized that as a smart, non-Catholic, female student of color who excelled in math in a predominantly White, Catholic context she was seen as an exception. She added, "We were considered a good Black family because we paid tuition." Yet the othering continued. In a high school religion class, a teacher had students raise their hands if they went to Catholic church on Sundays. Lutheran. Presbyterian. When Sage never raised her hand, the teacher asked her, "What are you?" She felt the layers of what she wasn't pile up. Her White boyfriend said he didn't think of her as very Black because she is smart and doesn't "talk Black." Meanwhile, Black students made her feel guilty for dating a White boy.

In the gymnastics world, Sage didn't belong either. She was from the city while her teammates lived in the suburbs. She was Black while most of them were White. Sage did have a few Black teammates throughout her career in Minnesota. One was adopted by middle class White parents. Another lived with her White mom and her Black dad was out of the picture. Other gymnasts and parents assumed Sage was adopted or that her mom was a single mom. When they met Sage's dad, they played into horrible stereotypes, anticipating that he would leave her or end up in jail. They treated Sage with pity, like a charity case. He came to every single meet in her career, proving their stereotypes wrong one day at a time.

Sage's junior year of high school, she sprained her ankle at a gymnastics meet in Missouri. On the eleven-hour ride home, her mom got very carsick. With her swollen ankle elevated, Sage tried to translate old road maps and find new containers for her mom to throw up in. They eventually pulled into a gas station to let her mom use the bathroom. Her mom fled the car, leaving her dad and her alone with a sinking feeling in their stomachs. There were confederate flags on trucks in the parking lot. White locals stared at them. Sage thought about the dream with the KKK and horses and riding on her dad's back. She would stay with her dad. She would let her mom go. She had been preparing for this. Her dad said to her in a dead serious voice, "Go check on your mother and don't you dare limp. Walk fast with your head up." Sage tried to object but he barked, "Go!" One of the men followed her inside. After throwing up more in the bathroom, her mom needed her help getting back to the car.

Sage didn't limp.

They got back on the road fast. Once safely on the highway, her dad glanced at her and simply said, "Good job." They never spoke about it again.

With high math scores on her standardized tests and a highly successful senior year in the gymnastics world, Sage headed to Ames, Iowa, to attend Iowa State, walking on to their gymnastics team. She had a few teammates of color and a Black beam coach who finally helped her feel less alone. "Ok, minorities," one teammate would joke, "let's take a picture with just us. Smile!" She tried to keep her head down and get her work done. When the head coach required that the gymnasts swim laps three days a week for endurance, her Black teammates pushed back and offered alternative aerobic activities. Sage and her Black teammates did not like how chlorine affected their hair. In a sport where appearance matters, this was a legitimate consideration. Their coach made fun of them, citing the stereotype that Black people can't swim. Sage and her Black teammates did a slow doggy paddle for their required twenty laps in defiance, not wetting their hair. Some of their White teammates joined them in the doggy paddle, and the others who finished quickly stayed to cheer them on. After that day, the head coach shifted their endurance assignment with neither a word of apology nor recognition.

In a women's studies class with a Black professor, Sage settled in a bit, hoping for a safe space to learn and discuss. One day, the topic in discussion was Black hair. Sage, having dealt with others' fascination with her hair her whole life, offered a story of a White Iowa State student petting her hair in the library without permission.

"Why would that happen to you?" the professor asked her in front of the full lecture hall. "Your hair isn't ethnic."

"Excuse me?"

"You're not Black."

"Yes, I am. I'm mixed."

"Are you regular mixed?" (By "regular mixed," she meant a White mom and a Black dad.)

"Yes," she mustered through her anger and disbelief.

Sage told the story to a graduate student in the Center for Multicultural Student Awareness. That student reported the incident as racial discrimination. Sage got a call from the provost and the professor with apologies. She let it go at that. She had been accepted to graduate school at the University of Chicago and hoped to leave Ames with her head high. In class, the professor asked students what they would be doing after graduation, and Sage said she was heading to the University of Chicago.

"The University of Illinois at Chicago?" the professor asked.

"No. The University of Chicago."

"Are you sure? That school is very hard to get into."

"Yes, it is. And I got in."

Maybe Chicago would be a more generative place to learn and grow.

Sage walks through the world aware of her skin all the time. Even her parents do not find themselves having to deal with the racial ambiguity of being light-skinned and Black. She feels like she is continuously telling people who she is. Her racial ambiguity has been seen as exotic and fetishized. Starting in her early teens, older male strangers have said to her, "I would love to make babies with you." In Haiti, she received unwanted attention for the combination of her "strong birthing hips, Black features, and light skin tone."

When George Floyd was murdered in her town, she felt the exhaustion of being both Black and not Black enough. Being asked "What are you?" others Sage again and again. People want to place her, to label her, and those labels are limiting. They give her a sense of dis-belonging. Of being inferior to the standard. She is a survivor in a broken system that not only advantages White, male, Christian bodies but is also actively anti-Black, anti-woman, and anti-non-Christian. She continuously overcomes, which is endlessly exhausting.

Telling the story of her skin counters the oppressive and binary master narratives of White superiority and creates space for her complex, interesting, and powerful person to expand in all directions. Sage only uses labels if they set her free. Even as a Division I athlete, she had and still has a tumultuous relationship with the idea of team. She avoids identifying with a single-minded group because she has been forced to span disparate groups from day one. Her people include her White husband, who loves her and is learning by the day, and her dad's sisters, who never question her Blackness.

"People still don't quite know where to place me," she sighs. "But I am learning to live in the margins. In the in-between. And I have an answer for all those people who asked me, 'What are you?'

"I'm human. I am who I am. I am enough."

> *Where do you locate yourself in Sage's story? What is one thing you can do to help dismantle the system that places Sage in the margins instead of the center?*

New Ways to Belong

Think about how your awareness of your body shifts as your context shifts. I am more aware of my body, how it moves, and how it is being perceived in a job interview than when I am hanging out with friends, for example. In the former, I am an outsider who wants to become an insider. The person across the table from me has the power to grant me that access. When I am with my friends, I'm in. I take my body for granted. There is a body ease that comes with belonging.

My awareness usually heightens when I am in a group of men. I'm the other. When I ask for a raise, watch election returns, or walk alone in the dark at night, I feel it in my bones. The patriarchy tells women that our bodies are inferior and are made to care for others first, so we engage in unpaid labor far more in our society, contributing to compassion fatigue and burnout. The patriarchy also tells me that the patriarchy doesn't exist. It wants me to believe that I am the problem so that I spend time fixing myself instead of dismantling the system. As my female body exists within the patriarchy—a rigged game—I can easily fall into learned helplessness.

When I step into an empowering female space, however, there is often room to reflect on the patriarchy and the pressure it puts on my body. I am in a small group with five other women. We experience physical relief naming inequality in salaries, parenting expectations, and harassment compared to our male counterparts. In that safe place of our female community, where I experience the ease of belonging, I can craft a counter-story that names the patriarchy as the problem and creates space for me to unlearn helplessness. It is important for me to tell stories around my female body's experience in the world. My identity shifts, I name my body as exceedingly resilient and worthy, and I engage in activities that prove my helplessness wrong.

The women in my group desperately want our male companions to see the patriarchy and leverage their power to help us dismantle it, but it's a struggle. They opt in now and then, but their default is resting in their privilege. They stay complicit and perpetuate the inequity—possibly not seeing the system, possibly leaning into the ease of belonging, possibly subconsciously believing their hard work earned their place of superiority, possibly fearing that more power for us necessitates less for them. It is a privilege to exempt yourself from the work and opt in when it is convenient.

I was born into the world as a girl. I was also born into the world with a body that is White, heterosexual, cisgender, and able. I can and do take my body for granted often. I can trust my disposition. I often don't have to recognize my body, the clearest mark of privilege. My social world allowed my body to come into its own. Crafting my body story as it pertains to my systemic power can help me become more aware, empty myself of the toxicity, and contend with the old, inherited, and new power I benefit from and that lives in my body. Our oppressive systems work better when people in power stay disembodied. Writing my body story is one path in.

While working at a day shelter for women in Denver, I went to work without my name tag one day. As women entered the room, they walked right up to me and talked to me as if they knew I was staff. I finally asked one woman how she knew I worked there. "You wear it. Life hasn't been tough on you."

She was right. My privilege lives in my body. I have the posture of an aristocrat. The structures, the game of life is working for me. The loop between my body and my habitat reinforces my ease in life. I matter. I am smart and good. I have power. My world imparts and confirms these inner beliefs. My body takes on that shape. The clients, on the other hand, must keep watch, consciously thinking about their behavior as they navigate a social service agency run by gatekeepers. That vigilance is tiring, adding fatigue to an already grueling life experiencing poverty. I can write my body story in a way that implicates myself in the structures that normalize and support my body, not being ashamed of my ease, but using my power to help build something more beautiful, living into new ways of belonging.

In this moment in history, tending to the Whiteness in my body feels urgent and paramount. In the United States, White-bodied supremacy is in the water, baked into our laws, statues, and history textbooks, alive in our school systems, prison systems, and brand of democracy. Back in colonial America, Whiteness was created to separate working European bodies from working African bodies to protect the elite from collaborative revolt, and it continues sowing racial division today. Heather McGhee writes, "Yes, the zero-sum story of racial hierarchy was born along with the country, but it is an invention of the worst elements of our society: people who gained power through ruthless exploitation and kept it by sowing constant division. It has always optimally benefited only a few while limiting the potential of the rest of us, and therefore the whole." I can take my White body for granted because it has been wrongly established as the standard body. The norm. Learning the history of Whiteness in our country helps me see it in my body and see how it operates in our current systems so I can opt into anti-racist action.

Whiteness wants me to stay disembodied. It wants me to dwell in my mind and ignore my body so that I do not contend with it. White-bodied supremacy will not end by thinking about it. It doesn't live in my thinking brain but rather is alive in my body. Whiteness tells me I don't have a race. I am defined by what I am not. I am White because I am not Black. I can write a body story that is a positive process to recreate myself as what I am, rather than what I am not. In Whiteness there is housed centuries of colonialism, imperialism, enslavement, and brutality. Being embodied and exploring my culture is my work to do if we ever hope to end the perpetuation.

Writing stories that name and contend with my White body expands my constricted eye to see what I have been taught not to see. It is learning about my ancestors and the system that pressured them to give up their Irish and Polish cultures to become White. I can do the work from the inside out, choosing to turn inward with a posture that is open, receptive, and ready to learn. I can implicate myself in racist systems, opting into anti-racist work on a moment-to-moment basis. I can empty myself of false self-importance, understanding how I have benefited from the work and lives of others, reassessing what belongs to me and what I deserve. I can build up my capacity to not be the hero of the story. I can remember that what I do with my body and where I show up with my body in dissent makes a difference. I can challenge White-bodied violence, letting go of White male protection in the name of my humanity and claim that my body does not need protection. I belong to Whiteness, and there is an ease to that. My humanity is on the line, however, if I do not build resiliency around opting out of toxic Whiteness, helping to dismantle it, and helping to build something that believes in interconnection and equality.

Chanequa Walker-Barnes writes, "The victims of racism within the United States have lacked any meaningful opportunity or resources for voice, validation, or vindication. Even within the racial reconciliation movement, there have been no large-scale attempts to provide people of color with space to tell their truths without worrying about the impact that such truth-telling will have upon the feelings of White people." It is my hope in action that being on the embodied path will deepen my inner life and ethical intelligence, creating more capacity to hold space for bodies that have been wrongly othered to speak their truths and listen hard. It is my hope in action that on the embodied path, we understand more deeply how our bodies take up space and interact in the world. We heal from the inside out. We listen to stories and tell our stories. We take on a new posturing in the world so that we can resist, repair, and help build more humane and life-giving systems to belong to each other.

> Where do you see Whiteness at work today? How can you be a part of dismantling that system and building something new?

Our systems are not broken; they are working exactly as they were designed to work, placing some bodies as superior to others. Our systems want us to think and act like trees. Roots and branches are simply variation of growth from the trunk of a tree, locking us into a linear, individual, and hierarchical model of growth within a set system. The trunk is assumed as perpetuated hegemony and any act of resistance still stems from the assumed norm. Yet reality is more varied, communal, complex, and interesting than that. Our becoming expands in all directions. An alternative model is the rhizome, which is a subterranean plant system that creeps horizontally, sending out roots and shoots in all directions from its nodes. There is no origin. No normal. No beginning and ending. At any point in the rhizome, it can be connected to any other rhizome. The multiplicity of our identities, expanding in all directions, calls us to think and grow in a decentered, nonhierarchical way that values connectivity and interdependence outside of a fixed order.

How you craft and share your body story and listen to the body stories of others can put pressure on systems to expand toward compassion and universal belonging. We can dismantle the linear systems and grow expansive new communities to belong to. We can turn toward our own bodies, name where we have systemic and inherited power, explore our complicity, and empty ourselves of the toxicity that comes from oppressive power. The work is not drudgery but humanizing. As Paul Wellstone said, "We all do better when we all do better."

Reflection Questions

* What did your body experience while reading these stories? Did any of them resonate with you and your body's story?
* Have you ever been labeled by someone else because of a choice you made about self-expression? Did that label feel accurate? Did it limit or expand your sense of identity?
* Has your body ever been the center of attention in a room of people? Did you feel safe?
* How have you felt pressure to behave, quiet down, or tone down your self-expression? How can you push back against that pressure in life-giving ways that support creativity and your true unfolding self?
* What binaries do you get put in? (man/woman, heterosexual/homosexual, Black/White, etc.) In what ways are you divided in half? Tugged at from two sides?
* What choices do you make daily to express your gender? How has your gender identity shifted over time?
* What is your favorite thing about being a woman/man/nonbinary person? If you could break one gender rule without any social consequences, which one would you choose?
* What identity groups do you belong to? Who are you with, what are you doing, and where are you when you feel like you belong? In what ways do you feel a sense of disbelonging?

* Talk about a time you were very aware of your race, gender, or religious affiliation (or lack thereof). Talk about a time your body was at ease in your context.
* Moving beyond passive empathy, how can you locate yourself in the body stories in this chapter? What are you sensing is your body work to move toward more healing and wholeness at the systems level?
* How do master narratives perpetuate racism, sexism, heterosexism, and xenophobia? How can your body story expand your freedom and agency while putting pressure on master narratives to expand?

Writing Prompts

Set a timer for seven minutes. Start writing about whatever is disturbing your peace. Don't pick your pen up, don't edit as you go, don't worry about sentences or grammar. When the timer goes off, don't reread it. Destroy the paper by tearing it up or safely setting it on fire. Don't direct the energy that came out of your body toward yourself. Your goal is to get feelings of dis-ease out of your body and let them go so you can access your body story with more neutralized energy.

Call to mind a piece of clothing or jewelry that is saturated with memories. Tell the story around that item. How does it express alignment between the inner and outer you?

Write about an early memory of realizing you were (insert a gender/race/religious/national/ability/class/sex/sexuality/ethnicity identity here).

Breath Practice

Find a comfortable seat free of distraction. Take a few moments to look around your space, noticing the windows and exits. Then settle in. Blink your eyes shut and create a posture that is alert and calm. Come into this moment. Bring your awareness to the top of your head and slowly move your awareness down to the soles of your feet, releasing any gripping in your muscles. Notice your thoughts without attaching to them, allowing them to float by like clouds in the sky.

Bring your attention to your breath. Do not alter your breath, just notice you are breathing. Notice if you are holding any tension, any gripping in the breath. Become effortless. Allow the breath to become full, deep, and steady. Visualize your inhales moving from your tailbone up your spine to the base of your skull. Visualize your exhales traveling down your spine from the base of your skull to your tailbone. Continue the loop, traveling up on your inhale and down on your exhale. Reaching. Grounding.

Now imagine the space one inch to the right and one inch to the left of your spine. Imagine your inhale filling that space as it travels up your spine from your tailbone to the base of the skull and down on your exhale from the base of the skull to tailbone.

After several breaths, do the same with the space one inch in front of your spine and one inch behind your spine. Fill that space with breath, traveling up your spine on your inhale and down your spine on your exhale.

Finally, picture the space one inch below your tailbone and one inch above the base of your skull. For several inhales and exhales, see your breath, your life force, expanding to create space in your body for what is next.

Allow the looping breath to be so smooth that it is as if you are painting the spine with a paintbrush. Allow the breath to continue to expand into the midbrain, and with a calm breath, notice your thoughts and your body calming too.

As you come to the end of your practice, notice the connection between your mind and your body, knowing you can come back to this feeling of connection anytime during your day you choose to be mindful of your breath. On your inhale, fill your lungs all the way up. Exhale slowly, and when you reach the bottom of your exhale, blink your eyes open and come back to the room.

Body Practice

Once or twice a day, notice your posture. Do you tuck your tailbone underneath you? Do you round forward at the shoulders? Does your chin jut out? Do you often cross one leg over the other while you sit? Our spines have three natural curves—concave curves in our lumbar and cervical spine and a convex curve in our thoracic spine. Improper posture can strain our spines in all three places. Our posture can tell us a lot about our relationship to our bodies and how we spend time in our bodies. Can you create a posture that is aligned and exudes confidence, calm, and a sense of center?

Your joints are more of an event than a location. Spend time gently rolling your joints, making sure to reverse the flow of your circles so you move in both directions. Slowly make circles with your head, then shoulders. One side at a time, roll your arm at the elbow, then wrist. Make circles with your hips clockwise, then counterclockwise. Roll each leg out at the knee and then ankle, both ways on both sides, using a wall or chair for support if needed. Notice sensations in your body before, during, and after your joint rolling. Do any images or urges arise?

Six

Bodies Remember
Welcoming Ourselves Back Home

Home is not where you are born;
home is where all your attempts
to escape cease.

—NAGUIB MAHFOUZ,
quoted in *Transnational Identity and Memory Making in the*
Lives of Iraqi Women in Diaspora

While teaching together at the same high school, one of the most beautiful women I know said to me, "I'm so glad I was not a pretty teenager." When I challenged her a bit, she said, "I was not stereotypically pretty or ugly. I didn't stand out. Watching some of these pretty students navigate the male gaze and the attention they get for their looks, now, looking back, I'm just lucky I didn't have to deal with that."

I was not stereotypically pretty in high school either. I never got made fun of for my looks, and I didn't get much positive attention for my looks either. I did not keep up on fashion, fads, or primping rituals. I didn't have great hair. My strong, athletic body kept me outside the slender feminine ideal. I didn't date much. I loved school and sports and enjoyed my friends. And as an adult, I also feel lucky. I was aware of the male gaze, but rarely paralyzed by or beholden to it.

Our master narratives around who and what is pretty are relentlessly cruel. The standard is impossibly high and ever-changing, driving our consumer society forward. Weight loss, fast fashion, exercise, and cosmetic companies use social media to make people feel worthless and believe that the next product will make them pretty and desirable to others, which will in turn make them enough. Other people tell you if you are pretty or not. You don't have much control, and you must keep changing to please different standards of what is pretty.

The stories in this chapter counter the dismissive master narratives around pretty. These are stories about humans who lived into their own beauty. They put down the drive for pretty and finally saw that they were, indeed, full of beauty. Our bodies are beautiful. They are. And if you don't feel beautiful, it may be in part because the world's loud master narratives have a tiny, boring, and limiting standard of pretty. Our work is to tell the story from the inside out. To seek beauty inside us and all around us—listen to beautiful music, seek out beautiful art, eat beautiful food, sit in beautiful nature—so we ingest beauty and exude beauty and thus make the world more beautiful with our easy presence. Beautiful people glow. They naturally remind other people of their beauty. They live out of their bodies as home.

This is part of the work of our lives—to put down the rigged game of striving for pretty from a place of not-enough-ness and fiercely commit to the slow process of turning inward, honoring our true selves, and filling up. Beauty in. Beauty out. We are not the subject of another's gaze. We are the one sitting in the front-row seat in a gorgeous world with beauty all around us. We are the beautiful main character of our own wild story. We take in beauty. We *are* beauty. We grow it and offer it around. When we put down pretty, we can continually welcome ourselves back home to our beautiful bodies.

A Walking Work of Art

Myrtle walks into Muddy Waters like they own the place, greeting three people on their way to an open booth. They shed their coat and infinity scarf and reach for their Moleskine in a satchel populated with punk feminist buttons. Our server knows their order—a dirty chai with oat milk—and chats them up about their upcoming wedding. I can't take my eyes off their fingers—in part because Myrtle emotes with their hands and in part because their fingers are covered in little tattoos. A crescent moon. A tiny crab. A feminist sign. I ask them about the tattoos, and in telling me the story of their tattoos, they tell me a story of their body.

"I was a very precocious child," they laugh. "My parents were older, and they took me to a lot of choir concerts when I was young. They brought me to a John Kerry rally the day before kindergarten." Myrtle has curly, sandy blonde hair and delicate retro glasses to match their high-waisted mom jeans and chunky sweater. Their luminous smile and playful wit make it easy to imagine Myrtle as this precocious child. Their adult face has retained the joy and animation of the kid who loved Elvis and Carole King and taught themselves to read. They are brimming with energy, story, and curiosity, residue from a magical childhood. Yet there was a middle time, between childhood and adulthood, wrought with fragmentation, hiding, and confusion.

Late in elementary school, Myrtle sensed a disconnect between their body and the ideal female body. Myrtle's mom, whom they adore, was a career-oriented person who wore clogs and overalls and wouldn't allow Myrtle to wear makeup. Part of them wanted to be just like their mom. Yet their peers started getting their periods, wearing makeup, and buying bikinis, and part of them desperately wanted that too. They asked their mom if they could buy a bikini and she replied, "No, honey. Bikinis aren't for girls like you." Their mom was trying to protect them, but the message was that Myrtle didn't get to do what other girls do, being too chunky to play the game. Skimpy clothes were forbidden. When Myrtle looked in the mirror, they saw a blob. They chopped off their hair to look like Elvis and sported Converse shoes and camouflage cargo pants.

"I had a huge growth spurt when I was in the sixth grade," they continue. "I was the tallest in my class and wore a C-cup bra." In a season when any abnormality is homed in on and exaggerated with social consequences, Myrtle was bullied for being different—first too chunky, then too tall. They responded by using their tall body to protect themself. They hung with the boys, throwing punches and wrestling them. Myrtle didn't see boys' affection as an asset. They played their violin and got good grades. And still, when they compared themself to their pretty, skinny friends, there was a quiet voice inside asking, *What's wrong with me?*

In high school, Myrtle became friends with a girl named Britney who was the same size as Myrtle but liked showing her body off. Britney lent Myrtle a bikini and they sunbathed together. Although it felt good to interact with their body, that is when Myrtle started picking it apart. Myrtle focused on parts of their body they despised and spewed hateful words at them. Meanwhile, their mother was losing a lot of weight fast. Myrtle felt anxious about their looks. They scratched their skin until it scabbed and scornfully grabbed pieces of flesh until they bruised. They lacked the knowledge and vocabulary around panic attacks and self-harm to know to ask for help.

By the time Myrtle arrived at college, they were viciously comparing themself to other people. "I refused to wear form-fitting clothes," they say. "Then I met Annie." Annie was very tall and very thin. They became best friends and soon started dating. Coupled, their differences were magnified, and Myrtle owned and embraced their butch identity in the pair. Annie struggled with eating disorders and body dysmorphia. She'd ask Myrtle what she looked like while only seeing herself as fat. Myrtle thought, *If you are fat, then what am I?*

Annie cheated on Myrtle, sending Myrtle into a tailspin of self-deprecating doubt. *Why did she cheat on me? Because I'm not pretty enough*, they thought. Myrtle was at an impasse. They wanted their self-hatred to recede. They wanted their anxiety to lose its hold. Their friends encouraged Myrtle to break up with Annie and start therapy. They found the strength to do both.

Despite all the pain with Annie, she did offer Myrtle a great gift—their first tattoo. "I'd draw with a ballpoint pen, and she'd stab me with a sewing needle on the back of a pencil." Their first tattoo is Saturn on one ankle and the second, a crescent moon on the opposite ankle. The moon is named Frank and is for Myrtle's father, who instilled in them a love of space and robots. While camping in Northern Michigan, their dad woke them up at 3 a.m. and brought a laser pointer outside to teach them about the constellations. He made sure Myrtle's glow-in-the-dark stars on their bedroom ceiling were as accurate as possible. Myrtle pulls down their wool socks to show me and smiles, "I love them."

The tattoo tour continues: a Myrtle flower done by their friend Lily in a Santa Fe kitchen. A bee for their middle name, Beatrice, passed down to them from their grandmother. A Taurus constellation, their fiancé's sign.

Before tattoos and before identifying as transgender and using they/them pronouns, Myrtle lived in the tension between binaries. Man or woman. Heterosexual or homosexual. Virgin or whore. It's a game of inches, and there are no winners. They suffered from the fragmentation, the forces pulling them to be something they were not. There was something about the tattoos Myrtle and Annie created that shifted the rules and the game. One of Myrtle's rules used to be that if they wore shorts, they must cover their arms. You can't show too much skin at once. Now they love their tattoos so much they invite Myrtle to love their skin. They thought, *I should get one on my arm. I don't like my arms, but maybe with tattoos I will want to show them off.* It worked.

Myrtle got more and more tattoos. A tomato, a raspberry, a carrot. Some were planned and some were spontaneous. One took five minutes and others took hours. Some used three-point needles and others five. Their fifth tattoo was the planet of Neptune because they find it geographically interesting and societally underrated. An opera singer, they add, "In the musical piece '*The Planets,*' Neptune is when the women come in." Myrtle has a sprig of lavender and a three-eyed squid. A shark from Seattle and a triceratops named Tina.

Myrtle started showing more skin not for others but for themself. They showed up to sexual encounters and could dwell in the pleasure of their body. They stood in front of the mirror and instead of picking body parts they didn't like, they'd discover parts of their body they did like and bought clothes to celebrate them. They took better care of their skin and was affectionate with their body. "I was always confident in my mind, but I finally became confident in my body too," they say. "I don't think I set out to tattoo the parts of my body that I didn't like, but it just happened that way. When I am texting or typing, the bee on my finger makes me happy. My left breast is my favorite breast because it has planets on it. I think, *Look at this cool art! It's mine!* I started cherishing my body because there's art on it."

After eight tattoos on their body, Myrtle wanted to tattoo others. They practiced on pillows and paper and stuffed animals. Then their friend asked them to tattoo a cat on her finger and a moon on her wrist. Then another moon and sun. Then a cup of coffee and a knife for their friend who loves true crime. Myrtle is building up their portfolio and claiming the practice of giving and receiving tattoos. The tattoos helping heal their body could also be a gift they give to others, growing the love, connection, and beauty. "There is something so cathartic about sitting down with someone and tattoo-ing your art on their skin permanently. That's a connection we will always share."

On the tour, when they get to their fourteenth tattoo, Myrtle's energy shifts. They rub their forearm and close their eyes briefly. "Marj is my second mom," they say. Marj was a friend of Myrtle's mom who lived in the neighborhood. Myrtle spent arguably more time at Marj's house than their own. "She helped raise me. She never had kids, fought for unions, and was a tyrant in the kitchen. After she died, I wore her necklace for a year. I took a sweatshirt and T-shirt of hers that still smell like her. I built a little shrine to her in my room with her pins and bracelets. I have her record player and some musi-cal scores, anything to keep her close. But I wanted something more permanent."

Marj and thus Myrtle loved using baby spoons to eat ice cream and yogurt. Myrtle brought Marj spoons back from their travels to Ohio and Niagara Falls. Marj sent spoons in care packages to Myrtle in college. The favorite of all the spoons was a smooth, red ceramic spoon. They fought over it regularly. Marj made Myrtle sundaes at her house with vanilla ice cream and warm, homemade hot fudge, and they'd trade off who got to eat with the red spoon. It was Marj's mother's hot fudge recipe, and she handed it down to Myrtle after an extensive two-year training and supervision process. Always a wooden spoon and only medium heat. Myrtle made the hot fudge for Marj's funeral. On Marj's first birthday after her death, then, it seemed fitting for Myrtle to get a tattoo of the beloved spoon on their forearm. "A little bit of her is on me. I can see it. I can hold it when I miss her."

Now Myrtle tattoos themself. "It is a restorative practice," they say. "I am in control."

I watch Myrtle tugging at their clothes and throwing their legs around to show off each of their tattoos. "I am never alone. I have all my little friends," they laugh. They are the embodiment of an artist who recognizes beauty and supports art. The tattoos have welcomed them back into alignment, integrated them back to dwell in their own skin. There is a wholeness and ease to their person that is compelling. They inhabit beauty that is owned, fought for, claimed, and reflected. Their tattoos tell a wild and beautiful story that is all theirs. They call Myrtle to reverence of the present moment and help them feel free.

"I feel like a walking work of art." They smile and shrug.

I met Myrtle while promoting my second book. Their theater was putting on *The Wolves*, a powerful play about a girls' soccer team, and they invited me as the author of *Play Like a Girl*, a story of a girls' soccer team in Kenya, to be on a panel about gender equity in sports. We hit it off right away. At a planning meeting about the panel, I asked about their finger tattoos, and Myrtle launched right in. We scheduled another date when they could tell me the longer version of their story. Their tattoos created plot points for their body narrative. They loved telling their story, and I loved listening to it. Myrtle understands counter-stories. They get how choices in what tattoo to get next and what shirt to wear, how to express gender, how to show up for connection, and how to talk about it all can all be acts of resistance and repair as they find a safe, loving, and beautiful home in their body.

> What messages did you receive about your body as a child? What is one thing you can do today to be kind to and affectionate with your body?

Returning Home

My feet were still painfully swollen a week after my son was born. The skin stretched taut, it looked like someone else's feet were attached to my legs. While Simon napped, Dan brought a small tub of warm, soapy water over to the couch. He gently placed my feet in the tub. At his first touch, I crumbled in tears. My body and spirit were tired. I felt ugly and unrecognizable to myself. The emotion kept coming out of my body in waves. Surrendering to my fatigue, I wondered if I would ever reach the bottom of my grief. I wondered if I would find myself again.

Dan slowly, deliberately dabbed my feet dry, then massaged and rubbed lotion into each bulging foot. The gentle, affectionate attention felt merciful. It reminded me that I had a body. After sharing my body for so long, it belonged to me again. I had to take stock of this new version of me, with new scars and memories, new milk, and primal feelings of mother love surging through me.

Dan rose and kissed me twice. "Thank you," I whispered, still crying softly. He unlocked a clog that was holding my sorrow hostage. I was unstuck. The next morning, he glanced down and said, "Look, your feet. They're back."

A few months later, I brought Simon into bed with me in the morning to watch him wake up. He was discovering his hands. He held his hands right in front of his unblinking eyes, rotating them slowly to study each finger in a way that invited me into the revelry.

"I know Simon, I know," I cooed. "Aren't your hands amazing? Aren't we just so lucky to have hands? You have two hands. One. Two. Me too. One. Two. You are going to do amazing things with those hands in your life. You have feet too! Look at your beautiful feet. I love your feet. And a whole body, and another day to play, play, play. Isn't it grand?"

My eyes filled with tears.

I believed it for him. I believe it for me.

Take a few moments to watch a baby or small child move and be in their body. Can children encourage you to turn toward your body with renewed wonder at its beauty?

Where Beauty Lives

Kathryn sits on her bed holding a bowl up to show me. There is an abstract profile of a pregnant woman etched in the bowl. "That's me," she says warmly, with nostalgic affection.

In 1996, Kathryn went to Holden Village for a women's retreat with her best friend, Emily. Emily had just miscarried a second time, and Kathryn was pregnant with her first child. A third friend, Meta, listened to the two women talking about fertility and children and asked if Kathryn would model nude for her. She had never seen a pregnant body nude and wanted to. Kathryn felt the risk but said yes. The pregnancy opened her up to the possibility. Fascinated with her own body, with the child moving inside of her, she understood Meta's curiosity. It took the focus off Kathryn.

Kathryn went to Meta's room and undressed. In a way, being pregnant was such a shift, it didn't even feel like her posing. Meta sketched Kathryn, then months later sent her the bowl with her image ingrained in it. Meta captured a beautiful fleeting moment.

Twenty-four years later, Kathryn studies the image. "I'm not cradling my body, I'm already cradling Dane," she says. "I was glowing."

Kathryn loved being pregnant and was mystified by the experience. "I radiated this otherworldly experience. I was myself and not myself. I knew my baby so well and yet not at all." She moved her gaze around the image. "I was always called flat-chested by boys in school, even by my mom, but here, look, I do have breasts." After a pause she adds, "As you can see, the most activity in the figure is in my hair."

The woman in the bowl is a form of singular, simple, curved lines. Her hair, in contrast, is a series of long, wavy lines alive with energy. With her fingers still on the bowl, Kathryn shares with me the story of her hair.

When she was small, Kathryn and her sister Karen, who was fourteen months younger, had bowl cuts. They looked like twins. It was a simple, no-nonsense haircut that deepened Kathryn's identity as an athletic tomboy, especially when compared to her older sister Lynette's long, beautiful hair. Lynette, sixteen months older than Kathryn, was regarded as the beautiful one. The princess.

People noticed and commented on Lynette's beauty, but that did not always work to her advantage. By high school, Lynette was a quiet and introverted caregiver whom people came to for protection. Meanwhile, Kathryn embraced her identity as brawny and brainy. She got good grades and excelled at volleyball, cross-country, and Nordic skiing. She shone brightest when she was hurdling. After a year of tripping and digging cinder out of her knees with a toothbrush soaked in rubbing alcohol, it clicked. In eighth grade, Kathryn was the fastest hurdler on the high school team. Eventually, she was one of the fastest hurdlers in the state. She never dated in high school or college. She was just too busy for boys.

Kathryn went to St. Olaf College, a small Norwegian Lutheran liberal arts school in southeast Minnesota. They have a program called Global Semester in which students travel around the world for five months. During her time abroad, Kathryn grew out her hair for ease and learned how to french braid. She laughs, "All the girls on the trip had me braid their hair. It was amusing to me that I became the one who managed everyone's hair because I prided myself on not being fussy about looks." Her shag cut turned into blonde spiral curls that bleached out in the summer. She instantly got attention, and thus began her tug-of-war between her commitment to ease and her attachment to beauty. When Kathryn's hair was long and curly, she received attention. When she cut it short, that attention faded.

Shortly after Kathryn posed nude at Holden Village, Dane was born. It was a hot summer, she had no air-conditioning, and Kathryn spent a lot of time driving with the windows down to stay cool. Ease trumped compliments. She chopped her hair short and kept it short for a long time.

In 2007, she and her husband and now two sons, Dane and Sigurd, received a fellowship to live in Tanzania and Israel/Palestine for nine months. Kathryn grew her hair out again. It was then, while living in Jerusalem, that she found a lump in her breast. It was April, a time she associates with dying and not dying. The grass is both brown and green.

"When I got diagnosed, I remember thinking I would probably lose my hair and my breasts and losing my hair may be harder." Losing her hair would feel like losing her uniqueness. Her thick, gold, curly, shiny hair gave her power like Sampson. She attached to stories of witches and powerful women who had long, curvy, magical hair. Her hair was deeply tied to her sense of femininity and beauty. Being a tall, athletic woman with short hair and no makeup, at times Kathryn is mistaken for a man. When strangers call her sir, old wounds from childhood crack back open. "I hated it when I was a child and I still hate it. I get choked up when it happens. To this day it still feels bad." Her hair protected her from shame.

Facing the possibility of losing her breasts inspired nostalgia. While pregnant with Dane, she wondered, "How will I breastfeed with such small breasts?" It was not a problem. Her body produced plenty of milk for her two big, hungry boys. Her milk dried up when Dane was six months while they both were sick, and she found it heartbreaking. With Sigurd, however, she cut him off when he was well over two. In 2008, her breasts were even smaller than they were when she got pregnant. She discussed her options with her husband. She worried about the impact it would have on their sex life. She calculated the risk and opted for a bilateral mastectomy. "That," she sighs, "was the beginning of the end."

At first Kathryn considered getting a large tattoo that would incorporate the scars. She dreamed of a big, blue water dragon across her chest. She decided against it in part because it was so odd to not have sensation in her chest. She chose reconstructive surgery and lives with small, cancer-free breast implants.

In September of 2008, two weeks to the day, almost to the hour, after starting post-surgical chemotherapy, her hair fell out. She was in the shower, and it started coming out in clumps. "I started howling," she says. "The boys were worried about me."

Kathryn felt like her breasts were taken from her and her hair was lost. Both translated into an absence of power and vitality. The losses were public, visible, intimate, and intertwined. "I was afraid of losing my hair, but ultimately I lost my husband." On April 20, 2012, three days before their twenty-sixth wedding anniversary, her divorce was finalized.

Kathryn's hair came back as lambswool, and then straighter, coarser, and no longer blonde. She receives comments about the beautiful color and texture of her hair—not gray but shining silver.

For the past eight years, Kathryn has felt asexual. She does not have much intimacy or tenderness outside of her grown sons, who remain affectionate with her. Now, during the stay-at-home order of COVID-19, she feels especially isolated. Her short hair is growing out yet again. She can't go to get her hair cut, and it's a challenge for her to not feel put together. "My hair is driving me nuts," she laughs, "but I'm getting my curls back again. I found a ringlet in the back the other day."

Kathryn's aunt was named Iduna after a Norse goddess. Like Kathryn, she was considered a bit manly as a young girl. In Kathryn's eyes, the older she got, the more beautiful she became. She grew into her beauty. "I wanted that," Kathryn admits, "and that is what happened. I always hoped I would grow into a beautiful older woman like Auntie Duna. We grow into who we are with all the weight and wisdom, experience, care, and love that come with living life." She can see a little Iduna inside of herself.

Kathryn looks at the bowl one more time. "I loved the bowl right away when I received it and still love it. It's so elegant. So beautiful," she pauses. "Me and not me." Kathryn, decades ago, on her way to becoming Kathryn here and now.

Our master narratives tell women their desirability is linked to a feminine ideal and that it depreciates as we age. Kathryn felt that pressure to be desirable most intensely through her hair. I was stand-ing next to Kathryn once when a stranger passing by called her sir. She became visibly upset. I didn't totally understand at first, but I stood six inches shorter than her, and my hair is a foot longer than hers. I was only mistaken as a boy once, when I was very young and had short hair. Since, I have kept my hair long, worn earrings, and painted my nails. I say these things are my choice, that I like pre-senting as femme, which I do, but I know part of it is also offsetting the muscles I had as a gymnast and still have as a yogi that can be considered masculine. I know that part of it is obedience.

Our limiting gender binaries are so strong I saw Kathryn shrink a bit when she was called sir. She felt shame and rage, which are real. And if I am honest, I put energy into avoiding those feelings by living up to the master narratives of society telling me what beauty looks like. Kathryn's counter-story of claiming her ever-unfolding beauty gives me hope. In our final Zoom conversation, she shared, "For the first time in my life I can talk about myself as a beautiful person. I see myself on a Zoom call now, I see my own smile and I recognize myself. I do light up. I see where beauty lives."

> *Have you felt your desirability wane with age? What is one thing you can do today to honor the beauty that emerges over time?*

Seeing Beauty Reflected

Beautiful
adj; pleasing the senses or mind aesthetically.
of a very high standard; excellent.
Or
an impossible standard to strive for but never achieve. Necessary for companionship and worth. Directly linked to

desirability. Exists outside of the self. Decided on by others. A means used to judge yourself daily as not good enough. White.

As a young girl, Michaela wanted to be beautiful. She intuited that beautiful was an important thing to be, an important thing to want, and a label to strive for. She thought of beauty as a standard set by others, outside her body, outside her control.

She was not old enough yet to apply feminist, womanist theory to beauty standards. She was not old enough yet to realize her mother never told her she was pretty because her mother thought it was more important to hear that she was smart. She *was* old enough, however, to master simple logic as it pertains to the lies of the dominant culture. White was beautiful. She was not White. Thus, she was not beautiful—or at least she didn't think she was.

Michaela's sense of beauty was deeply intertwined with her race. Her White mother wanted to send her to public schools, where she believed Michaela would have more contact with other children of color. Her Black father wanted to send her to private school, where he believed Michaela would receive the best education. In vital years of identity formation, Michaela roamed in mostly White spaces. Thin, feminine White women with long, straight hair held court. They seemed to float through the halls, disengaged from their studies. She thought they were beautiful.

Michaela is a well-read and whip-smart woman of color with curly hair. Being a good student of logic, she believed these truths restricted her from being wanted or desired, so she opted out of the game. Michaela played up her literary personality and enjoyed running intellectual circles around her peers. She cut her hair short, rocked big glasses, wore baggy cardigans, and presented as androgynous. She played the misfit card, joined the theater community, and didn't date. She looked down her nose at the popular girls while secretly longing to feel beautiful. For her beautiful remained elusive, outside herself, and decided on by White folks. She felt the pain of being required to be desirable to others.

Michaela could not control her skin color or contain her vibrant hair, but she could control her weight. In college, she leaned into thin as one criterion for beauty she could attain. She ate very little and flaunted her thinness with the desired effect. She started dating. Yet her desirability was tempered. Her boyfriend told her, "I wouldn't be with you if you were any darker." He qualified her beauty down to the offensive category of "pretty for a Black girl."

The airtight logic that kept Michaela entrenched in her own despicableness began to crack as her world expanded to include more diverse circles of people. She sobbed at a Beyonce concert watching this ambitious, gorgeous, talented Black woman own her power and beauty onstage. She watched more and more mixed families like hers on television and followed Michelle Obama's every intelligent and graceful move. She studied Tracee Ellis Ross and how she wears her humor, style, and charisma as power. As Michaela named these Black women queens, she had to explore her own dissonance around definitions of beauty.

When the African Student Union at Michaela's college recruited for a fashion show, Michaela begrudgingly signed up. The evening of the event came, and Michaela tried to back out. It was almost as if she knew stepping onto that runway in an African gown would challenge her to finally own, claim, express, and celebrate her own beauty. The event volunteers encouraged her to show up, and she did.

Her gown received the highest honor from the judges. She was glowing. Looking back at that moment, Michaela understands it was still a panel of judges that made her feel beautiful. She knows that beauty needs to come from within. And yet. That evening, she was at an event full of people who looked like her. She was wearing an African dress that felt like an extension of her gorgeous skin and curly hair. She felt Black and beautiful. The judges were simply confirming the truth she had lived into.

There is no arriving in this journey toward claiming our own beauty. Michaela does not think she has fully arrived. She thinks about the desirability of her Black body to White and Black men alike. She wears her hair long and natural. She is thin and healthy. She is a mentor to Black- and Brown-bodied students as a high school English teacher. In her classroom, she messes with logic, challenges traditional definitions, and plays with words. She shows her students pictures of herself in high school, points out her beauty then, and talks to them about beauty unfolding too. Sometimes we need to challenge our own limiting logic and definitions.

Michaela has always been beautiful, she just shifted who she listens to and who she believes. She shifted the definition and the importance of the label. Her students think she is beautiful. She believes them almost all the time and enjoys the moments she can hold her sense of intelligence, Blackness, and beauty all together in her skin, even if the moment is fleeting.

I taught Michaela in high school. She was breathtakingly smart and loved her friends with a loyal, fierce love you rarely see in someone so young. She thought big thoughts and took bold action. She reached out to me several times while she was in college, and we started meeting for coffee and walks after she graduated and took a high school teaching position nearby. I love hearing what she is reading and thinking about. I love watching her empower her students to think critically and push systems strategically.

I thought she was beautiful in high school, and I think she is beautiful now. Objectively beautiful. But it doesn't matter what I think, does it? It matters what Michaela sees and believes to be true. Over the years, it has been a delight to walk with her, literally and figuratively, as she lives into owning, claiming, and loving her body as beautiful so that her aligned inner and outer beauty flow out into the world with increasing ease.

> *What is one way you feel your body does not fit society's standard of beauty? Who are you with, what are you doing, or what are you wearing when your inner and outer beauty experience a sense of alignment?*

One of my professors in college who taught about communications and gender used to take the mail-back forms from the inside of fashion magazines on the rack at doctor's offices, dental offices, hair salons, and grocery store checkout lines. Without buying or reading the magazine, she'd mail the forms back with written notes, asking the magazines to stop perpetuating the harmful bikini industrial complex. It was a small gesture that made her happy. She liked that the magazine was paying for the postage whether they considered her feedback or not. It was a tiny, hopeful, clever, and subversive act that has stuck with me over the years.

While putting pressure on the beauty industries at the systems level, we can also turn inward and explore our internalized stories about our beauty. bell hooks writes about autobiography: "In writing about her, I reclaimed that part of myself I had long ago rejected, left uncared for, just as she had often felt alone and uncared for as a child. Remembering was part of a cycle of reunion, a joining of fragments, 'the bits and pieces of my heart' that the narrative made whole again."

We can redefine beauty, recasting the net to include ourselves. We can embrace our bodies as they age, soften, and soak in life. We can gaze at our phones less and at nature and each other more. We can ingest beauty and exude it, grow it, and share it. We can tell our body stories in a way that welcomes ourselves back home where we can remember that we belong as beautiful creatures in a beautiful world.

Reflection Questions

* What did your body experience while reading these stories? Did any of them resonate with you and your body's story?
* Have you ever adjusted your wardrobe to hide parts of your body?
* How did your family, friends, and people you dated affect your feelings and beliefs about your body and your beauty?
* Myrtle's tattoos have helped her feel beautiful and move toward wholeness. Are there people, things, ideas, or activities that help you align your sense of inner and outer beauty?
* Has your sense of your own beauty shifted over the years?
* How do you talk to your body? How do you talk about the bodies of other people?
* How do you (or don't you) live up to the impossible beauty standards of society? Does that affect your self-talk or your actions?
* How do you see the difference between pretty and beautiful? What holds you back from feeling beautiful?
* What are you doing, who are you with, and where are you when you feel the most at home in your body? The most beautiful?

* What do master narratives have to say about beauty? How do they get it wrong? How can your body narrative act as a counter-story?

Writing Prompts

Number your page from 1 to 15. Write 15 sentences that start with the phrase "I am from . . ." Finish the sentences with:

ordinary items
product names
home descriptions
plant names
family traditions
family traits
name of family members
description of family tendencies
something you were told as a child
representative of religion or lack thereof
place of birth or family far away
description of home
country or culture
food items
your choice

Read your "I Am From" poem aloud to yourself and notice how it feels in your body.

Write a list of things that bring you pleasure. Think about food, drinks, music, relationships, objects, and activities. How can you prioritize these things?

Find a picture of yourself as a child that conjures up some affection in you. Pick a photo at a specific age when you were dependent or vulnerable. Focus on the image in detail, allowing memories to surface. Practice tender compassion on your child self. Write a letter to that self. What did you need to hear then? Can you say these things to yourself now?

If the scars on your body could speak, what stories would they tell?

Breath Practice

Find a comfortable seated posture with a tall spine. Gently seal your lips and breathe through your nostrils. Notice air entering and leaving your nostrils without altering your breath. Simply notice that you are breathing.

Gently stack your palms and place them on your abdomen between your navel and pubic bone. Invite your breath down into your belly, expanding on your inhale and returning to neutral on your exhale. Create a supple belly, rising and falling without any hitches or clinging. Notice your palms rise and fall with your breath.

After several breaths, move your palms to the sides of your body, wrapping your thumbs around toward your back so your hands rest just under your bottom ribs. While continuing the belly breathing, also expand your lungs on your inhales, noticing your hands now moving out toward your side walls.

After several breaths, place one palm underneath your collarbones on your chest. This movement is subtle, but see if you feel your hand moving upward on your inhale and downward on your exhale. Notice the three-dimensional element of an expansive 360-degree breath as your belly moves out front, your lungs expand sideways, and your chest rises on each inhale.

After several breaths, release your hand, knowing you can return to this three-dimensional breath awareness at any moment in your day.

Body Practices

Rock. Sit in a rocking chair, hold a baby in your life, climb on a swing, or just spread your feet hip distance apart and rock yourself. Find the rhythm your body wants. Drop into your body and feel how the movement is self-soothing.

Go out into public and notice how your body reacts to other bodies. What assumptions do you make about other bodies? How do you have a reflexive judgment toward bodies that don't meet a certain ideal? Do you feel jealousy toward bodies that do? Practice saying to yourself, *That person is so beautiful*, and if dissonance shows up, notice it.

Our master narratives have a very limiting idea of what is beautiful. They tell harmful lies, like "Fat is lazy." We can be critical of these messages and expand our idea of beauty until it includes all people. Until it includes us. We can be less critical, release judgment, and find more joy by approaching bodies with curiosity and reverence.

In a place that is private and comfortable, spend some time naked. How does it feel? Is it hard for you or easy? Try doing a meditation naked where you scan your body and notice what sensations, thoughts, images, and memories come up for you while mindfully sitting naked. What messages have you received and internalized about your naked body?

Seven

Bodies Transcend
Dissolving Internalized Boundaries

> There are no shortcuts to wholeness. The only way to become
> whole is to put our arms lovingly around everything we've
> shown ourselves to be: self-serving and generous, spiteful and
> compassionate, cowardly and courageous, treacherous and
> trustworthy. We must be able to say to ourselves and to the
> world at large, "I am all of the above."
>
> —PARKER PALMER,
> *On the Brink of Everything*

A few months ago, I was uncomfortably tired. I went straight into
analysis and fix-it mode. "Why am I so tired? I'm getting enough
sleep, I exercise, I eat well. I shouldn't be tired. What's wrong?" One
day my friend said to me kindly, "You know, caring for little kids is
really tiring, especially while working at home during a pandemic.
Maybe that's reason enough." I wanted to dismiss her comment,
but I tried it on for size, and it fit. I was making my tiredness bigger
than it needed to be by fretting about it and turning it into a problem I needed to solve. I can work and parent well while tired. I can

fully enjoy my day while I am tired. Fatigue might be inevitable. The suffering around it is optional. I stopped fretting about my fatigue and just let myself be tired. I let myself feel tired with nothing extra around it. By dropping the story and judgment, the fatigue eased.

I tell myself stories about myself all the time, and some of those stories don't serve me. Some of them perpetuate suffering. Some of those stories limit my own freedom and agency. It's one reason I get on my yoga mat and practice. When I am doing yoga, I place my attention on the task at hand, and the rest falls away. The postures require enough attention that my body gets a much-needed break from the chatty, opinionated roommate in my mind. I drop the story and spend time with myself, letting myself feel what I feel.

Here's a story: I used to believe that my body would depreciate as I aged, getting weaker and less flexible over time. My yoga practice proved that story wrong. I am stronger and more flexible than I have ever been. I put my body in motion, travel to my edge, and dwell there. Now and then, when I'm not trying or striving or clinging, it feels like transcendence. This story-less attention used to happen practicing gymnastics, pitching a softball, and running a marathon. It happens when I write. By choosing tasks that envelope me in my own body, I can unlearn my learned helplessness, interrupt, prove my own limiting stories wrong. I get busy creating and transcend the spiraling.

This chapter contains stories about people entering their bodies more fully to dissolve real and perceived boundaries limiting their expansion. They subvert their own expectations of who they should be to become who they are, remembering their true selves and their bodies' connection to the world. In doing so, they find balance, rest, and peace. These are stories of transcendence, of traveling in and through.

Mind–body dualism would have us seek transcendence from our bodies by escaping our bodies and existing in the mind. We are learning more and more that we cannot think our way to healing and wholeness. An alternative framing is to turn toward our bodies, drop into our bodies more fully, live in our bodies and in the present moment as home. By becoming more embodied, we get access and connection to what is beyond the body. The only way out is through.

The Weight of Acceptance

When you step on a scale, be it digital or old-school, there is a moment of pause before a number presents itself. In that brief, fleeting moment, you can be anything, anyone. Thin. Healthy. Beautiful. Stable. Then, a number appears. An indisputable number. A number that you attach a story to, affecting how you tell yourself who you are and what you deserve.

Ben spent his childhood willing the number on the scale to be lower than it was so he could be someone else, something else. Eventually instead of changing himself, he changed the story he told himself about his worth, his wellness, and his humanity.

Prone to illness and injury, Ben broke his leg in seventeen places and was confined to a wheelchair when he was nine. Newly sedentary, he put on weight that he could not shed. Over 100 pounds, Ben became acutely aware of his body, what it could and couldn't do, and how others perceived him. The logic was easy: Fat is bad, and Ben is fat, so Ben is bad. He felt trapped in a body that didn't feel right, and the only way to live a life free of insult and self-loathing, a life so clearly only available to thin people, was to bring the number on the scale down.

Ben fixated on diets, fads, exercise, and fasting. His single mom, in hopes of toeing the line between promoting his health and not shaming him, had the whole family run laps before school. Nothing worked.

By sophomore year of high school, Ben made major life changes to lose weight. His goal was to lose 25 pounds. He joined the tennis team and changed his diet. He felt healthier, but every time he moved his mother's magazines off the scale and stepped on it, the number staring back at him remained the same.

Then, in May of that year, the weight started falling off. He weighed himself five times a week, and each time the number was smaller. It was the incentive he needed to drink more water, run more laps, and play more tennis. Finally, his dream was coming true. Life as a thin person was just around the corner. He hit his goal of 150 pounds. The person he was sure would be more likable was emerging. 145. 140. 137.

In June, on the day of his brother's high school graduation party, Ben bought two Mountain Dews on the way home from school. He plopped on the couch and turned on the television show *Scrubs*.

In the episode, Turk gets diagnosed with diabetes. The symptoms included intense thirst, increased urination, and inexplicable weight loss. Ben panicked, looked on WebMD, and called his mom. They went to the clinic, where a nurse drew blood. While waiting for the results, they went back home to the grad party. Friends and family commented on his weight loss.

"You look great! What is your secret?"

What he said was, "Tennis." What he thought to himself was, *I have diabetes.*

The clinic called and confirmed that he did have diabetes. Healthy blood sugar hovers around 100 mg/dl. Ben's blood sugar was 880. He packed a bag and headed to the largest hospital in New Hampshire.

At the hospital, a nurse explained to Ben that his pancreas was broken, not producing insulin to break down carbohydrates correctly.

Instead of turning into energy, his carbohydrates were going straight into his blood and urine. She said people with diabetes tend to live seven fewer years on average. There is no cure.

Once the shock eased and he settled in a bit, Ben realized he was in the pediatric intensive care unit. Surrounded by children with more acute (or even fatal) diagnoses, he quickly fell into a place of resolve. *I am chronically ill, but I am okay,* he thought. *I will be okay.* Humbled by his more hopeful diagnosis, he became a gold star patient, learning all he could about diabetes and doing everything he was told with a grateful disposition.

Before being discharged, Ben had to show a nurse that he could administer his own insulin shots. She advised him to find a fatty area. As he grabbed at his stomach, he remembered the fat that used to be there. He weighed 137 pounds, the lightest he had been since elementary school. A quiet voice in his head whispered, *Did I ask for this?*

By Ben's junior year in college, he became fluent in the mathematical language of carbs and insulin:

Kale Caesar, no croutons – 9 carbs (.2 units of insulin)
KIND protein bar, peanut butter – 18 carbs (.3 units of insulin)
One Double Stuf Oreo – 11 carbs (.25 units of insulin)
Two slices of pepperoni pizza – 59 carbs (1.3 units of insulin)

Ben controlled his carbohydrates while eating unhealthfully. He put the weight back on, and then some. He resigned himself to thinking that his body just wanted to be big, with or without diabetes. He wanted his body to be different, but he didn't feel unlovable. He settled into contentedness and headed to the University of Edinburgh to study abroad.

On his fifth night there, living in a flat full of strangers, he gave himself an insulin shot at 12:30 a.m. Instead of hitting fatty tissue, he hit a vein. Blood came spurting out, and insulin went straight into his blood. If your blood sugar is too high, it is bad over the long term. If it is too low, however, your heart races, you can pass out, go into a coma, or die.

140 mg/dl became 114 in five minutes. 89. It was dropping fast. 74.

Ben woke up a roommate and taught him how to administer an emergency shot if he passed out. He called 999 and spooned sugar into his mouth until a taxi came to take him to the hospital. At the hospital, he ate sugar until his blood sugar got back above 100 mg/dl. The doctors sent him home.

Ten minutes later, when he arrived back at his flat, he took his blood sugar one more time. There was a moment of pause before a number presented itself. In that fleeting moment, he could be anything, anyone. Healthy. Stable. Managing. Then, a number appeared. An indisputable number. A number that told him he was in immediate danger: 52. He boiled sugar in water and drank simple syrup until the number went back up to 100, then 150. He was so tired, but afraid to sleep. A bit before 7 a.m., his blood sugar reached 212 mg/dl. He slept for two hours before waking to check his blood sugar again.

From this episode, Ben developed anxiety around caring for his diabetes. He took more shots with smaller doses. He got nervous every time his blood sugar was not normal. Then when his blood sugar was not on the high end of normal. Then not high. He took less insulin. He ate less food. He was treating the anxiety, not the diabetes. He was also losing two pounds a week.

By the time Ben arrived back home to the States, he was 60 pounds lighter than when he left. He looked how he wanted to look, but it wasn't satisfying because he believed that he hadn't earned it because of his skewed view of health and wellness. He was thinner, but not well. He was no longer a good patient. The numbers told the truth.

Today, Ben is chronically ill and chronically anxious. He is managing both realities. He looks in the mirror and likes how he looks. He is proud of how well he takes care of himself. He also looks in the mirror and feels horrible. He is at the whim of his pancreas and will be until he dies. He has major scarring and loose skin. He no longer believes that skinny is the only way to be normal or good. He is finding ways to feel healthy that do not equate to his body weight. He is telling a body narrative about his health and wellness that is a counter-story to the master narratives thriving in our diet culture.

The doctors offered Ben a permanent insulin pump in 2010. He didn't get it until 2019. He was resistant to a constant, physical reminder to himself and the world that he is disabled. One of his vital organs is busted.

Before, he could draw blood or take a shot and then forget about it for a bit. Now, the tools keeping him alive are inescapable. Now, with the pump, he is visibly diabetic. There is a wire stuck into his body on his tricep and tubing that gets stuck on door handles. He can never fully be free of it. He wondered, *If I can't be mentally free of it, why should I be physically free of it?*

Ben will always have to pay attention to numbers and manage his anxiety around them. In claiming his health and wholeness, he is shifting his story around the numbers to loosen the embarrassment and shame. When the number appears, he acknowledges it, but it doesn't get to define his worth, his identity, or his story. He does.

> *Take a moment to think about the numbers in your life—your GPA, the number of hours you sleep, your blood pressure, your weight, your salary, your age. What stories and limiting beliefs do you attach to those numbers? How could your relationship to your body shift if you revised those stories?*

Interrupting Companions

Ingrid and her partner Paul both loved their jobs. They had interests and hobbies on hold, consumed with parenting a spirited firstborn child. Yet they could picture life with a second baby and opened themselves up to the possibility. Ingrid gave up drinking alcohol and eating sushi. When they conceived, they started asking typical logistical questions like, "How soon should we save a spot for our unborn child in daycare?"

Then, when Ingrid was five months pregnant, the global COVID-19 pandemic sent the country into lockdown. Ingrid is lead pastor of an ELCA Lutheran church in Minneapolis. In the month of March, the church went from fully operational to fully locked down in one week. One Sunday she and her colleague stood on the altar teaching congregants how to greet each other without spreading germs. The next Sunday they were worshipping online in their homes. Because Paul has a heart condition, they pulled their daughter from daycare and built an isolated life at home. Change was rapid.

Prenatal care consisted of telehealth sessions where nurses asked Ingrid, "Is the baby still kicking? Yes? Any changes it its movement? No? Ok, see you next time."

On May 25, 2020, George Floyd was murdered on 38th Street and Chicago Avenue in Minneapolis during an arrest. Derek

Chauvin, a White police officer, knelt on Floyd's neck for eight minutes and forty-six seconds even while Floyd pleaded, "I can't breathe." Protests erupted in Minneapolis, calling for justice for George Floyd and an end to police violence, especially aimed toward Black folks.

On May 26, Ingrid got a call late in the evening. The uprising had intensified. The temporary medic station was no longer safe. The person on the phone asked Ingrid if her church would open and serve as the temporary medic station for the protestors.

From March through May, Ingrid believed that Holy Trinity Lutheran Church was being faithful to the community by being closed. They locked their doors to protect the most vulnerable folks in the community. Now, in the wake of George Floyd's murder, was the commitment shifting to flinging their doors wide open again?

Ingrid and Paul watched the news unfold on television. Their neighborhood was burning. Paul looked at Ingrid and asked, "Is this a good idea?" She was eight months pregnant. How could he watch her go into tear gas and flames? Ingrid got on the phone with church leaders to discern the response of the congregation's faithful. They collectively decided to open the church. One member was protesting with a church key in his pocket. They went from doors sealed shut to doors propped open in twenty minutes.

Ingrid drove to join the leaders. Over the next few days, she was in proximity to the tear gas, rubber bullets, and flash-bangs being used on the protestors. Each night something new burned. She walked the line between being a responsible parent and a person willing to take risks on behalf of the whole community. She answered phones and organized donations while others who were not pregnant poured milk on burning eyes. Holy Trinity has never been a church obsessed with its building. They have always thought of their space as a tool for ministry. Any ounce of care about the aesthetic went out the window the moment it turned into a medic station where milk was constantly dripping off people and onto the floor.

Thousands of people entered the church over the first few days of protesting. Ingrid experienced beautiful moments of mutual aid amid the horror. Her very pregnant body often stopped people short, an invitation to a moment of empathy and connection. People offered her a chair to sit on or water to drink while she was trying to coordinate and facilitate a community response. At one point she thought, *I am a real liability here. If the National Guard raids this place, I am not at 100 percent.* Her growing baby reminded her of her own vulnerability. Her belly seemed to remind others of theirs as well.

When the fiery protests died down, Holy Trinity Lutheran Church morphed into a food distribution center. The neighborhood went from food-rich to a food desert. Days were long and very physical. With her first child, she was in labor for four days. With her second, it felt like she started labor a month early. Those days of food distribution were hard labor.

A snapshot etched in Ingrid's mind is a circle of people pressing in around diapers, or beans and rice, or cooking oil. Resources were so thin. There was an overwhelming feeling that there wasn't enough. Photographers in town covering the protests said that the area on Lake Street around Holy Trinity and the police's third precinct building felt like natural disaster sites they'd covered in the past. This was a social disaster that similarly put people in perpetual fight-or-flight mode. Tension ran high. Ingrid continued to search for the balance between being a responsible mom and a responsible community member.

Ingrid wasn't one to relish pregnancy. While pregnant with her first, she felt more like a container than a mother. Now, with her second, she felt like a vehicle, and he was a good, patient passenger. He allowed her to do what she needed to do and never once added to the turmoil. He gave Ingrid the freedom to react to the situation at hand.

Because of her extended first labor and the uncertainty of COVID, Ingrid and Paul decided to schedule a cesarean section. They also decided, because of Paul's heart condition, that Ingrid would go to the hospital alone. Seven days before surgery, Ingrid took a COVID test and went into isolation at home. On the day of the birth, Paul and their little daughter drove Ingrid to the hospital to drop her off. Paul said it felt like he was just dropping her at the airport, but he knew he wasn't.

Ingrid walked into the hospital alone. The security guard took one look at her and directed her to labor and delivery. COVID complicated everything. A nurse named Bintou approached Ingrid and while walking her to the triage room asked, "Is anybody going to be joining you?"

Ingrid said no and started to explain before bursting into tears. Bintou broke all the COVID protocols and gave her a hug. "Don't worry," she said. "We'll be with you the whole time. I promise to be near you." And she was.

Surgery was delayed a couple of hours. Ingrid distracted herself from contractions by talking with Paul and their daughter on FaceTime. She used WhatsApp to update her parents and siblings. When it was time for surgery, her anesthesiologist FaceTimed Paul. The OB's phone was used to film the birth. Unlike her first tumultuous birth, the cesarean section was routine and fast. Before she knew it, Ingrid was holding her baby boy.

The nurses were attentive and kind. The situation was not ideal, and Ingrid allowed herself to grieve that. But she never felt alone. It was a loving and miraculous experience. It wasn't long ago that men weren't expected to be part of the birthing process. Here, again, women were taking care of women. It was enough.

Ingrid went into the hospital with a list of names, but she wanted to spend some time holding the baby to confirm her suspicions about his personality. Both during pregnancy and after birth, the baby was patient. Where her first baby was a boxer, this baby seemed to move with grace and intention like a dancer. She named her calm, steady one Lars Anders. Two days later, Paul and their daughter came to pick up Ingrid and Lars and take them home.

Ten days after Lars's birth, Ingrid went back to work. She could not take a full maternity leave. Her neighborhood had burned down during a pandemic. They needed her.

Although it has been hard for Ingrid to find rest, Lars contributes to her ability to heal. He is a good sleeper and a good eater. He accompanies her, ever so gently inviting her to rest simply in his being. After Ingrid feeds him—when he is full and satiated, when she can feel the weight of his body on her shoulder and feel that deep stillness—that is when she finds a moment of peace, comfort, and stillness too. Our dueling pandemics have her in constant movement for the sake of people's lives. When she is home and he is still and satisfied, she can be the same. With him, she rests.

These days, Ingrid thinks a lot about privilege and rest. Knowing that the work of racial justice is a marathon and not a sprint, how does she pace herself? Living in constant anxiety is not sustainable. If she wants to be effective, Ingrid must have grounding times, and yet she knows the BIPOC folks in her community cannot disengage from the generational and personal trauma inflicted upon them. She also knows it may take a lifetime to work through the actual trauma her body went through during her pregnancy.

To Ingrid, pregnancy wasn't precious. She gave away her lung capacity and her abdomen for Lars. Carrying Lars while running Holy Trinity as a medic station and then food distribution center helped her see that faith, too, is a daily act of giving what you have for the sake of another. Whether growing a child or transforming a church into whatever the community needs it to be, her body has an incredible capacity to hold space. Like a container. Like a vehicle. It's not always precious, and yet, it is holy.

Ingrid paid attention to the baby growing inside her. It was part of her body and not part of her body. Simultaneously her and not her. Having Lars growing in her body shifted the story she told about her role as a pregnant woman. About work and rest. About giving and receiving. Ingrid paid attention to how her pregnant body shifted her role in her community. Having Lars growing in her body shifted the story she told about where her body stopped and her community started. She grew a sense of *I am because we are* in her body and beyond her body.

Ingrid could have escaped her body, living in her mind. She could have endured, not allowing the baby growing inside her to revise her story. Not allowing the burning community around her affect her life. Instead, she entered her body more fully to listen, learn, and revise her story to include deeper work and deeper rest, more love, and more justice, expanded *I am* and expanded *we are*.

> Have you ever felt more like a vehicle than a human? Have you ever entered so fully into your community that the boundaries between "you" and "us" dissolved just a bit? How might your body story help us imagine a world where interconnection and common good are the air we breathe?

Essence Unencumbered

Colin was born fast. He has body memories from when he was a small child, running unencumbered. Running fast was the purest, most natural expression of what his body could do.

"I'd add a thing to running like swinging a bat or shooting a ball. The add-ons never went well," he laughed, then added, "I felt like I didn't belong."

Colin grew up in a very poor town in Maine with few sporting opportunities. His high school only offered four sports. He ran track. The closest track was 40 miles away, so he trained on US Route 1, dirt roads, and paved driveways. He loved running. He loved being fast.

Then, as Colin started competing, layers were added to the pure, unencumbered nature of simply running fast. His parents, classmates, and teachers noticed he was fast. They expected him to win races, and their expectations felt like emotional agreements that changed his experience of running. He put pressure on himself to win races, and with that pressure came anxiety. Obligation kept him there. By the end of high school, he wasn't running for the joy of being fast. He said, "I ran because I believed it was the only thing that I was good at."

In the eighth grade, Colin's teacher told his parents that he would probably drop out of high school, and he'd never go to college. Only ten students from his high school went to college. He was one of them.

Colin received a track scholarship to attend Bryant University in Rhode Island. The scholarship added another layer of agreement and pressure to running. "It was a contract," he said. "I run fast, I get money." He kept his GPA just high enough to maintain his scholarship and running fast became his job. He ran the 100m, 200m, 400m, 4×100m and 4×400m. "Some people run to win once a day. I ran to place second through fourth, five times a day."

The financial pressure to keep running could have ruined Colin's joy completely had it not been for his college coach, Svetlana Kitova. Kitova was a world champion middle distance runner from Russia. She was tall, with blonde, wispy hair. Kitova walked around practice with a notebook and pencil, watching each athlete with quiet, thoughtful intensity. "She saw me as a complete person, not just a runner. She had a different approach for each athlete. She was astute. In tune," Colin laughed. "Beyond an empath."

In the middle of a rough practice, Kitova walked up to Colin and asked, "Did you have a caesar salad for lunch again today?"

"Yes."

"Don't do that," she replied. Then, notebook and pencil in hand, she turned and walked away.

Track practice was CrossFit before CrossFit existed. Colin dragged tires across the field with Svetlana's little daughter sitting in the middle. He box-jumped and ran tethered to parachutes weighted with sand until he collapsed. She worked Colin to failure, then offered him sips of rose tea from her thermos.

Kitova's practices honed Colin's awareness of his body. She had him run 100 meters, then guess what his time was. He continued to run 100 meters and guess his time until he came within 0.10 seconds of the correct answer. At first, it took him fifteen to twenty tries, which was a brutal workout. Over time, it became less about the speed and more about the symphony of his physical and energetic body. He learned to listen to the rate of his footsteps. He learned to hear the difference in sound from the impact of his feet when they were directly underneath him versus an inch in front of him. He listened to his breath rate and his heart rate as they came together. She asked him to notice how he was showing up to this millisecond in this specific space and time. She asked him to tune in and break down each movement. To pull apart what was happening in his body. He began to understand how the degree of tilt in his pelvis required a certain lift of his knee, which altered the length of his stride.

Eventually, Kitova could tell Colin to run a 12.1 or an 11.7 and he'd do it on the first try.

One day, Kitova approached Colin after practice and told him to take off his shoes. She asked him to walk barefoot around the track on the thin inner guardrail. When he finished, she simply said, "You are not graceful. You will go to yoga."

Colin found a power yoga class geared toward athletes. He attacked class like a track practice. He remembered, "My ego liked it right away. I thought I'd get praise for being good at something, but the praise didn't come. I thought, *Screw this, I'm quitting.*"

He had one more class in the series and decided not to waste it. During that last class, Colin had a yoga breakthrough. Because he had already quit in his mind, space opened for him in the lack of striving. The class felt easeful, like when he was a kid running fast through an open field. He bought a new class pack and returned to yoga again and again to recapture that easeful feeling.

While practicing yoga, he realized at a deeper level that his body moved at the request of his core. Something happened in his pelvic floor that made other things happen. He brought that easeful feeling and core awareness to the track, and he dropped seconds off his time. He went from the top 300 sprinters in the country to the top 75 in one week. His 200m time was faster than his 100m time doubled, meaning he was still accelerating in the second half of the race. He had access to a capability in his body that he didn't know was there.

More importantly, the layers of pressure that built up around running unraveled. Yoga gave him access to the unfettered joy of being in his body again. "In the yoga studio, as soon as I gave up the feeling of 'I must do this,' I could fully show up unencumbered. I found the orchestra of breath, heart, and body rhythms I discovered on the track on my yoga mat too. There is a musicality to it. It has nothing to do with strength or angles or being good. I could be alone or blindfolded. Class could be five minutes or ninety. It didn't matter. I could go until I wanted to stop. It wasn't an endurance event, but showing up to my breathing, my heartbeat, and my body moving one moment at a time. It was like running as a little kid. I stopped doing yoga to impress and did it for the joy of doing it."

Yoga, like running, had a way of stilling the fluctuations of Colin's consciousness. When you present your body with a series of difficult poses, it gives your mind an opportunity to go quiet. In a controlled setting, you can practice enduring and overcoming challenging situations. You can become more comfortable with being uncomfortable, turning toward your body and the moment instead of fleeing from it. Then, on the other side of resistance is the freedom that comes from pure awareness, and maybe—just maybe, for a fleeting moment—you can experience the bliss of your true nature and its connection to the divine.

On the track and on his yoga mat, Colin had these moments of complete freedom. He could see and feel his solid, physical body and yet transcend it, knowing his body was also a perception. Running and yoga poses were tools to enter more deeply into his physicality until he felt free of physicality altogether. Like water shifting from solid, liquid, or gas, his body became a recipe of energy that has different names attached to it. He was pure breath, heartbeat, feeling and sensation.

Yoga empowered Colin to disconnect with the agreements he made around running. The perception shift came at the right time. Colin got injured his senior year in college, and he knew he could stop running fast and be okay. He disconnected from competitive sprinting without clinging. That season of his life was over. Sprinting didn't serve him anymore; his body was capable of other things, and he could let it go.

———————◊———————

Today, Colin is still fast and takes joy in the sensation of speed. Colin's three-year-old daughter is also very fast and jumps very high. He hopes her unencumbered joy lasts a long, long time. Colin is a high-power executive helping to build the cannabis industry. He manages six companies with thousands of employees around the world. And he teaches yoga twice a week.

When Colin teaches yoga, he does not come in with a theme or choose the energy ahead of time. He sees physical bodies and gives physical cues, but he also sees before him a collection of energy labeled *breath* and *heartbeat* and *movement*. He cues from the pelvic floor, empowering people to move from their core. He guides toward connection where he sees it missing, encouraging yogis to plug leg bones into hip sockets like plugging a cord into a socket.

"I want you to connect, and it has nothing to do with your femur," he said. "I want you to connect to your four-year-old self before all the agreements were layered on. I want you to plug into your body in its pure form, when it moves unencumbered by expectations, out of sheer delight. Pure potential. Pure essence. I'll be here, cuing alignment in your body while that avenue opens. At some point in class, it is like a door opens and the class takes on an energy of its own. There is a communication then that happens between our bodies without words."

Colin speaks of sprinting and yoga, these moments of transcendence, true nature, and organized energy, in spiritual terms. While he was talking, I thought about all the bodies that might not be able to run fast or run at all. I thought of all the bodies that have no interest in practicing yoga. I asked him if it was only rigorous physical activity that led him to these moments of pure bodily freedom. He paused, looked away, seemingly turning inward, smiled and said, "Cooking. I feel it when I cook. The act of cooking is meditative for me. It brings me so much joy to give the gift of nourishment."

Colin's cooking has its roots in Southern Italy. He uses five simple ingredients and loves to create a harmony of flavor and texture in his dishes. Preparing and eating food, too, is a way to access transcendence through his physical body.

Colin started cooking as a young teenager. He needed a job and didn't want the popular yet grueling work of raking blueberries. Instead, he found a job in a restaurant. The owner told Colin to shadow him in the kitchen. Instead of writing down recipes, Colin absorbed the art. Not long after Colin started, the owner got sick and was faced with closing the restaurant. At age fifteen, Colin took over the kitchen. When the owner was discharged from the hospital, he stayed in the dining room and let Colin continue as head chef.

Similar to running, getting recognized for being a gifted child-chef took away from the pure joy of the act. An identity formed around it, adding intensity and expectations. Breakthroughs in running and yoga, where Colin dropped his ego and detached from the agreements, paved the way to do the same with cooking. Now, cooking for his family is a ritual that brings him joy yet again.

With work, yoga teaching, and parenting a spunky toddler, life was fast and full. Then Colin and his wife had a baby boy. Colin was traveling a lot for work, not getting enough sleep, and was spread terribly thin. His back went out and there was no room to heal. When Colin's son was five months old, he would smile at his dad if his mom was holding him. When Colin held him, however, he'd scream until he fell asleep. It was stressful and deeply disconcerting.

On a work trip, Colin talked with a shaman in the Sonoran Desert. The shaman invited him to sit with traditional medicine. Looking out over the expansive desert, Colin saw the trees, mountains, and sky stacked. Then they started to interchange until they were geometric representations in space. It felt familiar, like those moments of breakthrough running, doing yoga, and cooking. He was both in and not in his body. It brought him back to his pure essence, before the agreements, running unencumbered as a little kid.

"I was filled with an overwhelming sense of love," he said. "In my mind's eye, I could see moments from my life pass before me. My ancestors were there. I felt rooted and saw love expressed in different physical forms, but it was all the same. We were all stardust."

Colin traveled back home feeling in tune, reconnected, and plugged in. Yet again, releasing his grip on expectations created space to exude more pure love from his core. After setting down his suitcase, Colin greeted his wife and daughter. He picked up his baby boy, and for the first time in months, instead of screaming, his child nuzzled in against his chest. A few minutes later, his son fell asleep with his little cheek resting under Colin's left shoulder, against his heart.

Transcendence is not a one-time occurrence. It is available on a moment-to-moment basis. There is not a singular path to embodiment, and the path has no specific destination. Once Colin found an entry point, he could more easily access other pathways inward, to that place where he could drop the agreements; where his body ceased to be a body and became energy, breath, and movement; where he found the peace that comes with unencumbered freedom.

Colin found transcendence in running, yoga, and cooking. I find it in those things, and in writing too. I wrote this book in hopes that writing might be an entry point for some of you. bell hooks writes, "The moment when I whirl with words, when I dance in that ecstatic circle of love surrounded by ideas, is a space of transgression. There are no binding limitations; everything can be both held and left behind—race, gender, class. It is this intensely intimate moment of passionate transcendence."

Once we remember our bodies as home and live on the embodied path, coming back home will come with a greater sense of ease. We will recognize when we've been away too long, and we will know the varied paths back to ourselves, and maybe, if we are present and holding on loosely, back to transcendence.

What is something you loved doing in your body as a child? Have expectations and agreements taken away unencumbered joy in the activity? What is your body doing when you experience yourself as pure breath and energy?

Remembering and Revising

As we move toward an ending that will hopefully feel instead like a beginning, I offer a reminder that on the embodied path in and through our bodies, there is no arrival. No story is completely true or complete. We tell ourselves partial truths until we are ready to feel and tell a deeper truth. The stories in this book, including my own, are all ongoing, being revised as we remember who we are, expand, and unfold to a new layer of healing and wholeness.

Lest you believe that I have this whole "inhabit your body and gracefully walk on the embodiment path" thing down because I am writing a book about it, allow me to tell you a body story that will set the record straight.

At age forty, while writing this book, I am remembering how to breathe.

Something seemingly as natural and involuntary as breathing, something that I practice daily through meditation and yoga, something folks pay me to lead and teach, I had managed to do backward, maybe for decades.

When I was twelve years old, my softball coach asked me if I had a headache.

"Yes," I said. "How did you know?"

"I'm a chiropractor. I see a lot of headache pain. How often do you get them?"

"Every day." It had become my normal.

"Come see me. You don't have to live with them."

I did go see him. He took X-rays and did an assessment. My neck lacked curvature, acting like a pogo stick when I tumbled in gymnastics. The range of motion in my neck was limited from my muscles guarding and protecting my spine. His assistant asked me if I had been in a car accident.

"Nope," I said. "I just do gymnastics a lot."

After acupuncture, adjustments, ultrasound, stretching, reading glasses, a cervical pillow, increased water consumption, and a mouthguard to cut down on teeth grinding, my migraines came less often and were less pronounced when they did. I had my tools. I managed them well into adulthood.

Then recently, one day after practicing yin yoga, a horrendous migraine set in and lasted three days. It had been years since my last one, so I scheduled a session with my yoga teacher, Meghan, to see if she had any suggestions for me. I wanted yin yoga to keep my migraines at bay, not bring them on.

We talked about my posture, my diet, and my jaw. I felt like I had a renewed set of tools to try. Then at the end of the session, I was sitting on a tennis ball and talking about my pelvic floor. Meghan said, "Ok, get off the ball. This is exciting. Ellie." She paused and proceeded carefully, "You are a paradoxical breather."

"A what?"

"You breathe backwards. You are supposed to expand your belly on your inhale and return to neutral on your exhale, but you do the opposite. On your inhale, you suck in."

Instead of using my diaphragm to breathe while allowing my lungs to expand outward, I was pulling in my abdomen, restricting the inhale expansion to my chest. For the next several minutes, I tried to breathe, allowing my diaphragm and side lungs to expand.

I couldn't do it. I am a grown woman who syncs breath for a living, and I couldn't do it. On my inhale, I sucked in, and then released to neutral on my exhale. Eventually I got a breath or two where my abdomen expanded outward, but then my body switched back to its well-etched pattern. Meghan and I giggled, but I also felt like I was going to cry. I was confused and a little scared.

I shifted to my hands and knees. When I released my belly toward the ground on my inhale, it felt like all the organs in my torso were going to fall out of my body.

It felt like disobedience.

I felt vulnerable and exposed. Lazy and unkept. Like I got caught in a moment of aloofness, taking up more space than I deserved. And also like the floor was crumbling beneath me.

"OK, so that is your homework," Meghan said kindly. "Practice breathing. Watch your kids breathe, how easily their supple bellies expand on their inhales." And then she added, "A lot of people don't use the diaphragm much when they breathe. It's common for gymnasts and dancers to suck their bellies in.

"Usually, paradoxical breathers have been through trauma, and it's your body's way of protecting itself. Our bodies are amazing at coping and supporting our survival. Offer your body gratitude for protecting you while teaching it that it is time to let go and heal. You don't have to grip anymore. You're safe. Your breath can move out of fight-or-flight mode and drop into your diaphragm."

For the rest of the day, in the quiet moments, I practiced expanding my belly on my inhale and contracting it on my exhale. It was hard and felt foreign. Several times I started to cry. How long had I been breathing like this? From what was I protecting myself? I cautiously mined my memories for what could have inspired the gripping in my belly.

That evening, Meghan sent me an article on paradoxical breathing. While I was reading it, a memory came back to me. As a young teenager, after coming back from my elbow injury, the last tumbling pass in my floor routine was the one I crashed on, causing the injury and near amputation. I'd start wheezing right before the tumbling pass every time. I couldn't get enough air, and my legs felt shaky. Eventually the wheezing started earlier and earlier in my routine and grew more and more severe. I anticipated it, which made it worse. I always finished the routine, and it took several minutes of wheezing to regain my steady breath.

My coaches sent me to an asthma doctor. After several stress tests, he told me, "There is nothing wrong with you. You're a psychosomatic hyperventilator."

The diagnosis was not explained to me well. What I internalized was that I was crazy. I was doing this to myself, causing my own problem, making something up, and being dramatic. I just needed to push through and get over it. I stuffed my fear deeper down and carried on.

Sitting in my office, reading up on paradoxical breathing, with my kids sleeping upstairs and my spouse in the next room reading on the couch, I was filled with compassion for this young girl, standing in the corner of the floor mat, wheezing. My young body was trying to get my attention, pleading for me to stop. I was so scared of that tumbling pass.

Continuing to do the tumbling pass that almost took her arm away was not the only way to show her gratitude. She didn't need to prove anything to anyone. She had worth just being still, but she couldn't see it. That girl wanted desperately to please her coaches and not give in to her fear. She wanted to override stereotypes of girls being dainty and weak. She didn't allow room to grieve or be scared. Resting wasn't an option. Quitting gymnastics felt like quitting on herself.

The fierce, driven, intense kid pushed her fears down deeper and pushed through, claiming mind over matter. She overcame. She persisted. She went on to do amazing things with a bent left arm, and it made a great story. She told the story again and again, feeling proud and grateful every time. She could have had one arm, but she has two. She wrote the story in the introduction to this book, thinking it was complete.

Now, at forty, it's time to revise the story to include the cost of overcoming. Pushing trauma deeper will not make it go away. I began researching paradoxical breathing and slowly incorporated healing breath work into my days, learning to release, let go, and expand. Healing is hard, but so is not healing.

A few months later, Simone Biles got "the twisties" in the 2021 Tokyo Olympic Games and withdrew from of the gymnastics team and all-around competitions. The television coverage replayed Biles's vault in slow motion again and again. I recognized the look on her face and felt the petrifying disconnect in my body. I never flew as high or flipped and twisted as much as Biles, but it was the twisties that led to my tumbling fall and elbow injury. You are upside down and your mind and body feel disconnected. Your limbs don't do what they are supposed to do. You lose your sense of air awareness, and well-wired muscle memories are disrupted. You are forced to reckon with how truly dangerous what you are doing is. You second-guess yourself. The stakes are higher than for a baseball player who gets the yips. Once the mind–body trust is broken for a gymnast, it requires almost irrational courage to get up and try again.

If Biles had decided to push through the twisties, she would have put her life in danger, given the difficulty of her routines. Instead, she withdrew from the competition, causing a media buzz both in support and in criticism of her decision, quickly spiraling into a conversation about mental health, mental performance, and the pressure placed on elite athletes. She spoke eloquently about the burden of strength placed on her body over the years as a high-profile gymnast and abuse survivor. I watched in amazement and gratitude for her courage and maturity. When I was a child, pushing through *was* the work. I didn't fully realize that saying no and stepping away was an option. My hope is that Simone's holy "no" is a line in the sand in sports. My hope is that sexual and emotional abuse of young athletes stops forever. My hope is that young athletes, after watching Simone, realize they can listen to their bodies and summon the courage necessary to say, "No. Enough." For today or maybe forever.

I spent a lot of time in my childhood learning to conquer fear, learning how to ignore my body and repress the signals that something might not be safe. I loved doing gymnastics so much. I loved my coaches and teammates, and the character traits it instilled in me. I am proud of my career. And now I am also reflecting on the cost. Overriding fear was a badge of honor for me, and it was often accompanied by a locked jaw, squeezed glutes, a tongue pressed against the roof of my mouth, and clenched abs that kept my breath in my chest. It was the coaches' job to push us to our edge. When you were obedient and overcame your fear, you were met with accolades and approval. A mantra of mine, and a line of no-nonsense pride became, "You have to want it more than you're scared." It was as simple as that.

The tumbling pass I crashed on remained in my floor routine almost continually for the next eight years. I imagine that, somewhere early in the days of intense wheezing, I learned to breathe backward, bracing on the inhale instead of expanding.

I have a vivid body memory of that wheezing. It has come back on occasion when biking, swimming, or hiking. The muscles in my chest and upper back seize. My upper lungs can't get enough air despite stretching upward toward my throat for space. It feels horrible and often incites panic.

Part of my healing has been listening to the wisdom of the child inside me. She has seen me through it all. Part of my healing has been listening to the wisdom of my body, which often knows the truth well before my mind.

I marvel at our ability to function highly in the world with internalized trauma. I competed in two sports in college, ran four marathons, and birthed two children, possibly while breathing paradoxically. I taught embodiment, led meditation, and started writing a book about body narratives all while gripping in my diaphragm. I had unprocessed trauma living in my body, keeping my breath in my chest, unknowingly in fight-or-flight mode for years. And now that I know better, I can do better.

I am remembering how to breathe.

My childhood breath is inviting me to unclench my tummy. To uncross my legs. To untuck my tailbone. To take up more space. To unravel. To come out of hiding.

Our bodies take on the shape of our lives. The way we move through the world reflects the memories we are storing, unexplored. My breath journey has led me to my pelvic floor, an area where I clench for dear life. A tight, clenched muscle is not a strong muscle. There is a difference between strength and rigidity. A healthy pelvic floor subtly expands and releases with each breath too. The domes of our bodies—the pelvic floor, diaphragm, and roof of your mouth—talk to each other. At first, I was sure that if I released the muscles in my pelvic floor, my whole world would fall apart. Letting go requires a different type of strength and courage. I am peeling back the layers so I can more fully inhabit my body with freedom and agency. I am practicing the art of whole-body breathing. As I remember my easeful childhood breath, my story continues to be revised.

Meghan gave me a new mantra to try:

I am whole, complete, and protected. At my core, I am safe and still, and now is a good time to release, soften, and restore. I no longer need to grip and clench. It's okay to let go.

So dear reader, I am not a master at the pinnacle of embodiment. Rather, I am very much muddling through somewhere in the middle of this journey. I have a hunch that I will be muddling through the middle for the rest of my body's life. There is no arrival or destination. Yet I am committed to the work and find it deeply humbling and exciting. Writing my body story has created space to process and heal toward wholeness. If we approach our bodies and their stories with curiosity and reverence, there is so much to notice and explore.

Where do you clench and grip in your body? What do you need to let go of to live into more freedom and agency in your body and life? Which of your body stories might benefit from a revision?

Reflection Questions

* What did your body experience while reading these stories? Did any of them resonate with you and your body's story?
* Have you ever received a diagnosis that made sense of symptoms you had? What is your relationship to the label? Is it limiting? Clarifying? Depressing? Empowering?
* What is your relationship with numbers as they pertain to your body? Do you own a scale? If so, what words do you attach to the numbers that you see?

* How has your body been labeled by others? How have you labeled your own body? What labels, if any, set you free?
* Like Ingrid, has the presence of your body ever shifted the energy of a room of people?
* What people, places, and activities invite you to rest? How do you build a sustainable pace for your life?
* What activities help you more fully inhabit your body? Have you experienced moments of transcendence where time falls away and the boundaries between your body and the wider world dissolve, even if momentarily?
* Who are the coaches, healers, and friends in your life accompanying you to a new level of presence and awareness?
* When your body talks to you, what does it say? How does it get your attention?
* Wholeness is not perfection. Where in your life do you sense an opportunity to heal toward wholeness?
* What stories are you telling yourself that are limiting?
* What are the master narratives in your birth family, found family, place of work, media, and society at large around themes like weight, chronic illness, rest, speed, and winning? How are we taught to escape our bodies instead of deepening our relationship to them? How might your story join with these to challenge, diversify, and expand our canon?

Writing Prompts

Write about a time you broke a bone. A promise. A law. A heart.

Write about a time you realized your body is mortal.

Write about a time you transcended your body, not by avoiding it, but rather by entering it more fully. This often happens for people while doing things like having sex, playing sports, being in nature, or meditating. What did it feel like to be so in tune with your body that the boundaries between your body and the world faded just a bit?

Drop into your body and notice. What do you still need to say? What story in you is ready to be told?

Breath Practice

Take a few moments to look around at your space, noticing the walls, the ceiling, and the floor. Take note of where the exits and the windows are. Take any movement your body is calling for, working out kinks you may have acquired during your day or in your sleep. Maybe roll your shoulders and your head gently or take a full-body stretch. When you are ready for stillness, find a comfortable seated posture with a tall spine. Stack your shoulders over your hips and place your chin parallel to the floor. Gently seal your lips and breathe through your nostrils. Close your eyes and turn your attention inward. Notice air entering and leaving your nostrils without altering your breath. Simply notice that you are breathing. On every inhale, gently reach the crown of your head toward the ceiling or sky. On every exhale, gently ground your body through your sit bones into the floor, ground, or chair. This is the journey, reaching and grounding with every breath and dwelling in the space between. Continue for about ten breath cycles, then blink your eyes back open and return to your day.

Body Practices

Remember to laugh. Get together with a friend who makes you laugh. Be silly with the children in your life. Do something fun just for the sake of having fun. Watch a stand-up routine or funny movie and listen to your own belly laugh. Your body has been through a lot, and levity is important in the work to combat burnout. Inhabiting your body might not be easy, but it can be joyful.

Part of wellness is our ability to create homeostasis. We take in food and water, then sweat and eliminate waste. We inhale and exhale. We work and rest. Today, think about what you are taking into your body. Eat food that helps your body feel nourished and indulged. Drink plenty of water. Listen to beautiful music. Go outside and take nature in through all of your senses. Ingest good things, and sense what that does to your sense of wellness. How can you create a deeper sense of balance between input and output today?

Conclusion

The glorification of busy will destroy us. Without space for healing, without time for reflection, without an opportunity to surrender, we risk a complete disconnect from the authentic self . . . To combat this, we have to form the conscious intention to prioritize our inner life. To notice our breath, our bodies, our feelings. To step back from the fires of overwhelm and remember ourselves. It may feel counterintuitive in a culture that is speed addicted, but the slower we can become, the quicker we can return home.

—JEFF BROWN,
Hearticulations

On a Sunday morning in early October, I bike to the lake close to my house to watch throngs of runners participate in the Twin Cities Marathon. Waves and waves of runners with different body shapes, sizes, and ages pass by. Some are smiling, proud and playful. Others are struggling already. I've missed the leaders, running with ease and speed. These are the runners who run just to run, who run to finish.

T-shirts tell stories. One runner is running her 100th marathon. Another is running on his sixth continent. One runner is juggling and yet another is running backward. I see knock-knees, wheelchairs, and rainbow tutus. Perfectly imperfect bodies running.

Each runner has a different backstory. One runner is running in memory of her mother, another to raise awareness about diabetes. For some the training was easy and this will be just another day jogging. For others it is the pinnacle of a long and arduous road filled with self-doubt and struggle. The stories come together and meet in this moment on the journey, sharing the path for a few hours. The density and compression of their stories, converging and melding together into one collective event, carries a palpable weight. Each runner takes a risk in showing up, in their commitment, in their forethought. They risk by running in public, in community. They do not need their free shirt and participant medal to know they belong to this hodgepodge makeshift community of bodies.

I stand on the sidelines with the others, bundled up and holding coffee, toting cow bells and signs, witnessing and watching, enamored, impressed, and inspired. I cry a little at the beauty of it all and cannot help but cheer them on. Part of me desperately wants to jump in with them and run.

In reading this book, you are on the sidelines, maybe with a cowbell, maybe quietly observing. I hope you join me in honoring the risk of the participants. I hope you join me in seeing the beauty of it all. I hope you jump in with me and run.

Our bodies—all our bodies—are messy, beautiful, imperfect, and revelatory. It's what makes us human. Stories cannot contain them, but they can create space for our sense of identity to expand.

Many people don't write because they are intimidated by it. They don't identify with being creative or being an artist (which we all are in our own ways). They look at the blank page and don't know where to start or end. They think of writing as a to-do list item, and worry about people finding and reading their writing, which makes them feel vulnerable and shapes how they write. We craft our writing to please a vague, imaginative reader, and then it is no longer for us. It no longer serves a purpose of healing.

Pick up a pen. Start with the prompts. Set a timer. Don't overthink it. Write for you. Write to get deeper into your body and work through the stuck energy living there. You do not need to be a trained writer to understand the contours of your memories and comprehend what your body has endured. You can live into narrative repair. You can write your body narrative to bring healing and wholeness. You can unfold toward a sense of renewal, restored to your remarkable and beautiful body.

We can write our body stories to honor and remember. And in doing so, our stories can also witness and create a vision. bell hooks writes, "The function of art is to do more than tell it like it is—it's to imagine what is possible." We can write and share our body narratives in a way that casts us in a role of wholeness and in a way that shifts our master narratives. We can know more freedom and agency and help work toward that for others. We can live into a new society that values the wisdom of bodies and approaches all bodies with curiosity and reverence.

Visibility is not the same as belonging. The people in this book shared their stories knowing that visibility matters and hoping that we can all grow our capacity to listen to each other's body stories and work toward legislation that protects and advocates for all bodies. We all have a desire to belong, and it is our collective work to build new, more beautiful things to belong to as well as new ways of belonging. I believe our children are growing up in a more expansive narrative landscape that makes room for more body diversity with more visible paths forward. May our stories be the beginning—not the end—of our work for more belonging.

A common refrain from the collaborators in this project is that they felt seen when I asked them to share, when I listened to them sharing, as they read the first drafts and worked through the edits with me. My hope for you is that choosing the embodied path deepens your sense of feeling seen. I hope it brings healing and wholeness. I hope you find home in your body, a place you do not have the urge to escape from. And I hope that what emerges from our work to inhabit our bodies more fully is a more beautiful, varied, and thriving community of which to belong.

Recommended Resources

These are the kind of things we need for the tired spaces of our world. This is the way we need to move forward in a world that is so interested in being comforted by the damp blanket of bad stories. We need stories of belonging that move us towards each other, not from each other; ways of being human that open up the possibilities of being alive together; ways of navigating our differences that deepen our curiosity, that deepen our friendship, that deepen our capacity to disagree, that deepen the argument of being alive. This is what we need. This is what will save us. This is the work of peace. This is the work of imagination.

—Pádraig Ó Tuama,
On Being

The primary narrative act is reading. Keep seeking out and reading stories that counter our master narratives to improve our collective imagination and grow our collective freedom. If you want to dig deeper into the themes of healing trauma, counter-stories, and self-compassion through meaning making, try:

The Body Keeps the Score: Brain, Mind, and Body in the Healing of Trauma by Bessel van der Kolk, MD
Damaged Identity, Narrative Repair by Hilde Lindemann Nelson

My Grandmother's Hands: Racialized Trauma and the Pathway to Mending Our Hearts and Bodies by Resmaa Menakem

Remembered Rapture: The Writer at Work by bell hooks

Burnout: The Secret to Unlocking the Stress Cycle by Emily Nagoski and Amelia Nagoski

Breath: The New Science of a Lost Art by James Nestor

Writing as a Way of Healing: Telling Our Stories Transforms Our Lives by Louise DeSalvo

The Art of Solitude by Stephen Batchelor

I Bring the Voices of My People: A Womanist Vision for Racial Reconciliation by Chanequa Walker-Barnes

Pelvic Liberation by Leslie Howard

Man's Search for Meaning by Viktor Frankl

Wordslut: A Feminist Guide to Taking Back the English Language by Amanda Montell

"Identity: Skin Blood Heart" by Minnie Bruce Pratt

Andrew Solomon's TED Talk: How the worst moments in our lives make us who we are

The *On Being* podcast: Pádraig Ó Tuama and Marilyn Nelson; Bessel Van der Kolk; Resmaa Menakem; and Stephen Batchelor

Acknowledgments

The story of this book is beautiful. Thank you to the stunning humans who collaborated with me on this project—Kevin, Caren, Rebecca, Sawyer, Laura, Linda, Michaela, Kathryn, Myrtle, Stephane, Molly, Andrew, Fardosa, Justin, Sage, Cameron, Elizabeth, Melissa, Ben, Ingrid, and Colin. I learned so much from you in this process. I realized in interviewing you that this is one of the great loves of my life, to have an excuse to sit and listen deeply. Your courage makes me brave. Your creativity feeds my fire. It is an honor to work with you. Thank you for believing in this project and trusting the process. It has felt powerful and holy because of you. Look at what we built together.

Lisa Kloskin, thank you for developing this project with me; for taking a chance and giving it a second chance; for your advocacy, wisdom, and expertise along the way. You anchor me and make the project shine. And thank you to the team at Broadleaf Books. Your commitment to beautiful books gives me hope. Thanks to Enuma Okoro and my wonderful Collegeville classmates for workshopping my miscarriage story and *Inscape Magazine* for publishing a slightly different version of it in 2020 and allowing a reprint here. Thanks to Dr. Chanequa Walker-Barnes, Jonathan Wilson-Hartgrove, and my wonderful Collegeville classmates for workshopping a version of my throat story.

Juliet Farmer, thank you for being an early dreamer with me and continuing to support and accompany me and this project in myriad ways. Angela Denker and Emmy Kegler, thank you for telling me to keep writing about bodies. Lee Fisher, thank you for reading an early draft and supporting me every step of the way. Jevon Bolden, Anna Baeth, and Meta Herrick Carlson, thank you for such kind and true feedback as sensitivity readers. Traci McMurray, thank you for last-minute recruiting and support. Thank you to the very best launch team a person could wish for.

The work of a writer does not only happen when one is writing. The work I do away from the page inspires me and drives me back to the page. Thank you to my Up Yoga family—staff, EP 4 members, Wonder Women, and community at large. I have grown and unfolded toward flourishing as a teacher, yogi, and human so much in the care and warmth of this embodied community. It is a joy to be around such brave, beautiful, storied bodies day in and day out. Thank you to Lee Fisher and Kevin Lally. Our work together at the Minnesota Writing Project grounds and informs me continually. Your support is sustaining. Ruth Lin, I am so glad we found each other. To my people at The Loft, the Collegeville Institute, and Church Anew, thank you for providing the creative, generative spaces our world needs now more than ever.

Dan, thank you for truly co-parenting and making real sacrifices in our life together so I can live into my vocation as a writer. This one took a lot out of us, and I am grateful. I believe in us and all the things we continue to create together. Simon and Miles, you are the great loves of my life. I love belonging to you. You are the place I stand when my feet are sore. I wrote this book in the moments between playing with you, at times switching back and forth between you and it sentence by sentence. Closeness to you has brought so much healing and wholeness to my body. Your curiosity and reverence for life are contagious. It is amazing to live in a house of artists. Mom and Janet, thank you for loving the boys endlessly and offering me time to create. Dad and Julie, thank you for providing a desk where so much of this book was written. It takes a village.

Tina Green Krause, MJ Impastato, and Meghan Foley, thank you for being powerful intuitive healers in my life. My journey inward is deepened and joyful because of your attention and care.

To my sports teammates and coaches at Turners, Cretin-Derham Hall, and Gustavus Adolphus College, thank you for making the journey fun and being a constant found family to belong to. I am an embodied person because of exploring possibility playfully in my body with you.

Jen Larrick and Anna Baeth, thank you for running in the cold with me. Our triangle of love brings transformation to me. Emma Fox, thank you for your love and accompaniment in the work. You are a delight. Suds, I am continually grateful for our shared laughter and passion for the good. Stina Kielsmeier-Cook and Laura Fanucci, being in the trenches with you makes life bearable. You inspire me. Yi Shun Lai, Sally Franson, Heidi Barr, Caren Stelson, and Chris Johnson, thank you for your friendship and commitment to put beautiful things out into the world. Craig Parton, your kindness and care lift me up. What an unexpected gift. Tessa Lasswell, Jayne Pearson, and Ellen Weber, thank you for transcending from brilliant students to trusted friends. And speaking of students, it is you, my former and current theology, yoga, and writing students who inspired this book. Your body stories are remarkable, and I am paying attention.

And thank you, reader, for interacting with me and these stories as we travel toward healing and wholeness together.

Notes

Introduction

always someone who wants to confiscate our humanity . . .: Andrew Solomon, "How the Worst Moments in Our Lives Make Us Who We Are," filmed March 2014, TED video, https://tinyurl.com/24xjtpca.

"an underground—but perfectly manifest—network of multiple branching roots and shoots. . .": Elizabeth Grosz, "A Thousand Tiny Sexes: Feminism and Rhizomatics," in *Gilles Deleuze and the Theatre of Philosophy*, ed. Constantin V. Boundas and Dorothea Olkowski. (New York: Routledge, 1994) 199.

Menakem reminds us that our bodies hold the trauma: Resmaa Menakem, *My Grandmother's Hands: Racialized Trauma and the Pathway to Mending Our Hearts and Bodies.* (Las Vegas, NV: Central Recovery Press, 2017) 7.

It lives, as Bessel Van der Kolk says, outside "the tyranny of language": van der kolk, Bessel. "Bessel Van Der Kolk – Trauma, the Body, and 2021." The On Being Project, November 10, 2021. https://onbeing.org/programs/bessel-van-der-kolk-trauma-the-body-and-2021/.

bell hooks writes, "The longing to tell one's story . . .": bell hooks, *Remembered Rapture: The Writer at Work.* (New York: Holt Paperbacks, 1999) 84.

How to Use This Book

Deborah Siegel Acevedo asserts, "A certain kind of guided, detailed writing . . .": Deborah Siegel-Acevedo, "Writing Can Help Us Heal

From Trauma." *Harvard Business Review* (July 2021), https://tinyurl.com/j58j362v.

bell hooks writes, "Writing was the healing place . . .": hooks. *Remembered Rapture*, 7.

Bodies Persevere: Choosing Our Story

Minnie Bruce Pratt writes . . . "upheaval, not catastrophe . . .": Elly Bulkin, Minnie Bruce Pratt, and Barbara Smith, *Yours in Struggle: Three Feminist Perspectives on Anti-Semitism and Racism.* (Brooklyn: Long Haul Press, 1984) 29.

Bodies Transform: Embracing Our Ever-Unfolding Identity

They belonged to the Community of Christ the Redeemer. . . : "About Us." Community of Christ the Redeemer. Accessed March 16, 2022. https://ccredeemer.org/about-us.

Bodies Overcome: Surviving Oppressive Systems

Chanequa Walker-Barnes writes, "In any society, the most marginalized . . .": Chanequa Walker-Barnes, *I Bring the Voices of My People: A Womanist Vision for Racial Reconciliation.* (United Kingdom: Wm. B. Eerdmans Publishing Company, 2019) 13.

As bell hooks writes, "My writing was an act of resistance . . .": hooks, *Remembered Rapture*, 100.

Heather McGhee writes, "Yes, the zero-sum story of racial hierarchy . . .": Heather McGhee, *The Sum of Us: What Racism Costs Everyone and How We Can Prosper Together.* (United States: One World, 2021) 14.

Chanequa Walker-Barnes writes, "The victims of racism within the United States . . .": Chanequa Walker-Barnes, *I Bring the Voices*, 183.

Bodies Remember: Welcoming Ourselves Back Home

bell hooks writes about autobiography: "In writing about her, I reclaimed that part of myself . . .": hooks, *Remembered Rapture*, 87.

Bodies Transcend: Dissolving Internalized Boundaries

bell hooks writes, "The moment when I whirl with words . . .": hooks, *Remembered Rapture*, 45.

Conclusion

bell hooks writes, "The function of art is to do more . . .": bell hooks, *Outlaw Culture: Resisting Representations*. (United States: Taylor & Francis, 2015) 281.